SOCIAL CLASS IN AMERICA

SOCIAL CLASS IN AMERICA

A Manual of Procedure for the Measurement of Social Status

W. LLOYD WARNER

with Marchia Meeker and Kenneth Eells

with a new essay

THEORY AND METHOD FOR THE COMPARATIVE STUDY OF SOCIAL STRATIFICATION

by W. Lloyd Warner

HARPER TORCHBOOKS *The Academy Library*

HARPER & ROW, PUBLISHERS

New York

HARPER TORCHBOOKS / *The Academy Library*
Advisory Editor in the Humanities and Social Sciences: Benjamin Nelson

SOCIAL CLASS IN AMERICA

Printed in the United States of America

This book was first published in 1949 by Science Research Associates, Inc., Chicago

For the Torchbook edition, Chapters 16 and 17 have been substituted for the Appendix to the original edition. These new chapters appeared in different form in *Review of Sociology*, edited by Joseph Gittler, copyright © 1957 by John Wiley & Sons, Inc, and are reprinted by permission.

First HARPER TORCHBOOK edition published 1960

What This Book Is About

ALL OF us are trained to know and to cherish the ideals of democracy and to believe in the American Dream which teaches most Americans that equal opportunity is here for all and that the chances for success for anyone lie within himself. None of us is taught to know and understand the American status system which is an important part of our American Dream and often makes the success story a brilliant reality. We all are trained in school to understand democratic ideals and principles and to believe in their fullest expression in American life, but we only learn by hard experience, often damaging to us, that some of the things we learned in early life exist only in our political ideals and are rarely found in the real world. We never learn these things in school, and no teacher teaches us the hard facts of our social-class system.

It is time we learn all of the basic facts of our status system and learn them through systematic, explicit training which will teach at least the adult student much of what he needs to know about our status order, how it operates, how he fits into the system, and what he should do to improve his position or make his present one more tolerable.

This book presents basic materials about social class in America, tells how to identify the several levels, and describes the movement from lower levels to higher ones. Its fundamental functions are to tell the reader (1) how to identify any class level, and (2) how to find the class level of any individual. It makes it possible to learn by reading and study, rather than through the half-knowledge and confused emotions of experience, what social class is and how to study and measure it.

Social class enters into almost every aspect of our lives, into marriage, family, business, government, work, and play. It is an important determinant of personality development and is a factor in the kind of skills, abilities, and intelligence an individual uses to solve his problems. Knowledge of what it is and how it works is necessary in working with school records and the files of personnel offices of business and industry. What a woman buys to furnish her house and clothe her family is highly controlled by her social-class values. Keeping up with the Joneses and proving "I'm just as good as anybody else," although fit subjects for the wit of cartoonists because these slogans touch the self-regard of all Americans, are grim expressions of the serious life of most American families. The house they live in, the neighborhood they choose to live in, and the friends they invite to their home, consciously, or more often unconsciously, demonstrate that class values help determine what things we select and what people we choose as our associates.

This book provides a ready and easy means for anyone to equip himself with the basic knowledge of social class so that he can use this type of analysis whenever such factors are important in helping him to know a situation and adjust to it.

The reader is taught how to use two methods: one is called Evaluated Participation (E.P.); and the other, Index of Status Characteristics (I.S.C.). The first takes longer and needs more skill, but knowledge about it is necessary for using the second. The I.S.C. is easily learned, easily applied, and can be used by itself and without the use of Evaluated Participation.

The first chapter of this book tells what social class is and how it operates in the several regions of the United States. The next chapter gives an over-all view of the two methods. The chapters of Part II tell how to use the subtle techniques of E.P. Instruction and practice in the use of each technique are provided.

Chapters 8 and 9 instruct the reader on how to use the four characteristics of the I.S.C. to find anyone's social-class level; the development of the I.S.C. and its relationship to E.P. are traced in Chapters 10 through 13. Chapter 14 gives practical instruction and training to stratify a community, or, among other things, to work out the stratification of employees, of children on school records, of names on a customer list, or of subscribers to a newspaper or magazine.

The final chapter is a commentary on some of the more useful books and articles which can be read to provide background and sophistication about social class. The list of books commented on includes novels as well as scientific publications. It also demonstrates the use of the methods of Evaluated Participation and Index of Status Characteristics on Sinclair Lewis' *Babbitt* to show how the social novel can help to further our knowledge of social class and how the literary scholar can use social science to aid him in his profession.

This book on social status is a scientific tool with a detailed set of directions for understanding and measuring social class and making such knowledge useful to all social scientists, to class analysts, and, where necessary, to those who deal with more practical matters.

The businesses of men who make, sell, and advertise merchandise as diverse as houses and women's garments, magazines and motion pictures, or, for that matter, all other mass products and media of communication, are forever at the mercy of the status evaluations of their customers, for their products are not only items of utility for those who buy but powerful symbols of status and social class. This book will greatly aid them in measuring and understanding the human beings who make up their markets.

THE AUTHORS

Table of Contents

List of Charts

List of Tables

Part One

INTRODUCTION TO TWO PROCEDURES FOR ANALYZING SOCIAL CLASS

CHAPTER 1

What Social Class Is in America

THE AMERICAN DREAM AND SOCIAL CLASS

IN THE bright glow and warm presence of the American Dream all men are born free and equal. Everyone in the American Dream has the right, and often the duty, to try to succeed and to do his best to reach the top. Its two fundamental themes and propositions, that all of us are equal and that each of us has the right to the chance of reaching the top, are mutually contradictory, for if all men are equal there can be no top level to aim for, no bottom one to get away from; there can be no superior or inferior positions, but only one common level into which all Americans are born and in which all of them will spend their lives. We all know such perfect equality of position and opportunity does not exist. All Americans are not born into families of equal position: some are born into a rich man's aristocracy on the Gold Coast; some into the solid comfort of Suburbia's middle classes; and others into a mean existence among the slum families living on the wrong side of the tracks. It is common knowledge that the sons and daughters of the Gold Coasts, the Main Lines, and Park Avenues of America are more likely to receive recognition for their efforts than the children of the slums. The distance these fortunate young people travel to achieve success is shorter, and the route up easier, than the long hard pull necessary for the ambitious children of the less fortunate middle class. Though everyone has the common right to succeed, it is not an equal "right"; though there is equality of rank for some of us, there is not equality of rank for all of us.

When some men learn that *all* the American Dream does not fit *all* that is true about the realities of our life, they denounce the Dream and deny the truth of *any* of it. Fortunately, most of us are wiser and better adjusted to social reality; we recognize that, though it is called a Dream and though some of it is false, by virtue of our firm belief in it we have made some of it true. Despite the presence of social hierarchies which place people at higher and lower levels in American communities, the principles of democracy do operate; the Christian dogma that all men are equal in the sight of God because He is our Father and we are His spiritual children, buttressed by the democratic faith in the equality of men and the insistence on their equal rights as citizens, is a powerful influence in the daily life of America.

From grade school on, we have learned to cite chapter and verse proving from the lives of many of the great men of American history that we can start at the bottom and climb to the highest peaks of achievement when we have a few brains and a will to do. Our mass magazines and newspapers print and reprint the legendary story of rags to riches and tell over and over again the Ellis-Island-to-Park-Avenue saga in the actual lives of contemporary successful immigrant men and women. From mere repetition, it might be thought the public would tire of the theme; the names are all that vary and the stories, like those of children, remain the same. But we never do tire of this theme, for it says what we need to know and what we want to hear.

Among people around us, we sometimes recognize men who have got ahead, who have been successfully upward-mobile, and who have reached levels of achievement beyond even the dreams of most men. Many Americans by their own success have learned that, for them, enough of the Dream is true to make all of it real. The examples from history, from the world around us, and from our own experience provide convincing evidence that, although full equality is absent, opportunity for advancement is present sufficiently to permit the rise of a few from the bottom and a still larger number from the middle to the higher economic and social levels. Although we know the statement that everyone is equal but that some men are higher than others is contradictory, and although some of us smile or become angry when we hear that "all of us are equal but some are more equal than others," we still accept both parts of this proposition either by understressing one part of the proposition or by letting all of it go as a paradox we feel to be true.

Our society does an excellent job in giving us an explicit knowledge of, and good argument for, the equalitarian aspects of our life.

We have much scholarly knowledge about the workings of democracy, but we have little scientific knowledge about the powerful presence of social status and how it works for good and evil in the lives of all of us. Yet to live successfully and adaptively in America, every one of us must adjust his life to each of these contradictions, not just one of them, and we must make the most of each. Our knowledge of the democratic aspects of America is learned directly as part of our social heritage, but our understanding of the principle of social status tends to be implicit and to be learned obliquely and through hard and sometimes bitter experience. The lives of many are destroyed because they do not understand the workings of social class.[1]

It is the hope of the authors that this book will provide a corrective instrument which will permit men and women better to evaluate their social situations and thereby better adapt themselves to social reality and fit their dreams and aspirations to what is possible.

Our great state papers, the orations of great men, and the principles and pronouncements of politicians and statesmen tell us of the equality of all men. Each school boy learns and relearns it; but most of us are dependent upon experience and indirect statement to learn about "the wrong side of the tracks," "the Gold Coast and the slums," and "the top and bottom of the social heap." We are proud of those facts of American life that fit the pattern we are taught, but somehow we are often ashamed of those equally important social facts which demonstrate the presence of social class. Consequently, we tend to deny them or, worse, denounce them and by so doing deny their existence and magically make them disappear from consciousness. We use such expressions as "the Century of the Common Man" to insist on our democratic faith; but we know that, ordinarily, for Common Men to exist as a class, un-Common superior and inferior men must also exist. We know that every town or city in the country has its "Country Club set" and that this group usually lives on its Gold Coast, its Main Line, North Shore, or Nob Hill, and is the top of the community's social heap. Most of us know from novels

[1] Jurgen Ruesch, Martin B. Loeb, *et al.*, *Chronic Disease and Psychological Invalidism; a Psychosomatic Study* (New York: American Society for Research in Psychosomatic Problems, 1946). A research at the University of California Hospital by Ruesch and others which demonstrates that this can be literally true; their results show how certain serious physical and mental ailments are directly attributable to social class and mobility strivings and anxieties.

such as those of Sinclair Lewis of the Main Streets that run through all our towns and cities, populated by Babbitts or, more explicitly stated, by "the substantial upper-middle class"; and by now, thanks to another group of novelists such as Erskine Caldwell, we know there is a low road, a Tobacco Road, that runs not only by the ramshackle houses of the poor whites of the South, but by the tarpaper shanties of the slums and river bottoms or Goat Hills of every town and city in the United States.

The "superior people" of Marquand's New England, "the North Shore crowd," divided into a top level of "old families" with a set of values and a way of life rated above those of the "new families," are matched by Philadelphia's "Main Line" families in Christopher Morley's *Kitty Foyle* and by similar groups in many other novels which report on the dominance of "the upper classes" in all regions of the United States. Reading them, together with similar novels reporting on Suburbia and Main Street for the middle classes and those on the Tobacco Roads and the city slums for the lower levels, gives one the understanding that throughout the towns and cities of America the inhabitants are divided into status levels which are ways of life with definite characteristics and values. Talking to and observing the people of these communities demonstrate that they, too, know how real these status levels are, and they prove it by agreeing among themselves about the levels and who belongs to them in their particular city.

Although well aware of social class, social scientists have been more concerned with their theories and with quarreling among themselves about what social class is than with studying its realities in the daily lives of the people.[2] Until recently, they have lagged behind the novelists in investigating what our classes are, how they operate in our social life, and what effect they have on our individual lives.

But recent scientific studies of social class in the several regions of the United States demonstrate that it is a major determinant of individual decisions and social actions; that every major area of American life is directly and indirectly influenced by our class order; and that the major decisions of most individuals are partly controlled by it. To act intelligently and know consciously how this

[2] See Chapter 15 for a list of some of their publications and comments about each publication.

basic factor in American life affects us and our society, it is essential and necessary that we have an explicit understanding of what our class order is, how it works, and what it does to the lives and personalities who live in it. Our most democratic institutions, including our schools, churches, business organizations, government, and even our family life, are molded by its all-pervading and exceedingly subtle but powerful influence.

The researches on social class in the several regions of the United States [3] make it possible to fill in much of the missing knowledge necessary to give Americans such explicit understanding of social class and to answer some of the important questions we raise about it when adjusting to the realities of our existence. Reduced to their simplicities these questions are: What is social class? How are social classes organized? And how do they function in the individual and the community? How do we use such knowledge to adjust ourselves more satisfactorily to the world around us? What is the effect of class on buying and selling and other problems of business enterprise, on the problems of personnel, on school and education, on the church and religion, on the acceptance and rejection of the communications of mass media such as the radio, magazine, newspaper, and motion picture? And, above all, are there effective and simple techniques of studying and applying the social-class concept so that those who are not specialized class analysts can apply such knowledge to the practical problems of their business or profession or to the research problems of the scientist?

The answer to this last important question is "yes"; the answer to the others will be found in this volume. The authors believe that they present a sufficient description here of how to do these things to enable interested people to deal with problems arising from social class. They recognize that further refinement is necessary and that modifications and improvements will have to be made, but the fundamental elements are now known sufficiently well to provide this set of instructions adequate to the identification and measurement of social class in America. Most of the book—all chapters between this and the last—will deal specifically with these instructions.

THE STRUCTURAL IMPERATIVE—WHY WE HAVE A CLASS SYSTEM

The recognition of social class and other status hierarchies in

[3] For a commentary on some of these see Chapter 15.

this country comes as no surprise to students of society. Research on the social life of the tribes and civilizations of the world clearly demonstrates that some form of rank is always present and a necessity for our kind of society.

Just as students of comparative biology have demonstrated that the physical structure of the higher animals must have certain organs to survive, so students of social anthropology have shown that the social structures of the "higher," the more complex, societies must have rank orders to perform certain functions necessary for group survival.

When societies are complex and service large populations, they always possess some kind of status system which, by its own values, places people in higher or lower positions. Only the very simple hunting and gathering tribes, with very small populations and very simple social problems, are without systems of rank; but when a society is complex, when there are large numbers of individuals in it pursuing diverse and complex activities and functioning in a multiplicity of ways, individual positions and behaviors are evaluated and ranked.[4] This happens primarily because, to maintain itself, the society must co-ordinate the efforts of all its members into common enterprises necessary for the preservation of the group, and it must solidify and integrate all these enterprises into a working whole. In other words, as the division of labor increases and the social units become more numerous and diverse, the need for co-ordination and integration also increases and, when satisfied, enables the larger group to survive and develop.

Those who occupy co-ordinating positions acquire power and prestige. They do so because their actions partly control the behavior of the individuals who look to them for direction. Within this simple control there is simple power. Those who exercise such power either acquire prestige directly from it or have gained prestige from other sources sufficiently to be raised to a co-ordinating position. For example, among many primitive peoples a simple fishing expedition may be organized so that the men who fish and handle each boat are under the direction of one leader. The efforts of each boat are directed by the leader and, in turn, each boat is integrated into the total enterprise by its leader's taking orders from his superior. The

[4] See the reference to Hobhouse, Wheeler, and Ginsberg, *The Material Culture and Social Institutions of the Simpler Peoples,* in Chapter 15.

same situation prevails in a modern factory. Small plants with a small working force and simple problems possess a limited hierarchy, perhaps no more than an owner who bosses all the workers. But a large industrial enterprise, with complex activities and problems, like General Motors, needs an elaborate hierarchy of supervision. The position in a great industrial empire which integrates and co-ordinates all the positions beneath it throughout all the supervising levels down to the workers has great power and prestige. The same holds true for political, religious, educational, and other social institutions; the more complex the group and the more diverse the functions and activities, the more elaborate its status system is likely to be. We will amplify this point later.

The studies of other societies have demonstrated one other basic point: the more complex the technological and economic structure, the more complex the social structure; so that some argue (the Marxians and many classical economists) that technological advancement is the cause of social complexity and all class and status systems. It cannot be denied that economic and technological factors are important in the determination of class and status orders. We must not lose sight of the fact, however, that the social system, with its beliefs, values, and rules, which governs human behavior may well determine what kind of technology and what kind of economic institutions will survive or thrive in any given tribe or nation. In any case, social complexity is necessary for economic advancement. Furthermore, social complexity is a basic factor determining the presence or absence of class.

The Marxians have argued that the economic changes our society is undergoing always result in a class war in which "the proletariat" will be triumphant and out of which a "classless society" will result. The authors do not agree with them for several reasons. The principal reasons are: (1) the presence of a class order does not necessarily mean class conflict—the relations of the classes can be and often are amiable and peaceful; (2) classless societies (without differential status systems) are impossible where there is complexity for the reasons previously given. Russia's communistic system, supposedly designed to produce a pure equalitarian society, necessarily has citizens who are ranked above and below each other. Generals, there, outrank privates; commissars, the rank and file; and members of the Politburo, the ordinary comrade. Occupants of these higher ranks in Russia tend to associate together; those of the lower ranks form their own groups. Their children are trained according to the rank of their parents. This means that the younger generation learns these status differences, thereby strengthening status differences between levels and fostering the further development of social class in Communistic Russia.

All this has occurred despite the fact the Russians have removed the means of production from private hands and placed them under the control of the State ("the people"). The economic factor which by Marxian doctrine produced social classes is largely absent; yet social hierarchies and social classes are present for the reason that Russia is a complex society and needs them to survive.

These status trends in Russia will undoubtedly continue, for her population is vast, her peoples diverse, her problems immensely complex; and elaborate systems of co-ordination and control are necessary for such a nation to maintain itself. The Communist ideals of economic and political equality cannot produce perfect equality within the complexities of Russian life.

But let us return to the United States. We, too, have a complex, highly diverse society. We, too, possess an elaborate division of labor and a ramified technology. And we, too, possess a variety of rank orders built on the need of maintaining unity and cohesion in making our common enterprises successful. Men occupying high and low positions possess families. Their families and their activities are identified with their social position. Families of the same position tend to associate together. They do this informally or through cliques, associations, or other institutions. This social matrix provides the structure of our class system. Children are always born to their families' position. Through life they may increase or decrease their status. The family thereby strengthens and helps maintain our class order. Social status in America is somewhat like man's alimentary canal; he may not like the way it works and he may want to forget that certain parts of it are part of him, but he knows it is necessary for his very existence. So a status system, often an object of our disapproval, is present and necessary in our complex social world.

If we cannot eliminate the system of status, we can and must work to keep it as democratic and equalitarian as possible. To be successful we must see to it that each American is given his chance to move in the social scale. This ideal of equality of opportunity is essential for our democracy. To do this intelligently, we must know what our class order is and what can be done to make it conform most closely to the needs of the American people.

The remainder of this chapter will briefly summarize what we now know about our social classes and how they are organized and function in the towns and cities of the several regions of the United States. We will start with the New England Yankees and then go on to the Middle and Far West and end up with the South before we take up the question of the common features of American class and what it is as a status system.

CLASS AMONG THE NEW ENGLAND YANKEES

Studies of communities in New England clearly demonstrate the presence of a well-defined social-class system.[5] At the top is an aristocracy of birth and wealth. This is the so-called "old family" class. The people of Yankee City say the families who belong to it have been in the community for a long time—for at least three generations and preferably many generations more than three. "Old family" means not only old to the community but old to the class. Present members of the class were born into it; the families into which they were born can trace their lineage through many generations participating in a way of life characteristic of the upper class back to a generation marking the lowly beginnings out of which their family came. Although the men of this level are occupied gainfully, usually as large merchants, financiers, or in the higher professions, the wealth of the family, inherited from the husband's or the wife's side, and often from both, has been in the family for a long time. Ideally, it should stem from the sea trade when Yankee City's merchants and sea captains made large fortunes, built great Georgian houses on elm-lined Hill Street, and filled their houses and gardens with the proper symbols of their high position. They became the 400, the Brahmins, the Hill Streeters to whom others looked up; and they, well-mannered or not, looked down on the rest. They counted themselves, and were so counted, equals of similar levels in Salem, Boston, Providence, and other New England cities. Their

[5] See Chapter 15 for a description of the several volumes of "Yankee City Series." New and poorly organized towns sometimes have class systems which have no old-family (upper-upper) class.

sons and daughters married into the old families from these towns and at times, when family fortune was low or love was great, they married wealthy sons and daughters from the newly rich who occupied the class level below them. This was a happy event for the fathers and mothers of such fortunate young people in the lower half of the upper class, an event well publicized and sometimes not too discreetly bragged about by the parents of the lower-upper-class children, an occasion to be explained by the mothers from the old families in terms of the spiritual demands of romantic love and by their friends as "a good deal and a fair exchange all the way around for everyone concerned."

The new families, the lower level of the upper class, came up through the new industries—shoes, textiles, silverware—and finance. Their fathers were some of the men who established New England's trading and financial dominance throughout America. When New York's Wall Street rose to power, many of them transferred their activities to this new center of dominance. Except that they aspire to old-family status, if not for themselves then for their children, these men and their families have a design for living similar to the old-family group. But they are consciously aware that their money is too new and too recently earned to have the sacrosanct quality of wealth inherited from a long line of ancestors. They know, as do those about them, that, while a certain amount of wealth is necessary, birth and old family are what really matter. Each of them can cite critical cases to prove that particular individuals have no money at all, yet belong to the top class because they have the right lineage and right name. While they recognize the worth and importance of birth, they feel that somehow their family's achievements should be better rewarded than by a mere second place in relation to those who need do little more than be born and stay alive.

The presence of an old-family class in a community forces the newly rich to wait their turn if they aspire to "higher things." Meanwhile, they must learn how to act, fill their lives with good deeds, spend their money on approved philanthropy, and reduce their arrogance to manageable proportions.

The families of the upper and lower strata of the upper classes are organized into social cliques and exclusive clubs. The men gather fortnightly in dining clubs where they discuss matters that concern them. The women belong to small clubs or to the Garden Club and give their interest to subjects which symbolize their high status and evoke those sentiments necessary in each individual if the class is to maintain itself. Both sexes join philanthropic organizations whose good deeds are an asset to the community and an expression of the dominance and importance of the top class to those socially beneath them. They are the members of the Episcopalian and Unitarian and, occasionally, the Congregational and Presbyterian churches.

Below them are the members of the solid, highly respectable upper-middle class, the people who get things done and provide the active front in civic affairs for the classes above them. They aspire to the classes above and hope their good deeds, civic activities, and high moral principles will somehow be recognized far beyond the usual pat on the back and that they will be invited by those above them into the intimacies of upper-class cliques and exclusive clubs. Such recognition might increase their status and would be likely to make them members of the lower-upper group. The fact that this rarely happens seldom stops members of this level, once activated, from continuing to try. The men tend to be owners of stores and belong to the large proprietor and professional levels. Their incomes average less than those of the lower-upper class, this latter group having a larger income than any other group, including the old-family level.

These three strata, the two upper classes and the upper-middle, constitute the levels above the Common Man. There is a considerable distance socially between them and the mass of the people immediately below them. They comprise three of the six classes present in the community. Although in number of levels they constitute half the community, in population they have no more than a sixth, and sometimes less, of the Common Man's population. The three levels combined include approximately 13 per cent of the total population.

The lower-middle class, the top of the Common Man level, is composed of clerks and other white-collar workers, small tradesmen, and a fraction of skilled workers. Their small houses fill "the side streets" down from Hill Street, where the upper classes and some of the upper-middle live, and are noticeably absent from the better suburbs where the upper-middle concentrate. "Side Streeter" is a term often used by those above them to imply an inferior way of life and an inconsequential status. They have accumulated little property but are frequently home owners. Some of the more successful members of ethnic groups, such as the Italians, Irish, French-Canadians, have reached this level. Only a few members of these cultural minorities have gone beyond it; none of them has reached the old-family level.

The old-family class (upper-upper) is smaller in size than the new-family class (lower-upper) below them. It has 1.4 per cent, while the lower-upper class has 1.6 per cent, of the total population. Ten per cent of the population belongs to the upper-middle class, and 28 per cent to the lower-middle level. The upper-lower is the most populous class, with 34 per cent, and the lower-lower has 25 per cent of all the people in the town.

The prospects of the upper-middle-class children for higher education are not as good as those of the classes above. One hundred per cent of the children of the two upper classes take courses in the local high school that prepare them for college, and 88 per cent of the upper-middle do; but only 44 per cent of the lower-middle take these courses, 28 per cent of the upper-lower, and 26 per cent of the lower-lower. These percentages provide a good index of the position of the lower-middle class, ranking it well below the three upper classes, but placing it well above the upper-lower and the lower-lower.[6]

The upper-lower class, least differentiated from the adjacent levels and hardest to distinguish in the hierarchy, but clearly present, is composed of the "poor but honest workers" who more often than not are only semi-skilled or unskilled. Their relative place in the hierarchy of class is well portrayed by comparing them with the classes superior to them and with the lower-lower class beneath them in the category of how they spend their money.

A glance at the ranking of the proportion of the incomes of each class spent on ten items (including such things as rent and shelter, food, clothing, and education, among others) shows, for example, that this class ranks second for the percentage of the money spent on food, the lower-lower class being first and the rank order of the other classes following lower-middle according to their place in the social hierarchy. The money spent on rent and shelter

[6] See W. Lloyd Warner and Paul S. Lunt, *The Social Life of a Modern Community*, Vol. I, "Yankee City Series" (New Haven: Yale University Press, 1941), pp. 58-72.

by upper-lower class is also second to the lower-lower's first, the other classes' rank order and position in the hierarchy being in exact correspondence. To give a bird's-eye view of the way this class spends its money, the rank of the upper-lower, for the percentage of its budget spent on a number of common and important items, has been placed in parentheses after every item in the list which follows: food (2), rent (2), clothing (4), automobiles (5), taxes (5), medical aid (5), education (4), and amusements (4-5). For the major items of expenditure the amount of money spent by this class out of its budget corresponds fairly closely with its place in the class hierarchy, second to the first of the lower-lower class for the major necessities of food and shelter, and ordinarily, but not always, fourth or fifth to the classes above for the items that give an opportunity for cutting down the amounts spent on them. Their feelings about doing the right thing, of being respectable and rearing their children to do better than they have, coupled with the limitations of their income, are well reflected in how they select and reject what can be purchased on the American market.[7]

The lower-lower class, referred to as "Riverbrookers" or the "low-down Yankees who live in the clam flats," have a "bad reputation" among those who are socially above them. This evaluation includes beliefs that they are lazy, shiftless, and won't work, all opposites of the good middle-class virtues belonging to the essence of the Protestant ethic. They are thought to be improvident and unwilling or unable to save their money for a rainy day and, therefore, often dependent on the philanthropy of the private or public agency and on poor relief. They are sometimes said to "live like animals" because it is believed that their sexual mores are not too exacting and that pre-marital intercourse, post-marital infidelity, and high rates of illegitimacy, sometimes too publicly mixed with incest, characterize their personal and family lives. It is certain that they deserve only part of this reputation. Research shows many of them guilty of no more than being poor and lacking in the desire to get ahead, this latter trait being common among those above them. For these reasons and others, this class is ranked in Yankee City below the level of the Common Man (lower-middle and upper-lower). For most of the indexes of status it ranks sixth and last.

[7] The evidence for the statements in this paragraph can be found in *The Social Life of a Modern Community*, pp. 287-300.

CLASS IN THE DEMOCRATIC MIDDLE WEST AND FAR WEST

Cities large and small in the states west of the Alleghenies sometimes have class systems which do not possess an old-family (upper-upper) class. The period of settlement has not always been sufficient for an old-family level, based on the security of birth and inherited wealth, to entrench itself. Ordinarily, it takes several generations for an old-family class to gain and hold the prestige and power necessary to impress the rest of the community sufficiently with the marks of its "breeding" to be able to confer top status on those born into it. The family, its name, and its lineage must have had time to become identified in the public mind as being above ordinary mortals.

While such identification is necessary for the emergence of an old-family (upper-upper) class and for its establishment, it is also necessary for the community to be large enough for the principles of exclusion to operate. For example, those in the old-family group must be sufficiently numerous for all the varieties of social participation to be possible without the use of new-family members; the family names must be old enough to be easily identified; and above all there should always be present young people of marriageable age to become mates of others of their own class and a sufficient number of children to allow mothers to select playmates and companions of their own class for their children.

When a community in the more recently settled regions of the United States is sufficiently large, when it has grown slowly and at an average rate, the chances are higher that it has an old-family class. If it lacks any one of these factors, including size, social and economic complexity, and steady and normal growth, the old-family class is not likely to develop.

One of the best tests of the presence of an old-family level is to determine whether members of the new-family category admit, perhaps grudgingly and enviously and with hostile derogatory remarks, that the old-family level looks down on them and that it is considered a mark of advancement and prestige by those in the new-family group to move into it and be invited to the homes and social affairs of the old families. When a member of the new-family class says, "We've only been here two generations, but we still aren't old-family," and when he or she goes on to say that "they (old family) consider themselves better than people like us and the poor dopes around here let them get away with it," such evidence indicates that an old-family group is present and able to enforce recognition of its superior position upon its most aggressive and hostile competitors, the members of the lower-upper, or new-family, class.

When the old-family group is present and its position is not recognized as superordinate to the new families, the two tend to be co-ordinate and view each other as equals. The old-family people adroitly let it be known that their riches are not material possessions alone but are old-family lineage; the new families display their wealth, accent their power, and prepare their children for the development of a future lineage by giving them the proper training at home and later sending them to the "right" schools and marrying them into the "right" families.

Such communities usually have a five-class pyramid, including an upper class, two middle, and two lower classes.[8]

Jonesville, located in the Middle West, approximately a hundred years old, is an example of a typical five-class community. The farmers around Jonesville use it as their market, and it is the seat of government for Abraham County. Its population of over 6,000 people is supported by servicing the needs of the farmers and by one large and a few small factories.

At the top of the status structure is an upper class commonly referred to as "the 400." It is composed of old-family and new-family segments. Neither can successfully claim superiority to the other. Below this level is an upper-middle class which functions like the same level in Yankee City and is composed of the same kind of people, the only difference being the recognition that the distance to the top is shorter for them and the time necessary to get there much less. The Common Man level, composed of lower-middle- and upper-lower-class people, and the lower-lower level are replicas of the same classes in Yankee City. The only difference is that the Jonesville ethnics in these classes are Norwegian Lutherans and Catholic Poles, the Catholic Irish and Germans having been absorbed for the most part in the larger population; whereas in Yankee City the ethnic population is far more heterogeneous, and the Catholic Irish are less assimilated largely because of more opposition to

[8] It is conceivable that in smaller communities there may be only three, or even two, classes present.

them, and because the church has more control over their private lives.

The present description of Jonesville's class order can be brief and no more than introductory because all the materials used to demonstrate how to measure social class are taken from Jonesville. The interested reader will obtain a clear picture in the chapters which follow of what the classes are, who is in them, the social and economic characteristics of each class, and how the people of the town think about their status order.

The communities of the mountain states and Pacific Coast are new, and many of them have changed their economic form from mining to other enterprises; consequently, their class orders are similar to those found in the Middle West. The older and larger far western communities which have had a continuing, solid growth of population which has not destroyed the original group are likely to have the old-family level at the top with the other classes present; the newer and smaller communities and those disturbed by the destruction of their original status structure by large population gains are less likely to have an old-family class reigning above all others. San Francisco is a clear example of the old-family type; Los Angeles, of the more amorphous, less well-organized class structure.

CLASS IN THE DEEP SOUTH

Studies in the Deep South demonstrate that, in the older regions where social changes until recently have been less rapid and less disturbing to the status order, most of the towns above a few thousand population have a six-class system in which an old-family elite is socially dominant.

For example, in a study of a Mississippi community, a market town for a cotton-growing region around it, Davis and the Gardners found a six-class system.[9] Perhaps the southern status order is best described by Chart I on page 19 which gives the names used by the people of the community for each class and succinctly tells how

[9] Allison Davis, Burleigh B. Gardner, and Mary R. Gardner, *Deep South* (Chicago: University of Chicago Press, 1941). Also read: John Dollard, *Caste and Class in a Southern Town* (New Haven: Yale University Press, 1937); Mozell Hill, "The All-Negro Society in Oklahoma" (Unpublished Ph.D. dissertation, University of Chicago, 1936); Harry J. Walker, "Changes in Race Accommodation in a Southern Community" (Unpublished Ph.D. dissertation, University of Chicago, 1945).

the members of each class regard themselves and the rest of the class order.

The people of the two upper classes make a clear distinction between an old aristocracy and an aristocracy which is not old. There

CHART I

THE SOCIAL PERSPECTIVES OF THE SOCIAL CLASSES *

UPPER-UPPER CLASS

UU	**"Old aristocracy"**
LU	"Aristocracy," but not "old"
UM	"Nice, respectable people"
LM	"Good people, but 'nobody' "
UL	–
LL	"Po' whites"

LOWER-UPPER CLASS

UU	"Old aristocracy"
LU	**"Aristocracy," but not "old"**
UM	"Nice, respectable people"
LM	"Good people, but 'nobody' "
UL	–
LL	"Po' whites"

UPPER-MIDDLE CLASS

UU	"Society"	"Old families"
LU		"Society" but not "old families"
UM	**"People who should be upper class"**	
LM	"People who don't have much money"	
UL	–	
LL	"No 'count lot"	

LOWER-MIDDLE CLASS

UU	–	–
LU	"Old aristocracy" (older)	"Broken-down aristocracy" (younger)
UM	"People who think they are somebody"	
LM	**"We poor folk"**	
UL	"People poorer than us"	
LL	"No 'count lot"	

UPPER-LOWER CLASS

UU	–
LU	–
UM	"Society" or the "folks with money"
LM	"People who are up because they have a little money"
UL	**"Poor but honest folk"**
LL	"Shiftless people"

LOWER-LOWER CLASS

UU	–
LU	–
UM	"Society" or the "folks with money"
LM	"Way-high-ups," but not "Society"
UL	"Snobs trying to push up"
LL	**"People just as good as anybody"**

* Allison Davis, Burleigh B. Gardner, and Mary R. Gardner, *Deep South* (Chicago: University of Chicago Press, 1941), p. 65.

is no doubt that the first is above the other; the upper-middle class views the two upper ones much as the upper classes do themselves but groups them in one level with two divisions, the older level above the other; the lower-middle class separates them but considers them co-ordinate; the bottom two classes, at a greater social distance than the others, group all the levels above the Common Man as "society" and one class. An examination of the terms used by the several classes for the other classes shows that similar principles are operating.

The status system of most communities in the South is further complicated by a color-caste system which orders and systematically controls the relations of those categorized as Negroes and whites.

Although color-caste in America is a separate problem and the present volume does not deal with this American status system, it is necessary that we describe it briefly to be sure a clear distinction is made between it and social class. Color-caste is a system of values and behavior which places all people who are thought to be white in a superior position and those who are thought of as black in an inferior status.

Characteristics of American Negroes vary from very dark hair and skin and Negroid features to blond hair, fair skin, and Caucasian features, yet all of them are placed in the "racial" category of Negro. The skin and physical features of American Caucasians vary from Nordic blond types to the dark, swarthy skin and Negroid features of some eastern Mediterranean stocks, yet all are classed as socially white, despite the fact that a sizable proportion of Negroes are "whiter" in appearance than a goodly proportion of whites. The members of the two groups are severely punished by the formal and informal rules of our society if they intermarry, and when they break this rule of "caste endogamy," their children suffer the penalties of our caste-like system by being placed in the lower color caste. Furthermore, unlike class, the rules of this system forbid the members of the lower caste from climbing out of it. Their status and that of their children are fixed forever. This is true no matter how much money they have, how great the prestige and power they may accumulate, or how well they have acquired correct manners and proper behavior. There can be no social mobility out of the lower caste into the higher one. (There may, of course, be class mobility within the Negro or white caste.) The rigor of caste rules varies from region to region in the United States.[10]

The Mexicans, Spanish Americans, and Orientals occupy a somewhat different status from that of the Negro, but many of the characteristics of their social place in America are similar.[11]

The social-class and color-caste hypotheses, inductively established as working principles for understanding American society, were developed in the researches which were reported in the "Yankee City" volumes, *Deep South,* and *Caste and Class in a Southern Town.* Gunnar Myrdal borrowed them, particularly color-caste, and made them known to a large, non-professional American audience.[12]

THE GENERALITIES OF AMERICAN CLASS

It is now time to ask what are the basic characteristics of social status common to the communities of all regions in the United States and, once we have answered this question, to inquire what the variations are among the several systems. Economic factors are significant and important in determining the class position of any family or person, influencing the kind of behavior we find in any class, and contributing their share to the present form of our status system. But, while significant and necessary, the economic factors are not sufficient to predict where a particular family or individual will be or to explain completely the phenomena of social class. Something more than a large income is necessary for high social position. Money must be translated into socially approved behavior and possessions, and they in turn must be translated into intimate participation with, and acceptance by, members of a superior class.

This is well illustrated by what is supposed to be a true story of

[10] See St. Clair Drake and Horace R. Cayton, *Black Metropolis* (New York: Harcourt, Brace & Co., 1945), for studies of two contrasting caste orders; read the "Methodological Note" by Warner in *Black Metropolis* for an analysis of the difference between the two systems.

[11] See W. Lloyd Warner and Leo Srole, *The Social Systems of American Ethnic Groups,* Vol. III, "Yankee City Series" (New Haven: Yale University Press, 1945). Chapter X discusses the similarities and differences and presents a table of predictability on their probable assimilation and gives the principles governing these phenomena.

[12] Gunnar Myrdal, *An American Dilemma* (New York: Harper & Bros., 1944). For an early publication on color-caste, see W. Lloyd Warner, "American Caste and Class," *American Journal of Sociology,* XLII, No. 2 (September, 1936), 234-37, and "Formal Education and the Social Structure," *Journal of Educational Sociology,* IX (May, 1936), 524-531.

what happened to a Mr. John Smith, a newly rich man in a far western community. He wanted to get into a particular social club of some distinction and significance in the city. By indirection he let it be known, and was told by his friends in the club they had submitted his name to the membership committee.

Mr. Abner Grey, one of the leading members of the club and active on its membership committee, was a warm supporter of an important philanthropy in this city. It was brought to his attention that Mr. Smith, rather than contributing the large donation that had been expected of him, had given only a nominal sum to the charity.

When Mr. Smith heard nothing more about his application, he again approached one of the board members. After much evasion, he was told that Mr. Grey was the most influential man on the board and he would be wise to see that gentleman. After trying several times to make an appointment with Mr. Grey, he finally burst into Grey's offices unannounced.

"Why the hell, Abner, am I being kept out of the X club?"

Mr. Grey politely evaded the question. He asked Mr. Smith to be seated. He inquired after Mr. Smith's health, about the health of his wife, and inquired about other matters of simple convention.

Finally, Mr. Smith said, "Ab, why the hell am I being kept out of your club?"

"But, John, you're not. Everyone in the X club thinks you're a fine fellow."

"Well, what's wrong?"

"Well, John, we don't think you've got the *kind* of money necessary for being a good member of the X club. We don't think you'd be happy in the X club."

"Like hell I haven't. I could buy and sell a half dozen of some of your board members."

"I know that, John, but that isn't what I said. I did not say the amount of money. I said the kind of money."

"What do you mean?"

"Well, John, my co-workers on the charity drive tell me you only gave a few dollars to our campaign, and we had you down for a few thousand."

For a moment Mr. Smith was silent. Then he grinned. So did Mr. Grey. Smith took out his fountain pen and checkbook. "How much?"

At the next meeting of the X club Mr. Smith was unanimously elected to its membership.

Mr. Smith translated his money into philanthropy acceptable to the dominant group, he received their sponsorship, and finally became a participant in the club. The "right" kind of house, the "right" neighborhood, the "right" furniture, the proper behavior—all are symbols that can ultimately be translated into social acceptance by those who have sufficient money to aspire to higher levels than they presently enjoy.

To belong to a particular level in the social-class system of America means that a family or individual has gained acceptance as an equal by those who belong in the class. The behavior in this class and the participation of those in it must be rated by the rest of the community as being at a particular place in the social scale.

Although our democratic heritage makes us disapprove, our class order helps control a number of important functions. It unequally divides the highly and lowly valued things of our society among the several classes according to their rank. Our marriage rules conform to the rules of class, for the majority of marriages are between people of the same class. No class system, however, is so rigid that it completely prohibits marriages above and below one's own class. Furthermore, an open class system such as ours permits a person during his lifetime to move up or down from the level into which he was born. Vertical social mobility for individuals or families is characteristic of all class systems. The principal forms of mobility in this country are through the use of money, education, occupation, talent, skill, philanthropy, sex, and marriage. Although economic mobility is still important, it seems likely now that more people move to higher positions by education than by any other route. We have indicated before this that the mere possession of money is insufficient for gaining and keeping a higher social position. This is equally true of all other forms of mobility. In every case there must be social acceptance.

Class varies from community to community. The new city is less likely than an old one to have a well-organized class order; this is also true for cities whose growth has been rapid as compared with those which have not been disturbed by huge increases in population from other regions or countries or by the rapid displacement of old industries by new ones. The mill town's status hierarchy is more likely to follow the occupational hierarchy of the mill than the levels of evaluated participation found in market towns or those with diversified industries. Suburbs of large metropolises tend to respond to selective factors which reduce the number of classes to one or a very few. They do not represent or express all the cultural factors which make up the social pattern of an ordinary city.

Yet systematic studies (see Chapter 15) from coast to coast, in cities large and small and of many economic types, indicate that, despite the variations and diversity, class levels do exist and that they conform to a particular pattern of organization.

HOW CLASS OPERATES IN OUR DAILY LIVES

Because social class permeates all parts of our existence, it is impossible to do more than indicate how it enters consciously or unconsciously into the success and failure of business, professional, and other occupations or to show how knowledge of its effects is necessary for increasing the predictive qualities of much of the research done by psychologists and social scientists. Class is vitally significant in marriage and training children as well as in most social activities of a community. Status plays a decisive role in the formation of personality at the various stages of development, for if young people are to learn to live adaptively as mature people in our society they must be trained by the informal controls of our society to fit into their places.

Education is now competing with economic mobility as the principal route to success. Today fewer men rise from the bottom to the top places in industry and business than did a generation ago. More and more, the sons of executives are replacing their fathers in such positions, leaving fewer positions into which the sons of those farther down can climb from the ranks. Captains of industry educate their sons to take their places or to occupy similar places in other industries. Also, more and more top jobs in industry are being filled by men coming from the technical and engineering schools or from the universities. The route up for them is no longer through a hierarchy of increasing skill to management and ownership as it was two generations ago. The prudent mobile man today must prepare himself by education if he wishes to fill an important job and provide his family with the money and prestige necessary to get "the better things of life."

Social-class research demonstrates that our educational system performs the dual task of aiding social mobility and, at the same time, working effectively to hinder it. This ceases to be a paradox when all the facts are examined. In the lower grades, our public schools are filled by children from all walks of life. Since education is free in the public schools, since everyone has a right to it and our laws try to keep children in school, and since it is common knowledge that "if you want to get ahead you must get an education," it would be assumed that children at, and below, the Common Man level would stay in school and equip themselves for mobility. Such is not the case. The social and educational systems work to eliminate the majority of them and permit only a few to get through. It has been estimated that, whereas 80 per cent of the upper- and upper-middle-class children actually go to college, only 20 per cent of the lower-middle and five per cent of the lower-class children get there.[13] The evidence indicates that most, if not all, of the children of the top classes complete their preparation and go on to college, whereas those from the lower classes start dropping out in the grade schools and continue to do so in increasing numbers in high school. Only a very few of them go on to college. The educational conveyor belt drops lower-class children at the beginning and bottom of the educational route and carries those from the higher classes a longer distance, nearly all the upper-class children going to the end of the line.

If the teachers and school administrators in grade and high schools know the class positions of the children who enter their schools they can predict who will and who will not get to college. Furthermore, with such knowledge the educator can act to change a negative prediction to a positive one for the bright, ambitious lower- and lower-middle-class children, whose chances for higher education are now very slight.

The reason for the high mortality rate among the lower-class children becomes apparent when one examines the relation of the teachers and the other children to them. We now know that the intelligence of lower-class children is not responsible for their failures in school for often their I.Q.'s are equal to those of children higher up. Although inferior intelligence has been the most frequent and

[13] Robert J. Havighurst and Hilda Taba, *Adolescent Character and Personality* (New York: John Wiley & Sons, 1948).

plausible explanation,[14] I.Q. tests equated to social class demonstrate that differential intelligence is not the answer.

Teachers, it must be said, although one of the most democratically minded groups in America, tend to favor the children of the classes above the Common Man and to show less interest in those below that level. Studies in the Deep South, New England, and the Middle West indicate that they rate the school work of children from the higher classes in accordance with their family's social position and conversely give low ratings to the work of the lower-class children.

To illustrate how the system of rating the child's abilities and attainments is relative to his position in the social-class order, we will quote from *Who Shall Be Educated?* [15] on what happens in Old City in the Deep South.

"In some elementary schools where there is more than one classroom per grade there is a section system by which students are rated and put together into A section, B section, C section, and more if necessary. In Old City, we find such a system. Each grade is divided into three sections: A, B, and C. This division into sections pervades the whole school system but of necessity it has less formal characteristics in the later years of high school. The junior high-school principal says of these sections:

> When a child enters school he is put into one of three sections according to what the teacher thinks his ability is. When you have dealt with children much you soon find that you can pretty well separate them into three groups according to ability. Then if a child shows more ability he may be shifted into a higher group or if he fails he may be moved into a lower group.

"Sometime later when this same principal was asked whether there seemed to be any class distinctions between the sections, he answered:

> There is to some extent. You generally find that children from the best families do the best work. That is not always true but usually it is so.

[14] The unpublished studies of Allison Davis, Robert J. Havighurst, and their collaborators on the class bias *within* the I.Q. tests themselves provide strong evidence to show that the tests are not "culture free" but reflect the middle- and upper-class cultural bias of those who fabricate them. For example, the tests, being largely products of upper-middle-class people, reflect their biases and only middle- and higher-class children are properly prepared to take them.

[15] W. Lloyd Warner, Robert J. Havighurst, and Martin B. Loeb, *Who Shall Be Educated?* (New York: Harper & Bros., 1944), pp. 73-74.

The children from the lower class seem to be not as capable as the others. I think it is to some extent inheritance. The others come from people who are capable and educated, and also the environment probably has a great effect. They come to school with a lot of knowledge already that the others lack.

"Whatever one may think of this principal's theory in explanation of the correlation between social position and school section, this correlation holds true. There is a strong relationship between social status and rank in school. An analysis of the classes of three years in which the social position of 103 girls was known, shows that:

(1) of the ten upper-class girls, eight were in section A, one in B, and one in C
(2) of the seven upper-middle class girls, six were in section A and one in B
(3) of the thirty-three girls from lower middle and indeterminate middle class, twenty-one were in section A, ten in section B, and two in section C
(4) of the fifty-three lower-class girls, only six were in section A, twenty-eight in section B, and nineteen in section C.

"A teacher in junior high school was willing and able to talk more explicitly about these sections than was the principal quoted above. This teacher was asked if there was 'much class feeling in the school' and she said:

Oh, yes, there is a lot of that. We try not to have it as much as we can but of course we can't help it. Now, for instance, even in the sections we have, it is evident. Sections are supposed to be made up just on the basis of records in school but it isn't and everybody knows it isn't. I know right in my own A section I have children who ought to be in B section, but they are little socialites and so they stay in A. I don't say there are children in B who should be in A but in the A section there are some who shouldn't be there. We have discussed it in faculty meetings but nothing is ever done.

"Later on, she said:

Of course, we do some shifting around. There are some border-liners who were shifted up to make the sections more nearly even. But the socialites who aren't keeping up their standard in the A section were never taken into B or C section and they never will. They don't belong there socially. Of course, there are some girls in A section who don't belong there socially, but almost everyone of the socialites is in A.

"In Old City the ranking of students in their classrooms is clearly influenced by status considerations."

The democratically minded educator asks how this can be. The answer is that most of it is done through ignorance of social class and how it operates in our lives. To be more specific, part of the general answer lies within the teacher as a product of our class system. The teacher conscientiously applies his own best values to his rating of the child. The middle-class teacher, and over three-fourths of teachers are middle-class, applies middle-class values. For him, upper- and upper-middle-class children possess traits that rank high and are positive; lower-class children have characteristics that are negative and are ranked low.

Perhaps the most powerful influence of social class on the educational careers of our children, and certainly one of the most decisive and crucial situations in settling the ultimate class position of children from the Common Man and lower-class levels, is the influence of other children on the child's desire to stay in school. If the world of the child is pleasant, rewarding, and increases his self-esteem, he is likely to want to stay and do well. If it is punishing and decreases his self-respect, he is likely to do poorly and want to quit.

In a study of children's ratings of other children in a middle western community, Neugarten found that the children of the upper and upper-middle classes were rated high by all other children for such traits as good looks, liking for school, leadership, friendship, and many other favorable personal traits; lower-class children were ranked low or, more often than not, were given a negative rating and were said to be bad looking, dirty, and "people you would not want for friends." [16] When it is remembered that these children were only in the fifth and sixth grades and that each child in these grades was supposedly rated by all other children with no reference to status, we can see how quickly class values influence behavior and have their decisive effect in molding the personalities and influencing the life careers of Americans from their earliest years. School for the children of the populous lower classes is not the satisfactory place it is for the middle and upper classes. Given children of equal intellect, ability, and interest, it can be predicted by the use of class

[16] Bernice L. Neugarten, "Social Class and Friendship among School Children," *American Journal of Sociology*, LI, No. 4 (January, 1946), 305-13.

analysis that a large percentage of those from the lower classes will be out of school before the sophomore year in high school and that none of the upper-class children, except those physically or mentally handicapped, will quit school.

If our society is to use more effectively the brains and native talent of this great army of young people, it must learn how to train them. To do this, it must keep them in school long enough to equip them with the skills and disciplines necessary for them to function satisfactorily in our economic and social world. Children, as well as teachers and school administrators, must have a conscious and explicit understanding of social class and a simple and easy way to use such knowledge in solving problems. Personality and I.Q. tests are important instruments to guide the teacher, but unless they are supplemented with instruments to measure and count the effects of social class they are insufficient. We believe the instructions in this book for the measurement of social class provide much of the necessary information.

Studies of the relations of workers and managers in business and industry demonstrate how class continues to operate selectively when the young people leave school. Management is bringing college-trained men into the lower ranks of supervisors and promoting fewer from the ranks because it finds that the workers, while good men technically, do not have the necessary knowledge about handling men and relating themselves effectively to the higher reaches of management. Their education is often insufficient to make them good prospects for continuing advancement. The hiring of formally educated men effectively puts a ceiling over the legitimate aspirations of workers expecting to rise in the ranks. The blocking of the worker's mobility and the encouragement of college-trained men is the ultimate payoff of what began in the grade schools. Mobility for workers is becoming more difficult; this means for the United States generally that the American Dream is becoming less real.[17]

Studies of the personalities of workers and managers now being made demonstrate that the effects of social-class and mobility drives are clearly discernible and demonstrably a part of the personality of individuals.[18]

---

[17] See W. Lloyd Warner and J. O. Low, *The Social System of the Modern Factory*, Vol. IV, "Yankee City Series" (New Haven: Yale University Press, 1947), for a discussion of how many of the strikes and conflicts with management are determined by the factor of worker's blocked opportunity.

[18] The ordinary tests of personnel offices fail completely to account for social

In another area, studies of magazine subscriptions show that the class factor is of real importance in the selection of magazines. Readers from different class levels prefer various magazines on the basis of the different symbolic appeal of the stories and pictures. The Yankee City research showed that class entered not only into the purchase of magazines but into newspaper reading.[19] Later research indicates it has a decided effect on radio listening.

A casual examination of the advertising displayed in various magazines demonstrates that advertising agencies and their clients often waste their money because they are ignorant of the operation of class values in their business. This is not surprising since so many status factors have to be considered. The class distribution of readers of the periodicals published in America varies enormously. The readers of certain magazines are confined to the narrow limits of the classes above the Common Man, others to the lower classes, still others to the Common Man level, but there are some who are not confined to any one segment, being well distributed throughout all class levels. The editors of the magazines last designated, intuitively, by trial and error, or some better means, have chosen reading matter which appeals to all levels. The others, not knowing how to extend their readership or appealing deliberately to a narrow range, have a status-limited range of readers.

The readers to whom the advertiser is appealing may or may not be the potential purchasers of his product. The product may be of such a nature that it appeals to only a narrow segment of the total society; to advertise in those media which have readers largely from other strata or to pay for advertising in journals which appeal to every level is a waste of money.

Although advertising agencies often spend their money foolishly when judged by class criteria, the fault is not always theirs, for frequently the manufacturer or retailer does not know how his product appeals to the different classes. Sometimes the product will appeal to but one level, but often a product might appeal to, and be used by, all class levels, were the producer aware of how his product is

mobility and class factors, yet the predictive value of these factors for the success of managers in different kinds of jobs is very high.

[19] See Warner and Lunt, *The Social Life of a Modern Community*, Chapter XIX; and W. Lloyd Warner and William E. Henry, "Radio Daytime Serial: A Symbolic Analysis," *Genetic Psychology Monographs*, 1948, 37, pp. 3-71.

valued at different social levels. It is certain that the use and meaning of most objects sold on the American market shift from class to class.

The soap opera is a product of contemporary radio. The average upper-middle-class radio listener has little interest in soap operas; in fact, most of this group are actively hostile to these curious little dramas that fill the daytime air waves. Yet, millions and millions of American women listen daily to their favorite soap operas, and advertisers of certain commodities have found them invaluable in selling their products.

Research has shown that the soap opera appeals particularly to the level of the Common Man. The problems raised in these folk dramas, their characters, plot, and values have a strong positive appeal to women of this class level, whereas they have little appeal to women above the Common Man level.[20]

Other researches demonstrate that furniture, including drapes, floor coverings, chairs and other seating facilities, is class-typed.

Another phenomenon of class, social mobility, is enormously important in the daily lives of Americans and, to a very great degree, determines how they will act on the job or at home. Recent studies of executives in large business enterprises clearly demonstrate that the success or failure of all of them is partly determined by the presence or absence of a "mobility drive." Our research shows that when a family loses its desire to achieve and advance itself, this very often is reflected in the executive's "slowing down" or being unwilling to make the effort necessary for success as a manager. On the other hand, some men are too aggressively mobile and stir up trouble by their overly ambitious desires and their ruthless competition.

Tests combining knowledge of social class and personality demonstrate the necessity of knowing not only what the man's status level is, what it has been, and what he wants it to be, but how the class values and beliefs of his early training have become integral parts of his personality, and ever-present guides for what he thinks, what he feels, and how he acts. Those concerned with selecting executives need a personality inventory and a man's I.Q. to predict how a man will function in a given job; but they also need to find out what his experiences in our status order have done to his individuality and character structure.

---

[20] *Ibid.*

Every aspect of American thought and action is powerfully influenced by social class; to think realistically and act effectively, we must know and understand our status system.

We now face the task of giving exact and precise instructions on how to measure social class and how to identify and locate exactly the class position of anyone in our American society. The methods presented give the reader two techniques for establishing social-class position. The next chapter gives an over-all general set of instructions on how to use each of the two methods and how to combine them when necessary.

SPECIAL READINGS

Those who wish to know more about social class in America and about social stratification generally should read the last chapter (Chapter 15) of this book before continuing with the chapters on instruction for using the techniques for studying social status. It is a commentary on some of the more important publications on social class, color-caste, and other forms of status and rank. Some may prefer to study a few selected readings; for them, the following publications are suggested:

L. T. Hobhouse, G. C. Wheeler, and M. Ginsberg. *The Material Culture and Social Institutions of the Simpler Peoples.* London: Chapman & Hall, 1915.

This exhaustive study of hundreds of communities and societies of the world demonstrates how social stratification and rank are highly correlated with technological advancement and the increase in social complexity. See in particular pages 228-237.

Gunnar Myrdal. *An American Dilemma.* New York: Harper & Bros., 1944.

A study based on original research done by many of the writers listed in Chapter 15. Deals with the conflict between the values of democracy and the values of social status in America. Special reference: pages 667-705.

W. Lloyd Warner and Paul S. Lunt. *The Social Life of a Modern Community.* Vol. I, "Yankee City Series." New Haven: Yale University Press, 1941.

Read especially pages 127-201 and pages 422-450. The first readings are the "Profiles," which describe various kinds of personalities, their actions and values, and their social institutions as they are found in the several classes in a New England town. The last selection summarizes how various social characteristics, such as education, occupation, good and bad neighborhoods and houses, are distributed through the upper, middle, and lower classes.

Other books that might be read at this time are: *Deep South,* by Allison Davis, Burleigh B. Gardner, and Mary R. Gardner (University of Chicago Press), and *Plainville, U.S.A.,* by James West (Columbia University Press).

CHAPTER 2

Measuring Social Class and the Class Position of Individuals

THE research task confronting the social scientist when he studies the social and status structure of a community is similar to that the geographer faces when he discovers a new territory. The geographer identifies and describes the principal characteristics of the new regions and, by use of such concepts as direction and distance, locates them and measures their relations to each other and to previously determined points. From this body of knowledge, the cartographer constructs maps which are scientific representations of what he conceives to be the spatial relations in the new territory and their connections with the rest of the known world. Obviously, his map can represent nothing more about the territory than the knowledge he possesses.[1]

The scientist who studies the social and status structure of a community faces similar problems and falls victim to similar errors. He must identify, describe, locate, interrelate, and measure the facts about the structure of social interaction. To report on such analyses the social ecologist draws maps which represent the social use of physical space through time by human groups. Structural and status analysts construct scientific representations (or "maps") which represent their knowledge of the structure and status interrelations which compose the community's social system. The ecologist characteristically draws maps of people in physical areas; the structural and status analyst charts and diagrams the social and status interrelations of human beings.

[1] For further information see C. K. Ogden and I. A. Richards, *The Meaning of Meaning* (New York: Harcourt, Brace & Co., 1936); S. I. Hayakawa, *Language in Action* (New York: Harcourt, Brace & Co., 1941); Hugh R. Walpole, *Semantics; the Nature of Words and Their Meanings* (New York: W. W. Norton & Co., 1941); Albert M. Frye and Albert W. Levi, *Rational Belief; an Introduction to Logic* (New York: Harcourt, Brace & Co., 1941); P. W. Bridgman, *The Logic of Modern Physics* (New York: Macmillan Co., 1927).

Two systems for investigating and measuring social status in American communities are presented in this volume. Precise instructions for using each system are given. The several chapters tell how to use the two methods and their combinations, enabling the investigator to learn what the social-class system of any particular city is, to distinguish any given class level from those adjacent to it, and to find within reasonable limits the correct class position of any given individual or family in the community. It is, therefore, a manual of procedure for social scientists who wish to identify quickly and easily the class levels of a community or the social class of a particular individual or family.

The two methods are called Evaluated Participation (E.P.) and the Index of Status Characteristics (I.S.C.). Together they provide accurate procedures for measuring social class and the class position of individuals, for validating results obtained, and for translating social class and socioeconomic status categories into terms which are interchangeable.

The method of Evaluated Participation (E.P.), comprising several rating techniques, is posed on the propositions that those who interact in the social system of a community evaluate the participation of those around them, that the place where an individual participates is evaluated, and that the members of the community are explicitly or implicitly aware of the ranking and translate their evaluations of such social participation into social-class ratings that can be communicated to the investigator. It is, therefore, the duty of the field man to use his interviewing skill to elicit the necessary information and to analyze his data with the requisite techniques for determining social class, thereby enabling the status analyst to determine the levels of stratification present and to rank any member of the community.

The Index of Status Characteristics (I.S.C.) measures the socioeconomic levels of the community and, when related to Evaluated Participation (E.P.), makes it possible for the status analyst to say what is meant in socioeconomic terms by such class concepts as upper, middle, or lower class and, correspondingly, what is meant by higher or lower socioeconomic levels in terms of social class and Evaluated Participation.

Current procedures for class stratification,[2] while reliable, are

[2] Warner and Lunt, *The Social Life of a Modern Community*, pp. 81-126.

time-consuming and expensive, particularly in metropolitan communities, and require a large field staff of experts, often making it impossible for the interested student of human affairs to use a knowledge of social class to understand his particular problem. Educators, students of child development, guidance and counseling experts, specialists in social service, political scientists, psychologists, and public opinion and market experts, as well as status analysts themselves, require a simpler and quicker method for measuring status. Students learning how to study class need a more precise, more mechanical, and more explicitly communicable set of techniques. As knowledge about American social class accumulates, status analysts are increasingly aware that, if they are to make valid comparisons among the class systems of the cities and towns of our several regions and develop larger generalizations about the nature of social status, they must have a more adequate and explicit methodology for the study of this phenomenon.[3]

The methods of Evaluated Participation (E.P.) and the Index of Status Characteristics (I.S.C.) have been evolved to meet these several needs.[4]

Both methods can be used in any kind of community. The results obtained will vary, of course, from community to community; some cities may have many classes, some towns only a few; some may be rigidly organized, others very loosely.

This manual describes the techniques which comprise each method and gives detailed instructions as to how a technique is used by itself and in interrelation with the other techniques, how the Index of Status Characteristics was validated by Evaluated Participation, and, finally, for large samples, how the inexpensive and simply applied I.S.C. may be substituted for the other method and used largely by itself.

EVALUATED PARTICIPATION

Each of the rating techniques combined in the E.P. method for stratifying a community and for placing families and individuals at their proper level in the status system of a community can play a decisive part in the process of determining the social stratification of

[3] Some of the recent publications on social-class systems of America listed in Chapter 15 describe procedures which have been developed.

[4] The evidence for demonstrating the use of the two methods comes from a study of the middle western city of Jonesville.

a community or determining the status of an individual or family.

The status analyst uses six techniques for rating an individual's social-class position. They are:

1. Rating by Matched Agreements (of several informants on the placement of many people in the several classes). In interviews with informants of diverse social background the status analyst obtains a Social-Class Configuration (rank order) of named social classes from each informant. He first examines the rank orders recognized in the several interviews to determine the degree of correspondence among them. When this is done, and the correspondence is high (as it usually is), the next step is taken. Social-Class Configurations are ordinarily accompanied by lists of names of individual persons volunteered by the informants. The names on each list are always assigned to, and distributed through, the several classes. Many of the same names appear in two or more informants' interviews, thus making it possible for the analyst to match and count pairs of agreements and disagreements among the informants about the class positions of people in the community. When the correspondence between the ranking of classes by different informants is complete or very high, and when the count of matched agreements of informants on the class positions of a large number of people is also high, the analyst is assured that the class system he is studying has a given number of classes, is strong, and pervades the whole community; he also knows his class ratings of the individuals listed are likely to be highly accurate. For simplicity, this technique of matching class hierarchies and pairs of class assignments of subjects will be called Matched Agreements.

2. Rating by Symbolic Placement. An individual is rated by the analyst as being in a particular social class because he is identified with certain superior or inferior symbols by informants. We shall call this method of rating Symbolic Placement.

3. Rating by Status Reputation. An individual (or his family) is assigned to a given class by the analyst because (informants say) he has a reputation for engaging in activities and possessing certain traits which are considered to be superior or inferior. For convenience, this rating will be called Status Reputation.

4. Rating by Comparison. The subject (or his family) is rated by the analyst as being in a particular class because informants assert he is equal, superior, or inferior to others whose social-class

position has been previously determined. This technique of comparing the subject's status with the known class position of another will be called Comparison.

5. Rating by Simple Assignment to a Class. The subject (or his family) is rated by the analyst as being in a particular class because one or more qualified informants assign the individual to that particular class category; only one class is mentioned, and there is no explicit reference to the other classes which compose the whole system. We distinguish this technique from Matched Agreements first, because the analyst's operations are somewhat different from those used in Matched Agreements, and second, because the considerations of the informants are very different from those made in supplying information for Matched Agreements.

6. Rating by Institutional Membership. The subject is assigned to a particular status by the analyst because in the interviews of informants he is said to be a member of certain institutions which are ranked as superior or inferior. The institutions used for such a rating are families, cliques, associations, and churches. Hereafter, we will refer to this rating technique as Institutional Membership or Real Interconnectedness. The use of the latter term emphasizes the fact that memberships in these various institutions are interconnected and part of the class structure.

From the description of the six techniques of rating it is apparent that the analyst does not impose his ranking upon the people of the town but, on the contrary, must devise techniques of rating which will translate the criteria and judgments of the informants (townspeople) into explicit, verifiable results which will correspond with the class realities of the community. We must try to see the problem from the point of view of the informants, for they are the final authorities about the realities of American social class. At the risk of appearing repetitive let us briefly review the questions that the people of a town think about (and which appear in their interviews) when they rate each other (by Evaluated Participation):

Is the person included in the membership of a particular family, clique, association, or church, or is he excluded?

Is the status of an individual superior, inferior, or equal to the status of some other individual or family whose status has been previously established?

Is the person (or family) identified with well-known (and

easily used) symbols of superiority or inferiority (so that the attachment of the symbol to the individual places him in a particular social class)?

Is the person (or family) in activities or does he have traits that are superior or inferior which give him a superior or inferior reputation?

Those informants who are explicitly conscious of each social-class level and see all of them as a hierarchy of superior and inferior social levels ask: Which social class is the person in? Is it the upper, middle, or lower class? These are the questions which Americans ask and answer when they rate each other by Evaluated Participation.

Chapters 3 through 7 will describe these concepts in greater detail and will suggest specific procedures for using them to obtain E.P. social-class placements in any community.[5]

INDEX OF STATUS CHARACTERISTICS

The Index of Status Characteristics as a measurement of social class is posed on two propositions: that economic and other prestige factors are highly important and closely correlated with social class; and that these social and economic factors, such as talent, income, and money, if their potentialities for rank are to be realized, must be translated into social-class behavior acceptable to the members of any given social level of the community. This method is designed to provide an objective method for establishing the social level of everyone in the community and to do so by simple, inexpensive means. The skills involved are very few; the amount of information needed is small; the length of time necessary, brief. The data for each characteristic in the Status Index are easily acquired and do not necessarily require interviewing.

The Index of Status Characteristics is, primarily, an index of socioeconomic factors; but evidence will be presented later to demonstrate that it can be used with a considerable degree of confidence as an index of social-class position as well. Later chapters in this volume will provide more explicit instructions for the use of the

[5] Full instructions on the techniques of interviewing are given in the first volume of "Yankee City Series," *The Social Life of a Modern Community*. Instructions for getting the necessary information for Institutional Membership are also found in that volume. An examination of the present volume should provide the reader with a knowledge of what he should obtain from his informant during an interview and what he should gather by other field techniques for later status analysis.

Index in any community and will describe the procedures by which the I.S.C. was developed in the study of Jonesville and how its accuracy for the prediction of social-class position was tested. A very brief description of the general nature of the I.S.C. will be given here for those who may not have need for the more detailed account given later.

The four status characteristics used in the Index were first selected from the previous research on Yankee City,[6] and were chosen because they correlated highly with class and because they are easily obtained and capable of exact comparison among all American communities. They are: Occupation, Source of Income, House Type, and Dwelling Area. The basic criterion for choosing them was that they express in concrete form the two basic propositions which underlie the method of the I.S.C.

The most important fact to remember about using the I.S.C. as a measurement of social class is that, in order for it to be a reliable instrument and an accurate index of social class, each of the four characteristics and the points in their scales must reflect how Americans feel and think about the relative worth of each job, the sources of income which support them, and the evaluation of their houses and the neighborhoods in which they live. For it is not the house, or the job, or the income, or the neighborhood that is being measured so much as the evaluations that are in the backs of all of our heads—evaluations placed there by our cultural tradition and our society. From one point of view, the four characteristics—house, occupation, income, and neighborhood—are no more than evaluated symbols which are signs of status telling us the class levels of those who possess the symbols. By measuring the symbols, we measure the relative worth of each; and by adding up their several "worths," re-

[6] The methods of the I.S.C. and E.P. were first developed by Warner by re-examining the Yankee City material to see which social characteristics correlated most highly with class. Finding what they were for purposes of classification, he separated participation from social characteristics and developed the seven-point scale of the I.S.C. and the six techniques of the E.P. by testing them on a representative sample of Jonesville families. After the methods of E.P. and I.S.C. had been used and tested to determine their relations to each other, Meeker and Warner re-worked the seven-point scales for the several status characteristics and refined the Index. Meeker individually sharpened and refined some of the scales. When the two methods had been sufficiently tested to demonstrate their use for predicting social status by either of them, Eells was given the problem of the statistical refinement of the I.S.C., and he further helped sharpen the precision of the Index as a measurement of class. He also contributed significantly to the measurement of ethnic status. All three collaborated on the writing of this document.

flecting diverse and complex economic and social values, we get a score which tells us what we think and feel about the worth of a man's social participation, meaning essentially that we are measuring his Evaluated Participation or social class.

The first step in securing an I.S.C. for any given individual in a community is to obtain ratings for him on each of the four status characteristics—occupation, source of income, house type, and dwelling area—which comprise the Index. These ratings are made on seven-point scales which are described more fully in Chapter 9. The four ratings are then totaled, after assigning to each one a weight which expresses the importance of that particular status characteristic in social-class prediction. The resultant indexes will range from 12 (very high socioeconomic status) to 84 (very low status). A sample calculation for one individual follows:

Status Characteristic	Rating		Weight		Weighted Rating
Occupation	2	×	4	=	8
Source of Income	3	×	3	=	9
House Type	2	×	3	=	6
Dwelling Area	3	×	2	=	6
			Weighted Total		29

If the investigator wants only an index of socioeconomic status, he may use the Index in this numerical form. If, however, he wishes to use the Index for estimating social-class position, a conversion into social-class terms is necessary. This can be done in any one of several different ways, as will be described more fully in Chapter 8. As an illustration, the conversion data developed for Jonesville are given in Table 1.

TABLE 1

SOCIAL-CLASS EQUIVALENTS FOR I.S.C. RATINGS, JONESVILLE

Weighted Total of Ratings	Social-Class Equivalents
12–17	Upper Class
18–22	Upper Class probably, with some possibility of Upper-Middle Class
23–24	Intermediate: either Upper or Upper-Middle Class
25–33	Upper-Middle Class
34–37	Indeterminate: either Upper-Middle or Lower-Middle Class
38–50	Lower-Middle Class
51–53	Indeterminate: either Lower-Middle or Upper-Lower Class
54–62	Upper-Lower Class
63–66	Indeterminate: either Upper-Lower or Lower-Lower Class
67–69	Lower-Lower Class probably, with some possibility of Upper-Lower Class
70–84	Lower-Lower Class

It will be seen that in Jonesville the individual whose I.S.C. was computed at 29 points would very probably be in the upper-middle class. Data to indicate the degree of confidence which can be placed in this estimate are given in detail in Chapters 11, 12, and 13.

RELATIONSHIP BETWEEN E.P. AND I.S.C.

Two different methods of social analysis have been described very briefly in this chapter; full instructions for their use will be presented in greater detail in later chapters. While it will be shown that persons scoring high on the I.S.C. will almost always participate on a high level in the social-class structure (and have a high E.P. rating), the actual factors being directly measured by the two indices are quite different. The E.P. identifies the social-class group with which the individual actually is found to participate in community living, whereas the I.S.C. rates certain socioeconomic characteristics which, it is thought, (1) play a part in determining what that social-class participation will be and at what level it will occur, and (2) are in part themselves determined by the level of social participation.

Of the two methods, the E.P. is the more basic if social-class analysis is desired, since it is based upon an actual analysis of the social participation and social reputation of individuals in the community. The chief value of the I.S.C., for social-class purposes, is that it can be used to predict with a rather high degree of accuracy what the probable social-class participation (on an E.P. basis) will be and that it can be secured with less expenditure of time and money and with less highly trained personnel than is required for the E.P. process.

Actually, the E.P. and the I.S.C. can well be used to supplement each other. Preliminary use of the I.S.C. may make the interviewing for the E.P. simpler and more valid. This is particularly true in large metropolitan communities where the securing of a satisfactory sample of individuals for E.P. interviewing is a problem. The I.S.C. range from 12 to 84 can soon be established and a sufficient sample for each level quickly acquired. The establishment of this range gives great certainty to the researcher in that he has a representative sample of the status levels and, at the same time, reduces the problem of sampling when it is impossible to study all of the individuals in a community. Once the range has been worked out, subsequent spot interviewing can determine the general social-class levels by establishing the relation to their class position of the several points on the range of the I.S.C.

The use of the E.P. and I.S.C. methods, as we have said, gives the scientist a clear understanding of social class in a community and the place of any individual or family in this status structure. From one point of view, the use of E.P. alone gives the analyst the evaluated social participation of a community as it is categorized into the levels which comprise the social classes of the city. From another, the combined results of the E.P. and I.S.C. methods produce a larger configuration which gives a more rounded view of the class order for it includes both participation and the evaluation of it as well as the status characteristics.

No attempt has been made to make this introductory chapter complete in itself. Many special procedures and limiting qualifications have been omitted at this point for the sake of simplicity of presentation of the main ideas of the two procedures for social analysis. The instructions in the later chapters, dealing with each of the methods, should be read carefully by anyone interested in actually using either or both of the procedures.

Chapters 3 through 7 deal with the six techniques of the Evaluated Participation method and include a sample analysis of a case interview. Chapters 8 and 9 present the instructions and other material needed by anyone who is contemplating use of the Index of Status Characteristics. Chapters 10 through 14 describe the process by which the Index of Status Characteristics was developed in the study of Jonesville and present evidence as to its validity for estimating social-class position and further information on how to use it.

SPECIAL READINGS

This chapter is supplemented by the readings listed below: knowledge of E.P. is increased by the references to publications on symbols, meaning, and social interconnection; of I.S.C., by reference to how house type, area, occupation, and other economic factors relate to social class.

W. Lloyd Warner and Paul S. Lunt. *The Social Life of a Modern Community*. Vol. I, "Yankee City Series." New Haven: Yale University Press, 1941.

See pages 239-251 for material on the relation of the house type to social class; on dwelling area, pages 227-238; and occupation, pages 261-267. There are many other economic characteristics also analyzed in this volume (see Appendix). For Institutional Membership, see pages 301-365.

W. Lloyd Warner and Leo Srole. *The Social Systems of American Ethnic Groups*. Vol. III, "Yankee City Series." New Haven: Yale University Press, 1945.

See pages 33-102 for additional material on area and occupation.

C. K. Ogden and I. A. Richards. *The Meaning of Meaning*. New York: Harcourt, Brace & Co., 1936.

Contains background material on the analysis of symbols and meaning used in all interviews. A fundamental work on which the analysis of Evaluated Participation is, in part, based.

Part Two

INSTRUCTIONS FOR USING EVALUATED PARTICIPATION

CHAPTER 3

Rating by Matched Agreements of Social-Class Configurations

THE rating called Matched Agreements is based on an explicit effort by the informant to give an over-all status schema or Social-Class Configuration for the whole community. Research experience has shown that many observant and intelligent people in a town possess this knowledge as part of their adaptive equipment and can communicate it readily enough. It is a most satisfactory and rewarding technique to the status analyst.

The analytical operations connected with the technique of Matched Agreements are not difficult. There are four steps: (1) rank orders are abstracted from the interviews of those who contributed this kind of information; (2) by use of a table (see page 64) the several levels of each informant are compared for agreement and disagreement to establish, first, the class system of the community; (3) the names of citizens assigned to the several classes are compared for the amount of agreement among the rank orders in placing people; and (4) the agreements and disagreements for the several levels are counted to determine the degree of consistency in placement. If the agreement is high for placing people it indicates that the social-class system is a social construct operating generally in the community, giving its people a workable and consistent scheme for ranking those who live there. Moreover, the last procedure adds greater certainty to the analyst's construction of the class order of the city he is studying.

THE SOCIAL-CLASS CONFIGURATION OF A SUBSTANTIAL CITIZEN

The Social-Class Configuration (rank order) of a substantial citizen, Mr. Smith Brown, will be presented first. His description of the class structure of Jonesville and most of the other descriptions given in this section provide evidence that at least some of the people composing a most varied sample are highly conscious of the presence of a class order and think of it in terms of the status configuration which includes everyone. The present interview was made in the informant's home and recorded by the field worker while the informant spoke.

It will be apparent that the interviewer knew Mr. Smith Brown very well. A brief comment on the relationship is necessary to understand the interview. The first contacts with Mr. Brown were for research purposes; later, he became a friend and performed professional services for the interviewer. He was an excellent informant because his family had been in the community for a long time, he was interested in what made the wheels of the community go around, he had had college training, and under proper circumstances he was willing to tell what he knew.

"Since I made that crack about class to you the other day, Bill," Brown said, "I've done a lot of thinking about this class business. First thing, I want to say there's no use talking about people being in a certain class and in a certain portion of a class unless they are accepted by the people in that group as equals. If they are not accepted, they just don't belong. So acceptance is what I'm going to use, along with family, character, and money.

"Let's start with the top level and then work down. Now, I won't be able to tell you about everybody or the whole thing, but what I will do, Bill, is to tell you the main class groups and the main sections in some of these classes, and I will give you the illustrations and then tell you something about each one of these illustrations.

"The society class around here is the 400 class. In the main, it's rooted right over there in the Federated Church. It comes from the Federated Church. Now, Bill, a lot of these people are 398's, but they think they're 400's. With a few exceptions, no one who's not in the Federated Church is in this class."

Brown listed a large number of families and gave the reasons for their enjoying top status. Only a few of them will be mentioned.

"The Volmers from top to bottom are in; the Friedricks from top to bottom are in; the Caldwells—all of them are in. Now, there's a case of two families getting together and keeping the money in the family. You know, Ted Caldwell married the Volmers girl. As far as I can figure out, that was pretty well arranged by the old folks. You know, here for years, the Caldwells and Volmers have been close business associates. They worked out a lot of deals together."

Brown then listed some more families who belonged. Then he said, "Now, here's an example of a big boost up, Mrs. A. B. Henderson. Now, Mrs. A. B. Henderson is in and her daughter's family is in. . . . I'm going to tell you some details on that just so you can get the picture. . . . Don't get the idea I am just gossiping for gossip's sake. I am giving you the facts so that you will be able to fit in the picture. Now, Mrs. A. B. Henderson was clerk in a store here in town before her marriage. She married A. B. Henderson. The Hendersons were in around here, and they have been in [the 400] for a long time. . . . Oh, yes, she was a Stillwell. She has some sisters around here and some brothers who were down there, and they stayed there. They have never done anything.

"Some of the Stocktons do and some of them don't [belong to the upper class]. You've always got to make a division in the Stocktons." Then he said, "Here are the Stocktons who don't. . . . Mrs. Helen Cross, she doesn't. Now, she is Carl Stockton's sister, but she's not in. Now, there's the case of a girl who married down and stayed there. I'll have several illustrations of people who jump up or down because of marriage."

Brown continued to name families and constellations of intermarried families that were in the 400 of Jonesville, most of them having been there for several generations.

"I think that's just about all the society class. There may be one or two that I have overlooked, but that's all I can think of.

"The next class down is what we call the fringe of society around here." Brown then named a number of people who were downward mobile from the elite or had never been accepted. We will discuss their unhappy lot later. "The fringe of this thing has a lot of families on it who have had money and lost it.

"The Robert Claytons were former members of the 400, but they failed in business and he was dropped. Oh, hell, he got to owing everybody around town, and he just wasn't worth a damn, and they just got left out of things. Mrs. Tom Cooper and her sister, Mrs. Henry Gardner, are on the fringe, too. Mrs. Gardner is a nice person, but she had a cousin, Everett Roberts. He never was in. He was just a no-good-so-and-so. . . . They both inherited a lot of money. Hell, they both just ran through it. Just phlooey. Just threw it away. . . . Everett was no good from the beginning. . . . He was just never accepted. Just as I told you, the whole thing is based on money, but it isn't money alone. You've got to have the right family connections, and you've got to behave yourself, or you get popped out.

"Now, the Halls are another family who were never in. They never did move in that set, but they had a hell of a lot of money at one time. Old man Hall was never liked around here. I don't know just what it was, but he was just excluded. Oh, if they had big parties or something, they might invite him; but they were never accepted by the society class."

After naming a large number of families, he then said, "Then, there was the Adams family. . . . Arthur was the black sheep of the Adams family. He was just a wastrel; he never amounted to anything. . . . Now, Henry was a nice fellow, but he was tighter than hell. He was too niggardly and pinch-penny to be in. He could have been in the fringe, but he just didn't spend on anything.

"The next stratum starts with the fringe and takes in certain other elements. This is what you'd better call the upper-middle class. This level is made up mainly of the women who dominate the Country Club, along with some other groups, especially the top and the fringe. The top dominates the Country Club; at least they are in, but they're not active. They're the ones who, you might say, are behind the scenes and really control things. The fringe is pretty active, and this group of women are active, too. The women in this group just seem to split a gut to do things right. It's amusing as hell. We used to belong to the Country Club, but we don't any more. This Country Club is, of course, quite cosmopolitan. It's got a lot of people in it and diverse elements. Anybody who thinks he can afford to get in and play golf, and so on. But it's this bunch of women who really dominate the club and keep the activities going, although I'm pretty damned sure they don't have as much say-so in it as they think they do.

"Now, here are some illustrations of the people at this level." He then named quite a number of people who were safely in this position.

At an appropriate moment, the interviewer asked, "Well, now, Brown, where are you going to put yourself?"

Brown replied, "Hell, leave that out. Although we associate with this group most of the time, just leave me out of it. If you're putting me in, this [upper-middle-class clique] is where we belong.

But just leave me out of it, and you can make up your mind where we belong.

"Now, here is another group that's all about at this same level, and my wife and I are in this group some of the time. It's not in a different class from the others. Now, we don't have any money, and our being included in these groups is due wholly to my professional position and the fact that my wife and I belong to several good organizations. Hell, if it weren't for them we wouldn't be in anything."

Mr. Smith Brown had been previously placed in the class hierarchy by the research. Unlike many people, particularly the upper-middle class, he had scrupulously refrained from giving himself a higher status than he enjoyed and had precisely located himself in the position assigned him by others in the community and by the research.

"Well, now, that's about enough, Bill, of that middle-class group. That's not all of them. There are big gaps in there. But that will give you some idea of the people who are in it around here.

"Now, we come to the working class. The working class is made up of good, solid people who live right but they never get any place. They never get in real trouble. They are the ones who work down at The Mill and the other factories. They are the ones who work around as clerks in the stores, own little trucks and maybe little businesses. . . . These neighborhood grocers, and so on."

When Mr. Brown reached the level of what he called the working class, the number of names which he specifically listed was smaller than the others, demonstrating that in all probability he had closer affiliation with the upper-middle and upper classes and that he was more interested in them. However, part of the difficulty was that the hour was growing late, and he said that he would complete the list of names at some other time. But the fact that he made no differentiation between different levels of the working classes indicated that he probably knew less about them.

When he had completed his discussion of that level, he said, "Well, while they're fixing supper for us I just want to mention one more class. Now, this one is really a lulu. These are the families that are just not worth a goddam. Now, they're not immoral—they're not unmoral—they're just plain amoral. They just simply don't have any morals. I'll tell you they just have animal urges, and they just respond to them. They're just like a bunch of rats or rabbits.

"There's the Jones family. My God, that Jones outfit!" Brown gave a case history on the Jones outfit and on a large number of other members of the lower-lower class. "All their kids," he went on to say, "are tougher than hell. They never went any place in school, and they're always getting into jams. Another family that's in the making is that Kraig family. Those poor little kids are half-frozen and ragged all the time, and they come along one after the other. I've seen them go to the store with a nickel or a penny to buy some candy and that type of thing. Every morning they come down to the store and buy five or ten cents' worth of sweet rolls for breakfast.

"Now, another family that's in the same class is the Rain family. They're Kentuckians and, I'll tell you, they're really something. Then, there's the Jackson family that live down south of The River. Well, they're lulus, too. Then, there's that John Harding bunch that live in back of the tannery. Old John Harding and his family have been in more trouble around here than you can really think about. Then, there's the Kilgore family. Old Tom's got four or five girls. They've got into trouble. Some of them are about half-witted, and Harry himself is not any too bright. They aren't worth a damn."

Although the present account does not complete the directory of names which composed Smith Brown's list of people who belonged to the several strata, it does include all of the social classes which he recognizes as existing in Jonesville.

There are at least four of them and possibly five.[1] He first recognizes the 400 or the society crowd. Then, there is the fringe of the society class, which he recognizes as clearly not a part of the upper class, and he sometimes puts it slightly above the upper-middle and sometimes with the upper-middle class. The upper-middle class, with its several segments including those in the several churches and associations such as the Rotary and Country Club, is followed by the working class, which he does not take time to break down into divisions, and last, "the lulus" which, as we will see later, comprise what we will call the lower-lower class.

THE SOCIAL-CLASS CONFIGURATION OF TWO CHURCH MEMBERS

Smith Brown asserts that the churches of Jonesville are graded socially and that the Federated Church, favored by the local 400,

[1] See Table 3, p. 66.

ranks highest, and the others, including the Methodist and Baptist, follow in a serial order of decreasing status. The Pentecostal Church, imported to Jonesville by migrant southern hill people, falls at the lowest depth among the Christian churches. Moreover, Brown, relying on information collected by three generations of his family's residence in Abraham County, boldly states that the families in each of the churches are ranked into superior and inferior levels.

To make sure that Brown knows what he is talking about, and to increase the representativeness of those who speak about status in Jonesville, let us call in two expert witnesses, Mathew Carleton, member of the Federated Church, and John Wesley Withington, member of the Methodist Church, ranked below that of Carleton's.

Carleton, an intelligent, broadly educated man, was discussing the reading habits of the people of Jonesville. In attempting to tell who read the best literature, he said:

"I think generally you can put the people of this town into four groups and rank them socially so those in Group One are highest and those in Group Four are the lowest. In the first group, I would put such people as Mrs. Henry Coolidge and I would put Mrs. Joseph Coolidge in there, too." He then named a number of families who belonged to this level. "Now, all those people do sort of superficial reading, I think. They read light reading and magazines, but they don't do any serious reading. They don't do anything they have to think about much. The people in the top brackets, or the upper class probably, don't read at all. I would say probably the upper-middle class reads the most."

The interviewer asked if he would put the Volmers and Radcliffes in his top group. He said, "I think I would. Of course, I don't believe they read at all. They are so high up they're just social history around here now, and it doesn't matter what they do. They can do anything they want and don't have to worry about what people are going to think of them. They bought up the county early and own most of it. They have been here so long that it really doesn't matter what they do. And they don't care what people think of them because they know their position is all right anyway.

"Of course, I think that that whole group is pretty secure. They don't have to worry much about what other people think of them. But that isn't true of all of them.

"Then, in the second group I would put such people as Mrs.

Anita Gabel and Mrs. Jean Craig. I would say that the first group is more certain of itself than the second group. That second group hasn't gotten so far financially and they still worry about themselves and what people think of them. They're working to get some place, and they have to be more careful of what they do and what people think of them.

"The person I can think of that best typifies the third group is Mrs. Taft. I don't know her first name, but I know she is very active in the Methodist Church. That whole group I would consider as more religious than intelligent, if you know what I mean. They have a lot of principles such as loving each other as Christians even though there's a war on. But they are not very logical about their ideas. They don't think through anything very well. They're just religious."

Mr. Carleton then listed a number of people that belonged to this level.

"Then, the fourth class, well, they're all composed of poorer people, and I'd say they mostly read newspapers. That's just about all they read, I think. I think the husbands of most of them are laborers, or perhaps they have small office jobs. I saw some of them over at a Methodist women's group last night.

"Really, you can say that the first group and the fourth group are alike in a lot of respects. They're both absolutely secure in their positions. That fourth group is sort of at the bottom of the pile, to be crude about it, and they're perfectly secure and perfectly settled in their position. They've resigned themselves to it, and they know they won't get any place. It's only those people that are worrying about getting some place that think about other people's opinion."

Mr. Withington, of the Methodist Church, divides the people of Jonesville into several levels running from the "fancy crowd" he says he does not know to the very poor of the Church of the Nazarene whom he "knows little about."

Mr. Withington will speak for himself.

"If you look around town at all of the prominent and wealthy people, you will find that they all belong to the Federated Church. The Radcliffes, for example, the Lows, the Bascombs, the Bakers, John Madison, the Caldwells, and people like that—they all belong to the Federated Church. But most of them, I think, belong for social reasons. For example, they tell me that Caldwell used to be in the Methodist Church here, but that later he moved over to the Federated Church. He just learned what church it was his place to go to. In another case like that, at least so they tell me, they say that old Stewart Radcliffe's mother and father were in the Methodist Church. Of course, I don't know any of that fancy crowd at all; none of them are in our church, and I have never had occasion to have anything to do with them. Now, the Methodist Church here is primarily a middle-class church, although we do have a lot of poor people, too. But we don't have any of that fancy crowd that is in the Federated Church. You take a look at the prominent people in my congregation. There's Gordon Dalton, the architect, Dr. Newhouse, Forrest King, and Ted Smith—people of that sort. They are our most influential people, but they're all strictly middle class. So you see, we are a notch or two below the Federated Church. The funny part about it is that some of them could buy out three or four of a lot of those people who belong to the Federated Church.

"Now, the Baptist Church, they're a notch or two below us. You see, they have a lot of working people who go to their church. I guess that about the only person of any consequence in the Baptist Church is Paul Little. He's one of the big men at The Mill."

Before interviewing Mr. Withington, the interviewer had had several long discussions with the Baptist minister and learned that many of the Baptists were "Mill people" from the South. He mentioned this to Withington, who replied, "Yes, you see [a little jubilantly] that is why I said they were several notches below us. The Free Methodists," he continued, "don't amount to much. We don't see their pastor around very much. Their minister does pretty well though. He does remarkably well considering that he has no education and no background. He hasn't got much of anything. And, of course, you know there's the Gospel Tabernacle down here on Washington Street. They're very poor people with a persecution complex. I don't know very much about them. Then, there's the Church of the Nazarene. I think that one is even more radical, but I don't know anything about them."

Carleton (of the Federated Church), by listing the people of the upper and upper-middle classes and including only those from the Federated Church, puts his own church above the Methodist. He divides the town into an upper class and an upper-middle level which he separates from the common people. With only two or three exceptions, all the families named by Carleton and Withington as belonging to each of the several social levels agree with the ratings of these same families by Smith Brown. Withington, however, leaves most of the working classes and the very poor out of the Methodist Church and places them in the Baptist and the Free Methodist Churches; but when names are mentioned the correspondence between the class placement of these two church members is almost perfect.

The churches with large memberships and a variety of activities in community affairs present us with opportunities to learn what the Jonesvilles of America are like. The evidence in this section clearly demonstrates that the members of the churches are acutely aware of their class differences.

SOCIAL-CLASS CONFIGURATION OF A CITY OFFICIAL

The city government in Jonesville covers all parts of the community and recruits its membership from every segment of the town. Its members know and deal with all classes. The class analyst should secure information from them.

We will hear first from Mr. George Green, long-time resident in the town and a man who has kindred in Withington's "fancy crowd." Mr. Green divides the town into "social strata." These strata are "the top one," composed of old, wealthy families or "new people" who have a lot of money, the "upper-middle class," "a lower but middle stratum," and the "ordinary workmen, mostly ranked as lower class around here," who are not as low as "the canal renters and the older Poles" who are at the "bottom of the social structure." His rating, with few differences, corresponds closely with Smith Brown's and Carleton's.

"You'll find out there's a definite division between the men and the women in the upper stratum in this town. The men are common like us. They'll talk to you at any time. But the women draw the class line, and no one gets over or around it. I can see this just as clearly as I can you.

"We're in a unique position here because of my relation to a couple of families in this group. A cousin of mine married Jim Radcliffe. This relates us to several other people. We've been invited over to their houses to parties a few times, and I'm disturbed at how these people look down at others in town. They have several cliques within the larger stratum. Below this stratum is the one composed of prominent business and professional families. Some of these who have money and family are rated in the top group. However, if they have only family and not much money, they rank in the upper-middle class.

"The small business men and the foremen out at The Mill are in the lower but middle stratum. I mean a lower stratum than the one we have been talking about. I don't know much about their social life, but I know just about where they fit in here in town. The sub-foremen, machinists, several stationary operators, and people like that are in the lowest middle stratum. The ordinary workmen in the foundry and The Mill are mostly ranked as lower class around here. But they're not as low as the older Poles, the canal renters, and the people back of the tannery.

"The Poles and the poor Americans who work in The Mill are on the bottom. These poor Americans and Poles may be working side by side on the same job and getting the same income, but socially they're miles apart. You might say they're each an exclusive group. The several social strata in town are segregated into definite areas, and in each you generally find a class distinction.

"Now, that's about the way that the town is divided. That's the way it looks to me, and I am pretty sure that's the way it is."

Mr. Green's assistant, Mr. Alton, well acquainted with several midwestern communities and distinctly aware of the Who's Who of Jonesville, summarized Mr. Green's detailed statement when he asserted:

"I don't think that we have any more classes here in Jonesville than in any other American community of this size. The classes are not explicit. They're really implicit, if you know what I mean. If you would ask some of these people around here if they had a class system they would say no. They don't recognize themselves that they have one, but, nevertheless, these classes exist. You know, they like to pride themselves on being a democracy, but it's a democracy in word. When it comes to real behavior and social activities and selecting out your friends and so on, it's organized around class."

Before comparing the rankings of the several informants to ascertain how much correspondence there is among them, another kind of evidence is needed to round out the testimony about status in Jonesville. Until now, the witnesses have all been adult men and above the Common Man level. It might well be said that they are biased and, as older people and as males, feel the pleasant reward of looking down on those they put beneath them. This seems sufficiently cogent and valid criticism to inquire about what the younger people and men and women from the lower classes have to say about social class in Jonesville.

THE SOCIAL-CLASS CONFIGURATION OF AN ADOLESCENT GIRL

Americans generally believe that young people are more democratic than adults—that they are not aware of, and care nothing about, class distinctions. The present research indicates that this is not true or, at least, is not true categorically. Alice Little, the daughter of a substantial citizen of Jonesville, will tell about her experience with status and her understanding of the Jonesville class system.

"There's not supposed to be classes in this town, but actually there are," she said. "There's a higher class, and then there's a middle class, and then there's a lower class. Then, there are those in between. Well, families like us are in between the higher class and the middle class. We're not exactly middle class, and we're not higher class.

"Income, I guess, is the main thing in class, but—well, it's more than that, too. Part of it is the way you use your money, and the way that you act, and what you do in town. The things that you are in and stuff like that."

She divided the middle class into three levels—an upper, a middle, and a lower one. Her upper-middle people were the same as those listed by Mr. Smith Brown. She placed John Madison and his family in the same level as her own, in between the upper and the middle classes. She said, "Well, the Madisons belong with us. They are equal; they are just like we are. They've got money, and they've got a nice place. They're in community things."

However, the other people that she placed in her own class were those whom Smith Brown had put in the upper-middle and who, incidentally, our own research concluded were in the upper-middle class. We placed the family of the young lady who was our informant in the upper-middle class. All the people in the community who are informants on the class position of her family put them in the upper-middle class. The young lady, like most people, had in her own thoughts tried to lift her family to a higher position. To ascertain how well she had conceptualized her several levels, she was asked to describe each of them. Her descriptions, while in a different language from Smith Brown's, since they come from a young person talking to an older one and from a woman talking to a man, are not dissimilar from his.

"The kids in the lowest class," she said, "have to quit school and go to work. Well, let me see, then the kids are always away from home. They don't stay home much. They are out on the streets or they're wandering around somewhere. Besides, they are probably getting into trouble. Then, we judge them by the neighborhood that they live in. Anyway, the place they live in. We judge them by the appearance of their homes—how it is on the outside and how it is on the inside, by their furniture. This low class has very dirty homes. They don't seem to take any interest in the home. It's just some place to sleep and maybe eat. They're different in their recreation. They're not in the clubs in town. They're not in the churches. They drink a lot. This gang goes to the low-class taverns. They're always getting into fights. I guess that's about all.

"Now, the high-lower-class families—well, they usually keep their homes clean. They have a better type of home. They live in a better neighborhood. But they're not connected with clubs or churches. They don't stick around home either, but they keep their clothes better. They're neat and clean, but they don't have very much money.

"The low-middle-class families live in nice homes. They always keep their homes clean. They always have a neat yard. They may have a car, and they keep it in good shape. Their clothes are always okay. The husband, though, usually doesn't have any too good a job.

"You will find the higher classes and the lower ones don't have good family understanding. The middle class, though, has good adjustment between the members of the family, and the families are all pretty close together. The middle-middle class go to church. They're the leaders in the community. They belong to the clubs. Their kids go to school. They live in nice homes. They drink some, but they don't let the kids have it. In the high-middle class, the men and women belong to clubs. They belong to service clubs like Rotary, and the women to clubs like the Women's Club."

When she describes her own level, she uses terms ordinarily applied to the upper-middle class.

"I would say my own class belonged to churches and all the church clubs and the big clubs in town. We help in the Red Cross drives and things like that. There's a lot of community leadership here. We help any kind of association like the Boy Scouts and Girl Scouts. We associate with all classes but are careful of our friends. There's another thing about this group. The whole family doesn't have a good understanding of each other. They just seem to go their own ways—each one for himself and herself. There's little companionship in the family. The children have a better understanding with their father than with their mother. Dad and I get along just like that. [She grinned and held up her middle finger and index finger.] This class has nice homes, quite a bit of money. Most of them have two cars and belong to the Country Club.

"Now, the higher class, the Number One Class, I guess you'd call it. Well, they belong to churches, but they don't go very much. They just donate to everything in town. They don't have good family understanding. These people are in all the leading groups. They don't associate with the lower classes if they can help it. They associate with my class. This class drinks at its parties, but they don't go to bars to get it. They have it at home. They drink with the children in the family, too, but the children don't go out and get drunk—I don't know why.

"Most of them go to college. Most of the professional people and practically all of the bigger business people come from these classes [the top two]. I don't know why, but you just start looking at the town, and you'll see it's that way." [2]

The testimony of Miss Little clearly demonstrates that at least some of the high-school children are class-conscious and believe themselves capable of designating a number of class levels in Jonesville. Miss Little is from a level above the Common Man; testimony must be heard from the lower class of Jonesville.

THE CLASS SYSTEM AS SEEN BY A MILL LABORER

Mr. Tolman, a semi-skilled mill laborer and father of three children, is bitterly aware of the class differences. He is at the bottom

[2] See Chapters 8-14, which present statistics on occupation and other characteristics of the I.S.C.

of the Common Man level. He sees class as purely a matter of income and power. He draws a distinction between powerful landowners and wealthy industrialists and professional people, but he puts all of them at the top. Below the top, he sees a level of common people, of poor people like himself, and of poorer people below his family. His class lines are less clearly drawn than those of the others, but his feelings about status are deep and powerful for he has felt the punishing effect of it on his children and sees it operating in his own life.

"We are poor, but we are not as poor as a lot of people. Since I got this job down at The Mill, we've been doing all right. All this end of town is full of poor people. But I suppose the poorest people live on the far side of the railroad tracks.

"The Federated Church has more money in it than any other church in town, but it doesn't have so many members. Most of these old, landed families around here and some of the wealthy people belong to the Federated Church. The Methodist Church, I guess, has the next greatest number of wealthy people. That's where we go now. It's a good church. Poor people go to the Free Methodist. Maybe I shouldn't say the poorest people. There's the Church of God that's located down on West Washington over the furniture store or one of those places. They just have a room. I suppose you would say the poorest people go there."

Mr. Tolman conceives of power and prestige in terms of people who are "in rings." According to Mr. Tolman, these rings all interlock. "The school board's always on the inside ring. The courthouse ring and the lawyer ring here in town decide who's going to run on the school board. They pick out someone who belongs to their group, and then they run them. It's easy enough for them to always elect the people they want to have in there because practically no one will stop work to go vote in the piddling school election. Do you think that the workers at The Mill are going to take off two or three hours from work and get docked to go out there and vote? No, they stay at their work, and only those who are inside the ring vote.

"The inner ring is organized around the newspaper and the courthouse. Dr. Bowman is probably the leader of it. The banks and the lawyers and the big landowners—they're in on it, too. Dr. Bowman and this newspaper over here run this town.

"My daughter, Rose, and the Volmers girl, the younger one,

were in the eighth grade together. Rose had better grades than the Volmers girl right up to the last month. Then, one of her teachers gave her a B —. There had been some gossip around here that they were going to let that teacher out. Mr. Volmers was on the school board. They gave his girl A's that month. Well, she graduated with highest honors, and our girl was second. They didn't fire the teacher either. In high school Rose was Number One in the graduating class. The Smith boy was Number Two. His father knew some of the big people in town; I don't. They recommended him for the scholarship. Just think, those people kept my girl from having four years of college. The last year something about the same thing happened. Karl Schmidt and Will Madison were pretty close together in scholarship. Karl really had the best grades, and I know because I've seen them. Will's dad was a big politician and connected with the school board. He's in the lawyer ring around town. They recommended Will Madison for the scholarship. He's now in college. And Karl Schmidt, he's working down here at The Mill for about $18 or $20 a week. I don't think he'll go to college. You see, his father is a mechanic, and he can't afford to go. He's just about like us. You see, that's the way things go around here. If you're inside the ring, you're all right, but if you're outside, they keep you out."

Let us briefly review the instructions, with their several steps, necessary for using the Matched Agreement technique. To demonstrate the use of this technique, significant materials have been taken from a number of interviews which present Social-Class Configurations from upper-middle, lower-middle, and upper-lower informants, distributed from the top to the bottom of the status system.[3]

(1) Interviews which contain such schemata are taken from informants from several class levels, from the two sexes, from the old and the young, and from several occupational groups. Such a distribution of informants provides status information which largely checks itself and makes it likely that agreement among the informants assures the status analyst that the social-class system derived from their statements is reliable and an ever-present and all-pervasive social reality. (2) The class levels and their designations from each informant are next determined and charted; and

[3] Informants from the other two classes were available and used in the larger study of Jonesville. Similar interviews have been gathered from other communities. Social-Class Configurations for males and females, adults and adolescents, as well as the members of several occupations, have been included in the sample presented here.

each class level, for purposes of comparison and distinguishing between class levels and grades within a class, is given a serial number. Each informant, when using rating by Social-Class Configuration, always gives a list of names as examples of the several status levels; this leads to step three. (3) These names are then compared for agreement and disagreement on class placement. This helps the analyst align the class levels among the several schemata of his informants and gives him validation of his own conceptualization of class. To do this, the names on each informant's list are placed on a master list which contains all the names as well as their class placement by each informant. (4) Finally, each name with its class placement by a given informant is *paired* with its class placement by another informant and the amount of agreement and disagreement among the pairs counted. For example, when Informant A puts Mr. Smith in the upper-middle class and Informant B also places him there, such a pair is counted as one agreement. Should Informant C place Mr. Smith in upper-middle, this would amount to three pairs of agreements (A + B, B + C, and A + C). But should Informant C put Smith in lower-middle, he would disagree and, therefore, the count on pairs of agreements and disagreements on Smith's class position would be one pair of agreements (A + B) and two pairs of disagreements (C + A, C + B). Table 2 (page 64) gives the results of such a count for the ten informants used here. These ten class configurations and the names listed are not selected because of any factor except that they are good examples for illustrating rating by Matched Agreements as a method of determining the social-class system of a given community.

The amount of agreement and disagreement among several judges on the names common to two or more lists and their class placement found in each list is a good measurement of how pervasive the social-class system is, how well people are socially classed by their fellow townsmen, and how accurately the judges can socially class their fellow citizens and themselves. If only pure chance were involved in the placement of the names into the five categories, the amount of agreement between two or more judges about the class placement of any individual would be quite small.

The class placements of the names in the lists of the ten judges in Table 2 were compared to determine the amount of agreement and disagreement among them. There was a total of 340 individuals

TABLE 2

MASTER LIST OF AGREEMENTS AND DISAGREEMENTS

INFORMANT:		GREEN	CARLETON	WHITE	BROWN	BLACK	TOWNE	BALL	RIVES	WITHING-TON	LITTLE	TOTAL (D)	TOTAL (A)
Total No. Families		15	18	44	122	31	11	37	19	16	27		340
Green	A*	0	0	9	11	7	5	10	7	7	5		61
(profession)	D†	0	0	0	1	0	0	0	0	0	0	1	
Carleton	A	0	0	5	6	3	0	5	2	0	1		22
(profession)	D	0	0	0	1	0	0	0	0	1	0	2	
White	A	9	5	0	30	20	7	24	14	7	6		122
(merchant)	D	0	0	0	6	0	0	0	0	0	1	7	
Brown	A	11	6	30	0	22	11	34	17	9	16		156
(merchant)	D	1	1	6	0	2	0	1	0	2	0	13	
Black	A	7	3	20	22	0	4	14	13	3	5		91
(accountant)	D	0	0	0	2	0	0	0	0	1	1	4	
Towne	A	5	0	7	11	4	0	8	6	4	8		53
(politician)	D	0	0	0	0	0	0	0	0	0	0	0	
Ball	A	10	5	24	34	14	8	0	11	7	7		120
(laborer)	D	0	0	0	1	0	0	0	0	1	0	2	
Rives	A	7	2	14	17	13	6	11	0	4	7		81
(farm expert)	D	0	0	0	0	0	0	0	0	1	0	1	
Withington	A	7	0	7	9	3	4	7	4	0	4		45
(profession)	D	0	1	0	2	1	0	1	1	0	2	8	
Little	A	5	1	6	16	5	8	7	7	4	0		59
(school girl)	D	0	0	1	0	1	0	0	0	2	0	4	
Total	A	61	22	122	156	91	53	120	81	45	59		810
	D	1	2	7	13	4	0	2	1	8	4	42	

*A—Agreements
†D—Disagreements

in the ten lists. Some of the names were mentioned twice and others were mentioned only once (were on but one list). The names listed by each judge were selected by him from the many thousands of people who live in Jonesville. All things considered, the amount of duplication is surprisingly high. There were 426 pairs of "mentions" (from each of the two judges of a pair and when counted as in Table 2, it "doubles" the count of agreements and disagreements). We found overwhelming agreement: there were 405 pairs of agreements and 21 disagreements; 95 per cent of the names were in agreement, and only 5 per cent in disagreement. Clearly a well-defined set of status criteria and status categories guided their individual judgments and clearly these informants are conscious of class.

A careful inspection of Table 2 reveals an eloquent story about the use of rating by Matched Agreements for establishing the class position of an individual or family. The totals at the bottom of each column give the number of times each judge agreed or disagreed with all others. The figures in each square give the number of agreements and disagreements a judge had with one other judge. The totals range all the way from Towne, who had 53 agreements and no disagreements, through Rives and Green, with ratios of 81 to 1 and 61 to 1, to Withington, with 45 agreements and 8 disagreements. The ratios run: 53-0, 81-1, 61-1, 60-1, 23-1, 17-1, 15-1, 12-1, 11-1, and 6-1.

We can be sure, from an inspection of these figures, that class-consciousness exists, and we can have confidence that the rating system of a community is a vital and important social reality in the lives of its people.

The comparison of the placements of the judges is helpful in guiding the field worker in the selection of his class informants. Withington and Carleton, rather new to the community but well aware of social class, are not too sure of their judgments because they have yet to learn all that they need to know about particular families to place them correctly. Yet their judgments are still fairly reliable, and none of their placements was off more than one class. On the other hand, Mr. Towne, born and bred in Jonesville, knowing almost everyone in the community and meeting most of them every day, is highly accurate. Smith Brown, two generations in Jonesville, had a lower score than he deserved because six of his disagreements were with White, a comparative newcomer less sure

TABLE 3

Master List of Social-Class Configurations

	Class:	Carleton (church member)	Withington (church member)	Davis (doctor)	Little (school girl)	Brown (teacher)	Towne (politician)	
Above the Common Man	I. U	Group One—the highest People so high up they're social history around here People who feel secure	The fancy crowd The wealthy and prominent Federated Church people	The 400 The Society Class The 398's who think they're 400's Federated Church people	The High Class The No. I Class	Upper stratum People with family and money	The Top Families The Federated Church people	U
	II. UM	Group Two People who are working to get somewhere	Strictly middle-class People a notch or two below the fancy crowd	The fringe of society - - - - - - The upper-middle class - - - - - -	My class Second highest class - - - - - - Higher-middle - - - - - - Middle-middle	"Upper-middle"	The solid people but don't go in for social things The Methodist Church	UM
Common Man	III. LM	Third Group More religious than intelligent	Working people "Baptists"	The working class ↓	Low-middle	Lower, but middle status	The plain, common people Like most of the Baptists	LM
	IV. UL	The Fourth Group At the bottom of the pile ↓	Very low People with a persecution complex ↓		Higher-lower	Lower class	The little people The real poor people, but honest and fine	UL
Below the Common Man	V. LL			The lulus People just like animals, not worth a damn	The lowest class	Canal renters Older Poles The people back of the tannery	The poor, but not respectable	LL

TABLE 3 (*Continued*)

	Class:	Other Informants	
Above the Common Man	I. U	A group founded on wealth and ancient family People who look down on everyone else in town Snobs The silk stockings The landed gentry The aristocrats The Mainstreeters	
	II. UM	Not in the top group, but good substantial people The level just below the top group Prominent but not tops The strivers People who are in everything The community leaders Working hard to get in the 400 Above average but not tops	
Common Man	III. LM	Average people Ordinary people Working people, but superior Top of the working people Not poor and not well off Good common people	People with nice families but don't rate socially Nobodies (socially) but nice People just below the Country Club crowd Top of the common people
	IV. UL	The Mill people The poor but honest Poor people but nothing the matter with them The little people The younger Poles Poor but hard working Poor but respectable "We're poor [UL] but not as poor as a lot of people [LL]"	
Below the Common Man	V. LL	The poor and unfortunate The chronic reliefers Tobacco road Poor whites Hill-billies River rats	Peckerwoods Dirty and immoral (Those who) live like pigs People who scrape the bottom Goddamn yellow hammers

of his judgments, and three were with the two less expert and more recently arrived church members. If these were removed his score would have been excellent. A good judge ordinarily is someone who has been in the community all of his life, who thinks about the people in his town in status terms, and who has a vocation that relates him to all social levels.

To provide greater efficiency in obtaining lists from several informants with the same names on them, the field worker can prepare a list himself and redirect them to several informants for their judgments about the class levels of those listed.

We have presented the conceptions of the Jonesville class system of a few people who range from near the top to close to the bottom of the social heap in Jonesville. Throughout all their statements, there is the constant theme of social inequality and class difference. All of them recognize several classes. The status levels outlined by them are in general agreement. Perhaps the most critical and decisive proof of the general recognition of class in Jonesville is that all those who mention names not only place a large number of the same families but place these families in the same classes.

The chances that this agreement among them is purely individualistic and not a well-recognized social phenomenon are very few. It seems highly probable that the citizens of Jonesville know and think about class behavior and that this knowledge is one of the basic guides to proper and adaptive behavior for all of them.

The classes recognized in the Social-Class Configurations just reviewed have been placed in Table 3; class placements from other configurations have been added, including a politician's, and two columns from several other informants are also given. The two left-hand columns present the five class levels with the identifications given each class by the research; and the remaining columns, the class configurations of our informants.

All agree that there is an upper class. Some call it "Number One" or "The Top Class." Others describe it as "The 400" or "Fancy Crowd." But all recognize its existence. All of them clearly identify an upper-middle class, and several actually refer to it by this term, resting just below the top crowd and above the common run of men in Jonesville. Some of them divide it into grades, just as a few of them rank "The 400" into sub-levels.

All of these distinguish between the upper-middle and lower-middle classes, and most of them between the lower-middle and upper-lower classes. The two church members failed to distinguish between the upper-lower and lower-lower classes. It is possible that further interviewing of them might have demonstrated they were well aware of the differences, but that they were confining their attention to the dominant class differences among the churchgoers. A cross-section chart tells a vivid story about any given class. For example, the lower-middle people are said to be "top of the common people," "Baptists," "people with nice families who don't rate," "lower-middle class," "the working class," "people who are more religious than intelligent"; whereas the upper-middle are said to be "good, substantial people, but not in the top group," "a notch or two below the fancy crowd," "people who are working to get somewhere," and "above average, but not tops." The people in the lower-lower class, clearly marked and distinct, are called "people who live like animals," "people who live like pigs," "chronic reliefers," "tobacco roaders," "lulus," "the poor and unfortunate," and by many other terms of derogation.

The informants who give these Social-Class Configurations are explicitly class-conscious, and their presence in a society clearly demonstrates the existence of a class system; but class consciousness, as a critical concept for determining the presence or absence of social class, is largely unsatisfactory. More often than not, its use causes confusion and error. The term has more than one reference; the latter half of it, consciousness, may mean that an individual is explicitly conscious of class, that his behavior indicates the consciousness of class differences, and, consequently, that he makes such distinctions in his daily life in categorizing people. On the other hand, it may mean that the individual is not explicitly conscious of class differences but is implicitly aware of them and acts accordingly. Such a person sometimes actually denies the existence of class. Is such a person "conscious of class" or not, and, if he isn't, must we thereby deny the existence of class in his society even if others like him should agree verbally with him? Obviously, it would be nonsense and poor science to do so.

Few, if any, of the young children of our society are explicitly "class conscious"; yet their evaluations of their fellows show them to be naively applying class-determined evaluations. Indeed, one implicitly aware of class and unconscious of it in our status system may be dominated by class values more than one who is explicitly aware of it and can often control some of the influences of class motivation. The adult explicitly aware of class is less likely to judge all of the actions of an individual by class judgments than a child who unconsciously uses them in his judgments of his peers.

CHART II
THE FIVE SOCIAL CLASSES

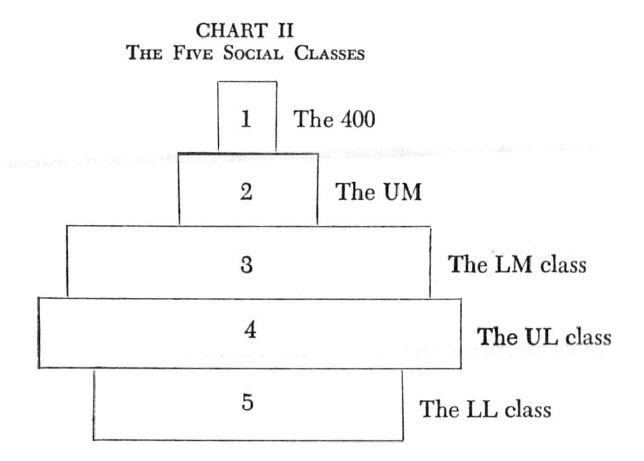

It is useful to the analyst for him to draw a diagram representing the position of the several classes. Chart II expresses the relative size and relative formation of the several classes abstracted from the information gathered from the summary of Social-Class Configurations in Tables 2 and 3. It is a representation of how the technique operates with status evidence. This chart is an over-all schema and not particularistic; it deals with categories of class more than with the placement of specific individuals.

SPECIAL READINGS

Social-Class Configurations are social maps of the informant's understanding of the social stratification of his city. As such they are evaluated schemes of who is, and who is not, who. To further his knowledge about these matters, the reader will be rewarded by reading:

Allison Davis, Burleigh B. Gardner, and Mary R. Gardner. *Deep South.* Chicago: University of Chicago Press, 1941. Pp. 3-59.

John Dollard. *Caste and Class in a Southern Town.* New Haven: Yale University Press, 1937. Pp. 99-187.

James West (pseud.). *Plainville, U.S.A.* New York: Columbia University Press, 1945. Pp. 115-141.

To understand rating by Matched Agreements certain readings from other societies are immensely valuable.

Ruth Benedict. *The Chrysanthemum and the Sword.* Boston: Houghton Mifflin Co., 1946.

Gives the action and value systems of Japan.

W. Lloyd Warner. *A Black Civilization.* New York: Harper & Bros., 1937.

See pages 244-411 for a detailed analysis of the Social-Class Configurations and symbolic structure of the religion of a primitive tribe.

The following three publications provide techniques for analyzing children's class beliefs and feelings.

H. Hartshorne and M. A. May. *Studies in Deceit.* Vol. I, *Studies in the Nature of Character.* New York: Macmillan Co., 1928.

Bernice L. Neugarten. "Social Class and Friendship among School Children." *American Journal of Sociology,* LI, No. 4 (January, 1946), 305-13.

J. L. Moreno. *Who Shall Survive?* Monograph No. 58. New York: Nervous and Mental Disease Pub. Co., 1934.

CHAPTER 4

Techniques of Symbolic Placement, Status Reputation, Comparison, and Simple Assignment

THE techniques of rating by Symbolic Placement, Status Reputation, Comparison, and Simple Assignment to a class are more often concerned with the placement of individuals and families than with locating class levels; however, they sometimes function in this latter capacity particularly to supplement the informant's use of rating by Matched Agreements or Institutional Membership.

SYMBOLIC PLACEMENT

Informants often refer to the social place of another individual by Symbolic Placement,[1] which can be divided conveniently into three common types: (1) symbolism by structure, (2) symbolism by region, and (3) symbolism by social traits.

Symbolism by structure includes such expressions as "The Cabot Lowell family," "the Astorbilts," or "the low-down John Doe tribe" (family and kinship symbols), and similar structural expressions or references to "the Union League crowd," "the Junior League," or "Garden Club" (association symbols), or "the High-Church Episcopalians." Such usage does not necessarily mean that the individuals participate in a given structure, but is a symbolic device for status placement.

Regional symbolism includes such phrases as "the wrong side of the tracks," "Hill Streeter," "Riverbrooker" or "Back of the Tannery," "Nob Hill," "Main Line," "North Shore," and many others. Every city has its list.

Trait symbolism covers the whole range of our social behavior, but usually only a few such terms are selected for symbolic use in any particular city or region. Often the reference is rather indirect:

[1] See W. Lloyd Warner, *A Black Civilization* (New York: Harper & Bros., 1937), p. 10.

for example, the terms "Yellow Hammer" or "Peckerwood" indicate low status. The yellow hammer or peckerwood is a woodpecker that lives in the piny woods of the South. In these regions it is associated with the "poor whites." Hence the symbolism. "The 400," meaning exclusiveness, is another such term. First invented in New York to indicate the exclusiveness of a relatively small number of people as compared with the vast mass in that metropolis, it was carried to all parts of the country and into such communities as Jonesville where the term is used for an exclusive top class in which there are fewer people than the number indicated. Occupational terms, such as "clam diggers," "ditch diggers," or more personal ones, such as "wool hats" and "high hats," are often used. To exhaust such terms is almost impossible.

At the beginning of a study, Symbolic Placements are particularly useful for placing people and establishing the extremes of high and low status in the community. Such a phrase as "he is one of the Lowells" or "one of the Astors" may be confusing at first to the analyst if he does not know that the person he is trying to place is not a kinsman of the person mentioned. However, when he learns that the Lowell reference means the person being placed is symbolically ranked by the informant as the social equal of the Lowells, it is very revealing and of great value in stratifying the individual in question. Persons may be referred to as "Nob Hillers" even though they do not live on Nob Hill. Such statements as "Smith is a Nob Hiller, but he does not live on Nob Hill" or "Jones lives on Nob Hill, but is *not* a Nob Hiller" tell their own symbolic story about status.

STATUS REPUTATION

Almost all interviews in which the informant talks about a number of people in the community are filled with conscious and unconscious, direct and indirect, references to the Status Reputation of one or more of the people being discussed. Status Reputation covers the whole range of American behavior. Anything which can be evaluated as superior or inferior is utilized. Moral, aesthetic, intellectual, educational, religious, ethnic, and personal behavior, as well as many other categories of social activity, are constantly being used. In reality the person referred to may or may not possess such traits but he is believed to have them and, therefore, they constitute part of his Status Reputation. One man is referred to as dirty, stupid, immoral, illiterate, and generally a low person. Another man is said to be a prominent citizen, active in all civic affairs, well read in the literature of the day, a leader in the Episcopalian church, and generally someone everyone looks up to. Such characterizations are definitely part of a person's Status Reputation. They help place the man. At the same time, they also help place the speaker because such remarks are often reflexive and must be understood in terms of the social position of the person talking. To return to our earlier geographical analogy: if the person doing the placing is in the lowest part of the "topography" he often talks differently about someone on the "plateau" than another informant talking about him from the top of a "mountain peak." Although the information gathered about him from the two will sometimes seem contradictory, each is telling the truth, from where he sees his status world, about the social position of the person under discussion.

The difference between Status Reputation and Symbolic Placement is clearly illustrated by use of Chart III. It must first be noted that Chart III analyzes two parts of the statement, "the society class around here is the 400." "The society class" is a Status Reputation term which refers directly, by use of the concept "highest status in the social system," to such concrete phenomena as: (1) an interactive organization, (2) a kind of highly evaluated behavior, (3) a kind of highly valued social characteristics, as well as, by inference, (4) a group of individuals.

In Chart III, depicting Symbolic Placement, the reference is indirect, and the fit between the term and the direct concept is not present for there is in the literal sense of the word no "400" in Jonesville. "The 400" directly refers to a numerical point in our counting system but indirectly to a relatively small number of individuals; by further reference, to an exclusive top position; and then to the organization, behavior, characteristics, and individuals mentioned for Status Reputation.

A number of examples of Status Reputation are listed below. They include materials from "judges" belonging to the several classes and are about people being judged from higher and lower levels.

The social reputation of upper-lower and lower-lower people will be given by an upper-lower informant. This material is presented to demonstrate how the division is made by Status Reputation between two contiguous classes. A woman is speaking. "Mr. and Mrs.

Dodd are very nice, hard-working people. They raised a family of ten or eleven children. The boys have all turned out to be pretty good workers and average citizens." The upper-lower informant is talking about respectable people who belong in the lower half of the society. She then states, "The girls have all been loose and heavy drinkers. The oldest girl became pregnant before marriage. There

CHART III

TERMS OF SYMBOLIC PLACEMENT AND STATUS REPUTATION

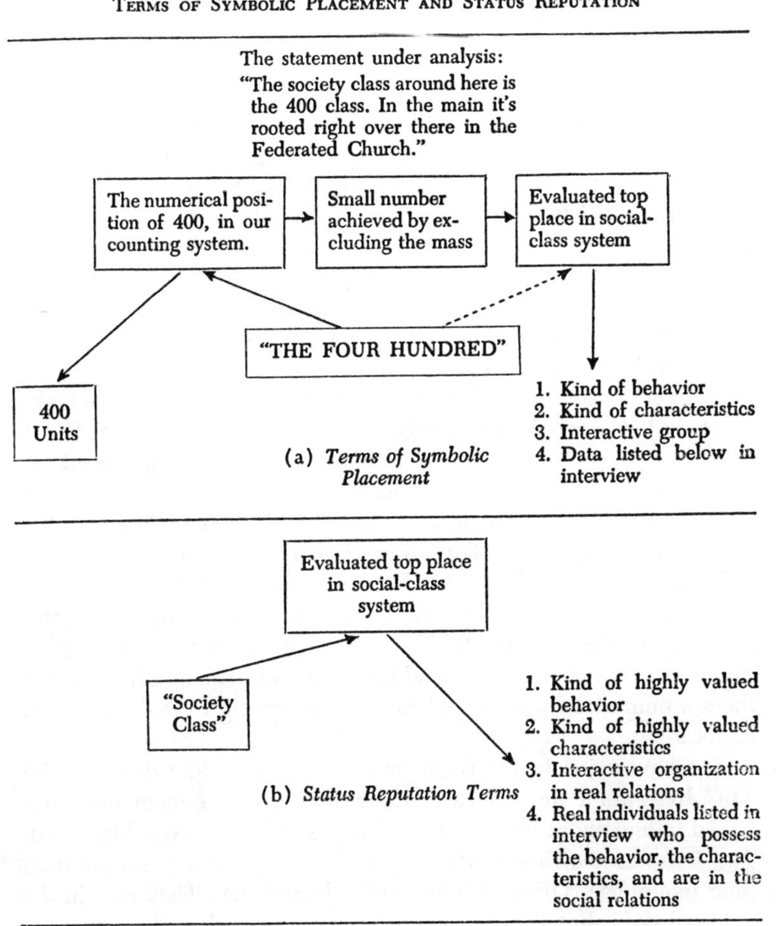

was considerable gossip as to how many men were involved. All the rest of the girls are like her. Ever since she was a young girl, the oldest girl has run around with several men. She's married now. It's a question whether her husband is the father of her child."

The married daughter and her husband are clearly non-respectable—below the upper-lower level. The informant distinguishes between the "nice, hard-working average people" (UL) and the "loose," immoral members (LL) of this kinship group. A comparison of the social reputations of the two parts of the family indicates strongly that by Status Reputation one belongs to the upper-lower class and the other to the lower-lower class.

Mr. Ranney, a minor city official, presents the Status Reputation of some lower-lower people and shows how Status Reputation operates in maintaining class. He was sitting in his office when he was interviewed. He was giving his attention to people of the lower level. His feelings about them are mixed. He says, "The class of people who come in here [lower-lower] aren't worth much. Most of them have been on relief the last ten years. Right now there's a lot of work, and a man can get ninety cents an hour for common labor over at the munitions plant. But ten years from now, I bet, those people will be right back in here.

"Every once in a while you will find someone who tries to make good. But if a family has a relief reputation, it's pretty hard in a town like this to get any place. I always tell these young people to get out of town—go somewhere else where their family is not known and they will have a chance. They don't have any here. You take the Kula family. It's a mess. Those women don't live right. That woman isn't raising those girls right. They never go inside of a church or anything. They're one of the really immoral families we have in this community. Now, this is a family that's got three or four grown girls. The father was in trouble several times around here, and he deserted them a number of years ago. The girls are trying to make an effort to get a job.

"I have tried to get them jobs. Now, the fellow down at the ABC Restaurant needed two girls recently, and I went over and talked to him about putting the Kula girls on, and he wouldn't do it. 'No, I can't have those girls in here,' he said, 'with the reputation their family has. Those girls just better leave town. They can do the work all right, but I just can't have them in my place.'

"I know that those girls are good, steady, honest workers, but they can't get work in this town.

"Now, some of the people aren't worth anything. Others try to help themselves, and they just can't because they have a bad reputation."

Mr. Ranney, a respectable member of the lower-middle class, distinguishes between the "poor but honest worker" who is trying to get off relief and the "chronic reliefers." He listed a large number of families "who are no good." They all belong to Smith Brown's "lulu" level. Our own research concluded they belong to what we call, less expressively, "the lower-lower class."

The study of the Status Reputation of children can be accomplished not only by interviewing but by combining Hartshorne's and May's "Guess Who" technique [2] with Moreno's "Best Friend" technique and relating them to social class analysis.[3] This procedure was followed in the Jonesville study to find out the social reputations of children at different class levels and to learn how children of the several strata use status values for judging their peers. The children were in two age groups, the fifth and sixth grades and the second and third year levels of high school.

Each child was asked to name peers who were good looking and not good looking, who liked and did not like school, who were popular and unpopular, clean and dirty, as well as many other judgments children make about each other, including those they would or would not like for friends. The papers of the judges were coded, permitting us to know the judge and thereby enabling us to establish his class position as well as the class of the person judged.

The results of this procedure give overwhelming proof that ordinary social reputation more often than not is a function of Status Reputation. Ordinarily, the low-status children are rated high for characteristics which are negative and of which the children generally disapprove and low for things the children approve, while the high-status children rank low for negative characteristics and high for those things approved by other children. These same techniques for establishing Status Reputation can be used in adult groups, par-

[2] See Bernice Neugarten, "Family Social Position and the Social Development of the Child" (Ph.D. dissertation, University of Chicago, November, 1943).

[3] See Neugarten, "Social Class and Friendship among School Children," *op. cit.*, and Warner, Havighurst, and Loeb, *Who Shall Be Educated?*, *op. cit.*

ticularly for associations and churches and, in general, among adults in a community where everyone knows everybody else.[4]

The Status Reputation of the upper class is well stated by an upper-middle-class woman in referring to certain families who belong to the upper level:

"I have been thinking about the requirements of being in this [top] group. I think there are two. First, there is no one with less than $5,000-a-year income who could belong to it. All of those who belong in it have a larger income than that except the David Blacks. But most of them come from 'old families' and have made it their business to be in this group. Around here, it's like in New York or Chicago. Only there, to get into the social registry, you have to have an income of $20,000 or more, but here the ante is lower. Yet, you have to have pleasant manners and a gentle countenance. But there's something else, also, because there are a number of people here in town with an income of more than $5,000 and yet they don't rate in the top group. I guess it must be a conformance to a sense of importance because they take it all very seriously; and you have to do things the way they do them, or you simply don't rate."

An example of Status Reputation for the lower-lower people is given by an upper-lower-class man: "Boy, some of those people live in awful places. Just like pigs. Have you seen that place along the Canal on Washington? This group of people living around here south of the Canal is the most adulterous bunch of people you ever saw. I don't think there is one of the men living with his original wife."

COMPARISON

All people in a community are constantly making comparisons between the social levels of other people in their environment; usually they are using the technique of rating by Comparison.

Frequently, a speaker places someone (with reference to his own status) as above, below, or equal to himself. He may or may not be conscious of what he reveals. If he discusses a number of people who have been previously placed and indicates that some are above, some equal, and some below him, a fairly close estimate can be made of where he places himself. The reliability of his own

[4] The status analyst who wishes to use these techniques in combination with a structural analysis should read Bernice Neugarten's Ph.D. dissertation, p. 55.

placement can be easily checked by examining his participation to ascertain whether his clique, family, and associational memberships validate what he says. More often than not, the informant will place someone by saying his status is above or below that of another person whose social status has already been established. This technique of placing people is called rating by Comparison. Sometimes the status analyst identifies a configuration of traits belonging to a person, family, clique, or association which is sufficiently similar to other constellations previously identified to be classed alike, and the analyst can assert that the person or group being placed belongs at a particular level. This method, however, is not the technique of rating by Comparison but is the technique of rating by Status Reputation.

An example of Comparison is taken from a comment of an upper-middle-class man: "Paul Little may associate with Dick Thornton." (Dick Thornton was previously placed by the researchers as upper-middle; he had also been placed there by the speaker.) The speaker continues, "That's where I put him anyway, whether he's in that group or not." In the first part of his statement, the status judge ranks Little by participation (Institutional Membership) on the basis of equality in an upper-middle-class clique. He, then, becomes uncertain of the participation and says that's where he would place him anyway, whether he's in that group or not. He thereby makes Little equivalent with the previously established status of Thornton.

The following is an illustration of Comparison between a lower-middle-class woman and an upper-class group: The field worker asked her, "Are you related to anyone here in town?" She replied, "Yes, Mrs. A. B. Henderson is my aunt [upper], and Mrs. David Black [upper] is my first cousin." The field worker said, "Do you associate socially with these people?" She said, "Well, no, we don't; they are differently situated than we are." Although the speaker and the Hendersons and the Blacks are "near" each other by kinship they are "distant" by class because the speaker says they are "differently situated," indicating that their statuses are nonequivalent and (by inference) that she is lower than the upper-class women. The field worker and the informant are also using the technique of Institutional Membership.

Most of the terms of rating by Comparison are expressed by the following formulas:

X = the unknown person
Y and Z = the known persons or institutions
X is equal to Y: X = Y

X is higher than Y: X ↗ Y (X above, Y below)

X is lower than Z: Z ↘ X (Z above, X below)

X is lower than Y and higher than Z: Y ↖ X ↘ Z (Y above, X middle, Z below)

SIMPLE ASSIGNMENT

Rating by Simple Assignment to a class, being the class placement of an individual or family and occasionally an association by assignment to a social class previously defined, explicitly states that the subject referred to is definitely in or out of a given class. Such references, more often than not, are found in an interview context where the larger discussion is about the social life of the family or individual. Simple Assignment is represented and best understood by the construction and inspection of charts.

Chart IV illustrates the expression, "He is in the upper-middle class." Here the informant places the subject in a particular class, and, by the use of the words, "married into" and "dropped by," tells how a person moves into or out of the upper class. Interviews which discuss the status of families are filled with similar expressions.

"Middle class," "top crowd," and "Society Set" are all Status Reputational terms used to refer to a general level, a level (by implication) that is one of several. The expressions, "He is in the upper-middle class," "married into," and "dropped by," categorically place a given individual in or out of a particular class.

If the informant has spoken previously of the class referred to and established what he means by it, or if the researcher by previous interviews with others is able to identify the general class to which the informant refers, he can easily stratify the name mentioned. Under these circumstances when the researcher places a particular individual or family in a given class, he is using rating by Simple Assignment to place the individual and Status Reputation (in the three cases on page 80) to identify the general class and to help place the individual or family.

The difference between straight Status Reputational or Symbolic Placement terms and those used with Simple Assignment is illustrated by the following statement, "She goes around with the Society Crowd." If one knows no more than this about the participation referred to ("goes around with"), then the statement is classed as Status Reputation. Such a statement is far less definite and much less clear than "She is in the Society Set" (Simple Assignment for the individual ["in"] and Status Reputation for the class and the individual ["Society Set"]).

CHART IV

SIMPLE ASSIGNMENT DIAGRAMS

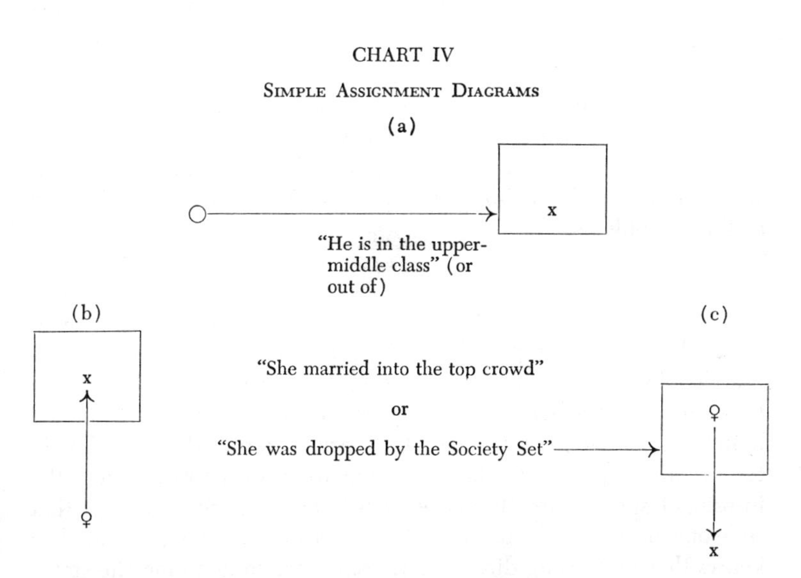

When the names of families or individuals are mentioned, Simple Assignment is ordinarily used with Social-Class Configuration. The classes having been established to the satisfaction of the informant, he then places people in them. Such statements as "He is in the upper-middle class" and "He is not in" (the upper class) are

Simple Assignments and almost always accompany Social-Class Configurations.

Simple Assignment often overlaps Symbolic Placement. When an informant says, "He belongs to the 400," he is obviously using Symbolic Placement; but when this is in part of a Social-Class Configuration and the informant has used "400" as his general term to refer to the top class and followed it by, "He belongs to the 400," he is using both Symbolic Placement and Simple Assignment: Symbolic Placement to refer to the general category, and Simple Assignment to refer to the place of the individual. When he says, "He is in the upper-middle class," after having established the upper-middle-class part of a Social-Class Configuration, he is using the technique of Simple Assignment to place the individual and Simple Assignment (a class previously defined by him) to establish the place of the whole class.

In general, the analyst will keep his procedure clear and simple if he will adopt the procedure of calling such expressions Simple Assignments when they are part of a Social-Class Configuration and Symbolic Placement or Status Reputation, as the case may be, when such expressions are used by themselves and out of a larger class context. The analysis of the interview in Chapter 6 and further instructions about the techniques in Chapter 5 give added clarification of these problems.

SUMMARY

Understanding how the techniques of Status Reputation, Symbolic Placement, Comparison, and Simple Assignment are used by the people of a community is largely a matter of analyzing the thought processes behind their expressions of stereotyped evaluated beliefs (social logics) through the various terms they employ in talking about people in the status hierarchy of a town. When the informant speaks directly and explicitly about status and says that someone he knows belongs to the upper-middle class, the analyst knows that he is using direct, literal reference in denoting the status of a person. But all of the symbolic and emblematic material and much of the use of rating by Comparison are something quite different.

The problem of meaning here is complex, and to accept any statement by an informant in its literal sense is to be misinformed and usually confused. An eleven-year-old boy comes regularly to school in clean, neatly patched overalls, with face washed and hair combed; his school playmates say he is dirty. His teachers report he enjoys his school work; his age peers say he does not like school. When this same boy's handsome face and well-formed body are described as "bad looking," it is clear that another kind of analysis is necessary to understand the truth his agemates are trying to tell. For here we are dealing with Status Reputation, emblems, and symbols, and with indirect reference rather than direct reference. Chart V tells the whole story of the meaning that children are attempting to communicate when they talk about a person's being dirty who is by actual observation clean. The case of a boy described by a large percentage of the class as dirty, when our own observation indicated he was not, will be analyzed. When a check-up is made to see what his other ratings are, it is found that for the great majority of them he is rated on the negative and inferior side. Chart V shows what happens when the children of the superior classes rate this boy and others like him from the lower classes as being dirty. The speaker's status is superior; the status of the person referred to is inferior. The trait, dirty, is classed as inferior. It is placed in a constellation of other negative traits. These traits are felt to be part of the way of life of children of low status and are made equivalent with low status in Jonesville. Therefore, if a child is said to be dirty, he is usually of low status. Very often he is also believed to be not good looking and to dislike school, is considered unpopular and has many other unpleasant characteristics attributed to him.

CHART V

REPUTATION AND SOCIAL STATUS

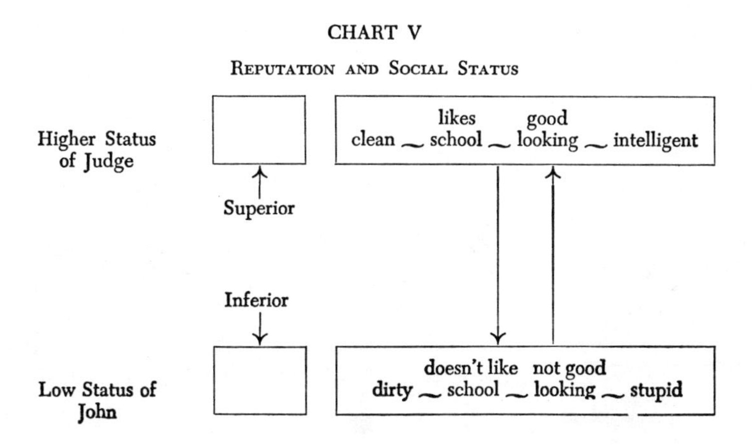

SPECIAL READINGS

The reading for this chapter, largely a continuation of Chapter 3 and selected for the same basic reasons, includes among other selections the great basic work on public symbols, Durkheim's study of "collective representations," a somewhat different treatment by a semanticist, and some novels which use class symbols, for the upper classes and the lower-lower class.

Émile Durkheim. *The Elementary Forms of the Religious Life.* New York: Macmillan Co., 1915.

A. R. Radcliffe-Brown. *The Andaman Islanders.* Cambridge: The University Press, 1922.

Charles Morris. *Signs, Language and Behavior.* New York: Prentice-Hall, 1946.

John Marquand. *The Late George Apley,* 1937; or *H. M. Pulham, Esquire,* 1941; or *Wickford Point,* 1939; or *Point of No Return,* 1949. Boston: Little, Brown & Co.

Erskine Caldwell. *Tobacco Road.* New York: Chas. Scribner's Sons, 1932.

CHAPTER 5

Technique of Institutional Membership (Real Interconnectedness)

ALL people in a community belong to one or more social institutions, ordinarily to several, whose social standing is known and evaluated by other members of the city. Instructions are given in this chapter on how to use Institutional Membership for the study of social class. Among the several types of institutions present are the family, clique, association, church, as well as political, governmental, and economic institutions. Ordinarily, economic, political, and governmental institutions cannot be used for Evaluated Participation because simple membership in such an institution is not significant. It is necessary to know the specific job or office an individual occupies and its relative rank to place him. Furthermore, jobs and offices are part of the occupational characteristic used in the Index of Status Characteristics. Knowledge of membership in a family is ordinarily sufficient to establish what that particular family contributes to an individual's class position, but knowledge of a man's employment without any information on what his job is in a factory tells very little about his social-class position. However, his specific type of job or occupation as manager or unskilled worker tells a great deal. Accordingly, occupation, a category which cross-cuts economic institutions, is treated as an independent factor and is one of the several characteristics which comprise the I.S.C.

Political and governmental institutions, not including associations engaged in political activities, are largely useless for Evaluated Participation because they spread through the whole status structure. Furthermore, official positions in the governmental structures are occupations and become part of the occupational characteristic of the I.S.C.

A man's memberships in his family, clique, associations, and church are evaluated, and such participation, when evaluated and rated by his fellows, contributes to, and largely establishes, his social-class position in his community.

Institutional Membership we sometimes call relations of Real Interconnectedness.[1] For membership in an institution is real, observable by the field worker, and connects the individual in real relations with other members of the institution and ultimately with other members of the larger community.

Institutional Membership is studied by use of interviews, observation, schedules, membership lists, particularly of associations and churches, and newspaper accounts of associational participation. Instructions for the use of family, clique, association, and church membership for the study of status will now be presented.

FAMILY MEMBERSHIP

The elementary family of orientation is the structure which first socially places the newborn individual in the community; and, as far as kinship can, the elementary family of procreation, later established by marriage and parenthood, ordinarily completes this placement. In our society, as in most, the new individual is identified with the social place of his parents and family. If the parents' status is high, his is high; if theirs is low, his is low. Since one may marry at his own social level or above or below it, or by social mobility move up or down the class ladder, the class level of the family of procreation often varies from the original one. Although the child and adolescent may be acquiring behavior preparatory for placement higher or lower than that enjoyed by his family, until he has moved out of the family of orientation and established a family of his own and achieved economic and social autonomy, he tends to be identified with the general status of his family. In other words, the family acts as a unit within the community.

There are secondary considerations, however, that are important if one uses the family of procreation or orientation for placement of the individual. The analyst should ascertain if the individual is living in the same household with the other members of the family. If he is, the chances are overwhelming that he has the same status as they have. If he is not, the analyst often finds that the individual is not of the same status as the other members of the family.

[1] A. R. Radcliffe-Brown, "The Nature of a Theoretical Natural Science of Society" (Department of Anthropology, University of Chicago, 1937 [Mimeographed]).

When an individual is found outside his family household, certain things become significant for diagnosis. He may be participating in cliques, associations, and informal groups far below or above those of the other members of his family; but the very fact that he is known to belong to the family and is partially identified with it by the community helps pull him up or down towards the level of the family itself. The problem of the analyst is to determine how much the downward or upward pull of the rest of the individual's social participation affects the pull of his family. It should be added that the study of such individuals is very rewarding for a status analyst.

When one uses the families of orientation and procreation for the purpose of status analysis, the place of the individual in the family becomes important. One must know if he or she is a spouse, parent, child, or a sibling. If the individual is a spouse, it is important to know if he or she has been married for a long or a short period. If recently married, the process of status identification of the two people may not be complete, as they have come from different families. If it is known that the families were of the same social status before marriage and that neither spouse has been upward or downward mobile, then the social position in the recent marriage will be the same. However, if one of them occupied a higher or lower status, the status of the two will be different for a period of time until the married couple, through participation and by community evaluation, are given a single social status. In very rare instances and under extreme circumstances, the two may keep separate statuses (as judged by participation and the social evaluation of informants).

However, this is so rare and depends upon the presence of so many factors and the absence of so many others, that for all practical purposes it can be disregarded. If the family of orientation of either spouse is solidly placed in the community and its general status better known than the family of the other spouse, the strong family will tend to determine the place of the family of procreation of the newly married couple.

If the family of orientation of each is well known, then many other considerations may enter. If both are the same, their own family's status is firm and strong. If the parental families' positions are different and the couple are mobile and conscious of status, their struggle for higher placement may end in open family conflict between the new family and that of the lower-placed spouse. There will be reorganization of cliques, dropping of some and strengthening of ties with others, and in general a period of disorganization and reorganization. This, however, becomes more a problem for clique and association analysis than for that of the family. The emphasis on the male side of our society (with the patronymic, etc.) often helps decide this issue. On the other hand, the greater consciousness of class by American females often outweighs other considerations.

A family check list is useful for summarizing interviews and to direct the field man who is interviewing for data on family membership and its status implications. The several questions are based on the present discussion. The rating of each family can be made only when most of the data are present (see Family Check List below).

CLIQUE MEMBERSHIP

The clique ranks next to the family in contributing to the placing of individuals in the class order. Of first importance in using the clique for status placement is identification of its type. The social clique (the group or groups of friends) contributes more than the occupational or technical clique, and the social clique which engages in reciprocal home hospitality is to be given more attention than those in which participation is outside the home. In the first case, the whole family and its identifying symbol (the house and home) are more fully involved than when the social living is away from home (recreational cliques, for example). The clique which is primarily organized around the exercise of certain techniques may be of only slight help in identifying the social place of the individual.

Men who habitually get together to play poker more often than not tend to be of the same or near social group. But if the exercise of skill is paramount and the dominating motive is the pleasure which a good player derives from playing with other competent players, men of the highest social level may play with men of the lowest social level. The place they play is likely to be indicative. If it is outside the home and away from their families, the class differences are more varied than if they play in their own homes. Some of the other cliques organized around the exercise of techniques are athletic cliques, such as tennis, golf, bowling, etc. The analyst should

FAMILY CHECK LIST

Family of Orientation

1. At what social level do other members of the family generally participate?

Very High	High	Above Average	Average	Below Average	Low	Very Low

2. Same for all......Different......Which members......What levels......
3. Are they all in the same......or different households......?
4. Are the others in the same community......?

Family of Procreation

1. What is the social level of other members of the family, or of the family generally?

Very High	High	Above Average	Average	Below Average	Low	Very Low

2. Same for all......Different......Which members......What levels......
3. With what family member do they participate as equals, inferiors, superiors......?
4. Are they all in the same......or different households......?
5. Are they in the same community......?
6. Is the status reputation of the Family of Procreation above or below that of the Family of Orientation?

   Far below......Below a little......Same......

   Far above......Above a little......Same......
7. Rating with what other families, cliques, etc., for which status has already been established.

Class Rating for F.O.:......

Class Rating for F.P.:......

know whether the group has strong motivation for exercise of techniques since, in social cliques, games are often used to provide form to the organization when the individuals are together.

The position in the clique is important since those who belong to the core of the clique[2] tend to be more easily identifiable than those who are in the periphery. The sex of the clique is also important since women tend to draw stronger class lines than men. If the social clique is mixed, the women will more likely be dominant in making distinctions than the men. Since, unlike participation in the family, the individual can participate in several cliques, it is important to evaluate how much the different cliques contribute to the social placement of the individual. Ordinarily, the interviews provide the necessary cues. When it is found that a known individual participates in several lower-placed cliques and in only one higher-placed clique, the chances are very high that his identification will be with the lower groups (see Clique Check List).

ASSOCIATION MEMBERSHIP

The use of associations, such as the club, the fraternity, and a great variety of similar organizations characteristic of American life, for status analysis is very similar to that of the clique. The association tends to be larger and less precise in giving the individual his social status. Ordinarily, the smaller the association, the greater the likelihood of exact placement of an individual; the larger the association, the less likelihood of exact placement.

Certain "social" associations are sometimes organized and function to "draw lines" around large groups of people who are above the others in the community. Cliques are too informally organized and often too difficult to identify for these purposes. Associations, such as discussion groups, dining clubs, and the like, are organizations which emphasize status distinctions. They provide the best material for the placement of individuals by associational means.

Church associations tend to spread through several classes, but ordinarily they are filled with people from the lower half of society. Sometimes in "status churches," women of the higher classes organize what amounts to a formalized clique to perform services for the church, such as providing flowers for the altar or controlling philanthropy. Secret societies usually are lower than occupational

[2] Davis, Gardner, and Gardner, *Deep South*, pp. 150-70.

CLIQUE CHECK LIST

1. How Many?...... Social level of other members of each clique:......

	Very High	High	Above Average	Average	Below Average	Low	Very Low
Clique 1							
Clique 2							
Clique 3							
Others							

Frequency of participation in Clique (a little (1); some (s); much (m)):....

Clique 1...... Clique 2...... Clique 3......

What is position in each clique?

	Cl. 1	Cl. 2	Cl. 3	Others
Core Member				
Peripheral Member				

General Score:
(Very high, High, etc.) ....

CHECK LIST FOR ASSOCIATIONS

How Many......

	Social	Civic	Church	Secret Society (lodge)	Athletic	Patriotic	Auxiliary
Rating and Social Level							
Sex							
Size							

General Score:......

CHECK LIST FOR CHURCHES

Ideology and Ritual

Emotional	
Literal Interpretation	
Formal Ritual	
Little Emotion	
Free Interpretation of the Gospel	

Status Reputation...... (Very high, High, etc.)

Amount of Participation by Member

	H	M	L
Goes to Church			
Pays Dues			
Secular Activities			
Other Activities			

and social groups. Athletic societies need to be carefully scrutinized to be of use for the placement of individuals, for if the exercise of techniques is dominant, class is of little importance.

If societies organized about the individual's participation in wars are purely "patriotic" and not identified with genealogical considerations (such as the D.A.R.) they tend to be democratic and spread through the whole society. For example, the American Legion more often than not has members from all social levels. Patriotic societies being formed since World War II include all levels. As the men grow older and a large number of deaths occur, the association tends to become lower-middle and lower class; the original higher-class members usually disappear before all of the larger number of the more lowly placed die. Furthermore, lower-class people maintain membership because they derive more satisfaction out of patriotic organizations. Upper-class people often drop out or, by refusing to participate, maintain no more than a paying membership.

Associations which emphasize history tend to be more highly placed than patriotic and church societies. On the other hand, auxiliaries, particularly female ones, tend to be low. Auxiliaries ordinarily have a larger number of members who are lower in class than the parent organization. For example, in the American Legion Auxiliary and the various auxiliaries of other war societies, the members tend to come from lower classes than in the main organizations.

Where the status of the membership of an association has been largely determined, it can be hypothecated that the other members' status is more likely than not to be within the range established and usually at the level of highest concentration. For example, if the association runs from upper class through lower-middle, and there are only a few members in the upper group and a large number in the lower stratum, the presumption is that the unknown members are likely to be lower-middle class. They can be placed there temporarily, to be checked with further material from Evaluated Participation and from the Index of Status Characteristics. After a number of the more important associations have had the status of their membership generally established, charts can be made representing the proportionate class distribution of membership to be used for ranking those members not yet placed. Each association can be given an approximate rating which can be placed on the E.P. status card of each individual member. [These cards are fully described in Chapter 7, p. 115.]

There are three criteria for the classification and rating of associations for purposes of class analysis. They are concentration of the core membership in a social class, the direction of the spread from the core, and the comparison between spread of membership and size of the core concentration. The concentration of membership usually tends to be in one and not more than two classes. The spread from the core can be upward, downward, in both directions, or there may be none at all. The membership spread can be conveniently categorized as strong, moderate, or weak. With these criteria in mind, class distribution of each association can be inspected for rating.

The concentration of membership should be taken account of first. In Chart VI on page 95 the Monday and Rotary Clubs are ranked very high (I) because, in our first, tentative placement of known members, all of them were concentrated in the upper two classes, meaning that members of unknown class position would probably be in these classes. Since no more than 15 per cent of the total population of any American community is ordinarily located in these classes, it is clear that the criteria of membership used by these clubs are quite definitely class-controlled and that the Monday Club is very likely an organization that makes a point of being class-conscious since 50 per cent of its membership is upper-class and not more than 5 per cent of such a community's population is upper-class.

The D.A.R., Hospital Aid, and Country Club are rated as high (II) on the scale because, while the concentration of membership is still heavily upper-class, their membership extends into the lower-middle level. The direction of the spread is downward and quite strong. The Masons and the Lions Club are rated as above average (III) because the concentration is at the lower level of the membership and the spread is from moderate to strong in an upward direction.

The next rank, the run-of-the-mill, average type (IV) is composed of four sub-types. All four of them have a very strong membership in the lower-middle class. The first sub-type spreads through all classes except the lowest one. The second's membership is concentrated in the lower-middle or upper-lower class with weak upward and downward spreads. The third has a very strong concentration in the lower-middle class with a small upward spread. And the fourth is concentrated in the lower-middle with a spread stronger downward than it is upward (see Odd Fellows, American Legion Auxiliary, Eastern Star, and Girl Scout Mothers). The group which is below average (V) includes those associations with a strong concentration in the upper-lower class or those with a strong downward spread from a lower-middle-class concentration (Royal Neighbors and Baptist Mission). The next level (VI) has heavy concentration at the upper-lower level (Polish National Alliance). The lowest level (VII) is entirely upper-lower or lower-lower (Free Methodists and Gospel Tabernacle).

If it is discovered that a person belongs to the Country Club in Jonesville, the chances seem favorable for placement somewhere above the Common Man, since over half of the known membership is above that level. But when we learn this person is a member of the Western Star, where almost all the known membership is lower-middle, and we later find out that he is a Royal Kinsman, the chances are overwhelming that his real placement will be lower-middle—lower-middle because the previously established lower limit of the Country Club is lower-middle and the upper limits of the Royal Kinsmen are lower-middle, while Western Star is entirely lower-middle and has no membership below that class.

Similar comparisons among associational memberships yield

CHART VI

Preliminary Class Distribution of Selected Associations and Churches

		U	UM	LM	UL	LL
I	Monday Club	50%	50%			
I	Rotary	16.7%	80.6%		2.7%	
II	D. A. R.	57.1%	4.3%	28.6%		
II	Hospital Aid	51.6%	32.8%	15.6%		
II	Country Club	29.9%	27.8%	42.3%		
III	Masons	14.7%	19%	65.3%		
III	Lions	4.8%	23.8%	71.4%		
IV	Odd Fellows	2.2%	20%	42.2%	35.6%	
IV	American Legion Auxiliary	1.6%	11.1%	63.5%	22.2%	1.6%
IV	Eastern Star		8.3%	91.7%		
IV	Girl Scout Mothers		9.3%	50%	35.2%	5.5%
V	Royal Neighbors			69%	28.2%	2.8%
VI	Polish National Alliance			8.3%	83.4%	8.3%
VII	Free Methodists				100%	
VII	Gospel Tabernacle				87.5%	12.5%

(Size of membership in each class is represented by the squares.)

good evidence for social-class placements. For example, membership in the Monday Club, D.A.R., and Hospital Aid, despite the fairly strong upper-middle membership in some of these associations, is almost certainly upper-class because only under extraordinary circumstances would it be possible for an upper-middle-class person to have sufficient influence with the upper-class control group to acquire position in all these high status associations. A comparison of Odd Fellows, Lions, and Masons tells a similar placement story but for a different class. And when it is learned that a man is a member of the Gospel Tabernacle, a likely tentative placement is upper-lower with the precautionary note which must always be emphasized about institutional membership. The status analyst always feels safer if he has other techniques to rely on to give final placement to a particular family or individual.

CHURCH MEMBERSHIP

The church is not very reliable for exact placement of an individual because it spreads through too many social levels. Almost all class points about denominations must be accepted as rule-of-thumb information. However, the church can be important and useful to the analyst. If it has an ideology and ritual which are informal, emotional, and literally interpret the Bible, the chances are high that almost all the people in the church will be from the lower half of society, and probably from the lowest part. On the other hand, if the church is formalistic, if the emphasis is upon interpretation rather than literal acceptance of the gospel, and if individual expression at meetings is at a minimum, the chances are it is middle-class or higher.

Denominations tend to be socially evaluated, but regional differences must be carefully considered. Episcopalians and Unitarians generally rank higher than the Methodists and Baptists. Congregationalists, Presbyterians, and Christian Scientists are centered in the middle class. Communities in the South do not always follow this pattern. There the Methodist Episcopal Church often enjoys a position like that of the Episcopal Church in most other communities.

The evidence from the use of Matched Agreements (Chapter 3) and the other techniques indicates that it is possible to assign grades within the several class levels according to the probable position of an individual or family in a class. For example, in Smith Brown's interview, the "fringe of society" tends to be rated above the ordinary middle class. Furthermore, he reckons certain people as the bottom part of the ordinary upper-middle class. Inspection of the other interviews shows that many of the references were such that the analyst could make a sufficiently fine discrimination to assign a *grade* as well as a class level to the individual.

Each class level is divided into three "grades," the top one designating those individuals whose position within the class level is strong or high (symbol ++), the middle one including individuals whose position is ordinary or "solid" (symbol +), and the bottom one for those individuals whose class position is weak (symbol –). By the use of grades, it was possible to make fine distinctions about status position within any given class. The grades assigned by Evaluated Participation do not always prove valid, but they are useful in training the status analyst to exercise care and continually to refine his analysis. Evidence will be presented later to show that the E.P. placements in the "plus" or "solid" grades are predictable by means of the I.S.C. with a much higher degree of accuracy than placement in the other two grades.

SPECIAL READINGS

The several instructions used for the analysis of social class and institutions including families, associations, cliques, and churches have a vast literature. Only a few works have been selected, particularly those which have examined the relation of the institution to social class.

Ruth Cavan. *The Family.* New York: Thomas Y. Crowell, 1945.
An account of the family in our class system is given on pages 429-461.

Allison Davis, Burleigh B. Gardner, and Mary R. Gardner. *Deep South.* Chicago: University of Chicago Press, 1941. Pp. 137-228.

W. Lloyd Warner and Paul S. Lunt. *The Social Life of a Modern Community.* Vol. I, "Yankee City Series." New Haven: Yale University Press, 1941.
See pages 301-365 for associations and churches.

St. Clair Drake. *Churches and Voluntary Associations in the Chicago Negro Community.* Chicago: Work Projects Administration, December 1940. Pp. 1-29.

William F. Whyte. *Street Corner Society*. Chicago: University of Chicago Press, 1943. Pp. 3-52.

CHAPTER 6

Analysis of an Interview to Demonstrate How the Several Techniques Are Used

WE HAVE defined, described, and given illustrations of the several techniques of Evaluated Participation in the last several chapters. To equip the status analyst properly with the necessary instruction for analyzing interviews to assign status to individuals, families, and institutions, a sample training analysis of a few pages of one interview is given.

The interview is Smith Brown's. Part of it, previously used to show how the class system of a city is established, is now being utilized to demonstrate how the several techniques for status placement are used by him and the authors. (See Chapter 3 for the portions of the interview used for the method of Social-Class Configuration.) Because of space limitations, all thirty-six pages of the original document cannot be presented here. The method used is to present several lines of quotation and to follow them by analysis.

Those who wish to use social-class analysis professionally should read this chapter several times and (after reading the whole book) study it. Those who wish to know how it is done but not use it professionally should read to page 105, perhaps thumb through the rest, and go on to Chapter 7 where final instructions are given for assembling the results from the use of the several techniques of E.P.

The informant had been interviewed several times previously and good rapport had been established between him and the field worker. In previous interviews, he had introduced the subject of social class. The present interview took place in the informant's home. No other persons were present in the room. The interviewer took full notes as the informant talked.

Page 3, lines 10-12: "Let's start with the top level and then work down," Brown said.

Analysis: Reference to Social-Class Configuration, with the use of social distance concepts: down and up, top and bottom, "work down"—indicating that there are levels in between.

Page 3, lines 12-21: "Now, I won't be able to tell you everybody or the whole thing, but what I will do, Bill, is tell you the main class groups and the main sections in some of these classes, and I will give you the illustrations and then tell you something about each of these illustrations, if you want that. I know what the system is and I'll try to tell you how it operates. Let's start out with the first class."

Analysis: Social-Class Configuration; also there is a recognition of basic and general levels with grades and divisions within a class. The statements are explicit and direct rather than implicit or symbolic.

Page 3, lines 22-26: "The society class around here are the 400 class. In the main, it's rooted right over there in the Federated Church. It comes from the Federated Church. Now, Bill, a lot of these people are 398's, but they think they're 400's. With a few exceptions, no one who's not in the Federated Church is in this class."

Analysis: "The 400" is a symbolic term because, when taken literally, it means 400 individuals or families but its real reference, the meaning it conveys to the listener, is to the highest social level in the community. In the present context it is also made equivalent with the "society class." The "society class" here is a Status Reputational term for it denotes a kind of people, a kind of "superior" behavior, and a group of people. In other words, the whole term refers to people who are a superior kind behaviorally and who herd together.

The triangle of reference (see Chart III) is direct for the "society class" and indirect for "the 400" (the term, "the 400," does not fit the object but the term "society class" does).

The expressions "rooted right over there in the Federated Church" and "comes from the Federated Church" are an effort by the informant to give church structuring to the top class to show that they are interconnected by church as well as by clique and family. Again, this is use of Institutional Membership. He also goes on to say that no one who is not in the Federated Church is in that class. Once again, he uses Institutional Membership to locate the status of people. It is clear that both of these references imply high status for the Federated Church itself. The reference to "398's" but "they think they're 400's" is again Symbolic Placement. Parenthetically, it might be said that the use of "they" indicates the speaker probably puts himself below the top class and thereby rates himself by Comparison.

The type of information given by the informant in the last several lines establishes the category of a general class (a differentiated higher and lower status for the general community). After he generally establishes the status system, he then denotes a specific one, the upper class, which to him is the "society class," "the 400," "the high class," etc. He also establishes the principal characteristics for the Status Reputation of the class, such as money and family. He then gives the basic criteria used by him in naming who belongs and tries to demonstrate that the same criteria are used by the members of the class, namely the criteria of Real Interconnectedness of the members of the level. In other words, who accepts whom. He says ultimately nothing else matters. "If you aren't accepted, then you don't belong."

Later on in the interview, he indicates that other characteristics, while less apparent, are present and powerful. They have to do with morals and manners and, in general, conforming to the norms of behavior accepted at that particular level.

Having established the class largely by Social-Class Configuration, but aided by Status Reputation and Symbolic Placement, he puts various people in it and excludes others. He usually does this by the technique of Simple Assignment. By so doing, as we have discovered, he adds further evidence in proof of his major propositions about the existence of class and of the existence of the upper class of his community.

Page 4, lines 1-7: The informant has just said that there are exceptions to the rule about the Federated Church. He continues: "There's Dr. Bowman's family and Mrs. Laura Radcliffe, who's the widow of Norman Radcliffe. Dr. Bowman is a Catholic, but he's in that group. Laura Radcliffe was a Catholic who married a Congregationalist. She was accepted into it by the fact that she married Norman Radcliffe."

Analysis: By depending upon the previously established class created by Social-Class Configuration, the Bowman family and Mrs. Radcliffe are put by Simple Assignment into the upper class. There are also implications that Catholics ordinarily do not rank as upper class.

Page 4, line 8: In this next line all of these points are brought out more clearly when he says, "All the Radcliffes are in the 400."

Analysis: Once again, Symbolic Placement in the upper class which has been previously established; once again, placement of a family in the upper class by Simple Assignment by saying they are "in," "out," or, as we shall see later, "almost in," "almost out." Furthermore, there is use of Institutional Membership by family interconnectedness.

Page 4, lines 8-15: The informant now modifies his statement about the Radcliffes' all being in the 400. "Now, wait a minute, there are some of them who are not. Now, let's see. Oh, yes, there are the Newton Radcliffes out west of town, there's Kenneth Radcliffe and his son, Kenneth, Junior, he was out to Rotary one night. Were you there?" The field worker said, "Yes, I met him there." He said, "That family has lost most of its money. They are just about fourth or fifth cousins of Norman Radcliffe and Harley and that bunch. Well, they're not in the 400."

Analysis: The exceptions show that the people spoken about are close to, but not in, the top class (tentatively upper-middle, the next class down). The techniques used again are Simple Assignment and Status Reputation. He also indicates that he thinks they are downward mobile. General placement by the analyst of the exceptions, upper-middle class.

Page 4, lines 15-16: The informant continues listing people. "The Albert and Gregg Thompson families are in it. Now, there's a case of money that's taking them in. They are accepted, and that's all."

Analysis: Again, Simple Assignment to a class previously established by Social-Class Configuration. Their Status Reputation is also given, and there are indications that he grades them near the bottom of the upper class because if he says, "It's a case of money that has taken them in," the status analyst suspects that there has been recent upward mobility; if the money had come to the family much earlier nothing would have been said about money "taking them in." Institutional Membership is also used here.

Page 4, lines 17-22: The informant continues listing families and their class levels. "Let's see now. We come to the Stocktons. Some of the Stocktons do and some of them don't [belong to the upper class]. You've always got to make a division in the Stocktons. Now, this is the group who do belong. They're in. Carl Stockton and his wife, Corey Stockton and family, that's Bill Stockton's father, well, you had better put Bill's family in as a separate family—I guess that's all of the Stocktons that are in."

Analysis: When he says that "some of them do belong and some of them don't," "you've always got to make a division in the Stocktons," he is using Simple Assignment to a previously established class and Institutional Membership combined. He sees the family structure as a unity and divides it by class—those who belong and those who don't belong to the upper class (those who do not, tentatively upper-middle). When he says, "Now, this is the group who do belong. They're in," he once again uses Simple Assignment and, by implication, Comparison because he makes some of them coordinate and others unequal.

Page 4, lines 22-25, and Page 5, lines 1-9: The informant continues with his analysis of the Stocktons. "Here are the Stocktons who don't. Now, let's see. Mrs. Helen Cross, she doesn't. Now, she is Carl Stockton's sister, but she's not in. Now, there's the case of a girl who married down and stayed there. I'll have several illustrations of people who jump up or down because of marriage. Now, there's the Chester Stockton family way out on the end of Fremont Avenue. They used to own a big farm east of the River there just north of the Radcliffes, but they lost it in some kind of a deal and they were dropped. The Stockton down at the City Hall is the sister of Chester Stockton. Then, there is Mrs. Blake Reynolds. She is another Stockton who doesn't belong. She's the cousin of Nick Stockton."

Analysis: Again, Simple Assignment and Institutional Membership for people who are in or out of "The 400"; they have stayed in or they have been dropped, or they belong or do not belong. The Real Interconnectedness of the class is again stressed. The informant also uses Comparison, and Status Reputation is used by reference to to the loss of money and the consequent loss of real interaction by the family that is dropped. The use of Comparison is more by implication than by direct statement. He, in effect, is saying that X is the same class as, or in a lower or higher class than, Y. Y's place has been previously established. Ordinarily, this informant, as other informants when they use Comparison, rates people in the following manner: Let us think of X as the person whose status has heretofore not been established and is now being rated. The propositions run somewhat as follows: X is higher than Y (this usually means, but he is sufficiently near to make the comparison important), X is the same as Y, or X is lower than Y (this also usually means that the status of X is fairly near that of Y).

Page 5, lines 15-16: "The Volmers from top to bottom are in; the Friedricks from top to bottom are in"

Analysis: This use of Simple Assignment for the two family names places a number of elementary families. The fact that the members of both of these extended families are all securely and highly placed upper-class people makes it easy for the informant to use Simple Assignment. Other informants use these families' names for Symbolic Placement to place other people by the use of such expressions as "they are the same kind of people as the Volmers."

Page 5, lines 17-22: "The Caldwells—all of them—are in. Now, there's a case of two families getting together and keeping the money in the family. You know, Ted Caldwell married the Volmers girl. As far as I can figure out, that was pretty well arranged by the old folks. You know, here for years, the Caldwells and Volmers have been close business associates. They worked out a lot of deals together."

Analysis: The expression, "all of them are in," using the method of Simple Assignment, again indicates that several elementary families are involved and that the position of each is sufficiently well defined that Simple Assignment can be easily used. The method of Real Interconnectedness is also used by showing that the families are interconnected. The method of Status Reputation is also used.

Page 5, line 22, to Page 6, line 3: The informant continues talking about the Caldwells by speaking of the marriage of young Ted's brother. "Now, Roger Caldwell married down. He married Harry Gear's sister. Now, Harry is just a paper maker over at The Mill. Harry is a nice fellow, but there's nothing there." This was said with a grimace to the face. "Roger's wife is accepted though by the fact that he is a Caldwell. Here is the case of a big pull up. No family background—nothing—but she's a nice girl, so she's accepted."

Analysis: Clearly, the informant is attempting to draw a strong social distinction between the family of the groom and the family of the bride. The family of the groom is clearly upper-class. The family of the bride, we know, is much further down but how far is not too clear. However, the informant's use of two contrastive references by

Status Reputation gives us some indication of the probable place of the Gear family. We hear that he is "just a paper maker over at The Mill" and that there is "no family background—nothing." But at the same time we also hear that "Harry is a nice fellow, but there's nothing there," and that the bride is "a nice girl, so she's accepted." The informant is using the method of Status Reputation. We learn from this that the Gear family is not at the bottom because they are respectable and nice people. We know that they are not upper-middle-class because we are told that they have no family background and "there's nothing there," indicating that they do not have the Status Reputation of being the kind of substantial people usually associated with the upper-middle class. Furthermore, and implicitly, the informant is rating himself above the Gear family. We shall see later that he places himself as upper-middle and that the other informants also give him an upper-middle-class position. This implicit method of rating by the informant is by Comparison. From this analysis we are certain that the Gears are either lower-middle or upper-lower-class—probably lower-middle, because the girl is accepted by the upper class which would be easier if she were lower-middle than if she were upper-lower; however, this is only a probability and not a certainty. (The Gear family's I.S.C. places them as lower-middle. Other interviews substantiate this placement by Evaluated Participation.) It might be noted that the Gear girl has been rapidly upward mobile by marriage and that in all probability she was prepared for this mobility by education.

For purposes of brevity we will pass over several pages of interview material where many more upper-class people are mentioned.

The reader who is learning *what* is done with the techniques of E.P. to analyze an interview might very well stop here, skip the remainder of this chapter, and go on to the next one. Those who are concerned with learning *how to do the E.P. analysis* should continue reading it; in fact, as we said earlier, after the book has been completed, this chapter should be re-read several times.

Page 10, lines 10-14: "I think that's just about all of the society class. There may be one or two that I've overlooked, but that's all I can think of. The next class down is what we call the fringe of society around here. The fringe of this thing has a lot of families on it who have had money and lost it."

Analysis: This summary statement continues what the informant began at the first of this interview and continues with until the end, namely, the use of Social-Class Configuration. The expression, "fringe of society," symbolically places the new level that he is talking about just below the top one. The expression, "society," again is a technique of Status Reputation. The context, "who have had money and lost it," uses the technique of Status Reputation. It will be noted later that he includes a number of people in the fringe of society class who have recently come from a lower level rather than people who have dropped from the top class. There are also people whom he includes in the fringe of society who have not been mobile upward or downward.

Page 10, lines 15-18: "The Robert Claytons were former members of the 400, but they failed in business and he was dropped. Oh, hell, he got to owing everybody around town, and he just wasn't worth a damn, and they just got left out of things."

Analysis: The informant uses Simple Assignment when he speaks of the Claytons' being dropped from the 400 but depends upon Social-Class Configuration (see the statement immediately above) for placement. He also uses Status Reputation combined with the others to indicate why he places the family at this particular class level. In saying that "they just got left out of things," he indicates that they no longer have relations of Real Interconnectedness with the people of the 400 to give them top-status ranking.

Page 10, lines 10-15: "Now, the Halls are another family who were never in. They never did move in that set, but they had a hell of a lot of money at one time. Old man Hall was never liked around here. I don't know just what it was, but he was just excluded. Oh, if they had big parties or something, they might invite him; but they were never accepted by the society class."

Analysis: The expression, "another family who were never in," is a statement of Simple Assignment. This is followed by another Simple Assignment when the informant says, "they never did move in that set." The speaker continues by saying, "they had a hell of a lot of money at one time," but that "old man Hall was never liked around here," indicating by Status Reputation that several factors are involved in addition to money and that money as money did not give him top position. His reference to the big parties to which they were occasionally invited is one of Institutional Membership or Real

Interconnectedness. It shows that they were somewhat connected with the top class but not sufficiently to be included there.

Page 11, lines 15-26, to Page 12, lines 1-11: "Now, a family that's definitely on the fringe right now is Austin Hale and his wife. Old Austin is a nice old fellow, harmless enough, but they never were on the inside. Mrs. Hale is a sister of Dr. Otto Friedrick. He's dead now, but when he was living he was a prominent society physician of Chicago. He moved around in the big swim up there. His father and Mrs. Hale's father was a first cousin of Ernst Friedrick. That makes Mrs. Hale and Ernst Friedrick second cousins. I guess Mrs. Hale's about a third cousin of Herman Friedrick."

Analysis: By connecting the Hales with the Friedricks, who are securely upper class in the town, the speaker gives the Hales a very high-status position through Real Interconnectedness. But, then, he says categorically that the Hales were never "on the inside." He also indicates that they are part of the "fringe of society" and thereby uses Social-Class Configuration and Symbolic Placement.

Page 13, lines 21-26 to Page 14, lines 1-15: "John Madison is kind of on the fringe, but he's not exactly on the fringe either. He's not in the next strata, but he's not exactly on the fringe—he's kind of in between. It's hard to put him just where he belongs. But John's family is in a way on the fringe, but they're not in the society class. In a way, though, he belongs in the next strata. The answer to John's social position is cultural and not money or anything else. Now, the cultural position of the Madison family comes through Mrs. Madison. She is very suave and urbane—is well liked. She's accepted in circles where John is just left out. We know them probably as well as any family in town. They've been here at the house a number of times. We've been over there, and we've been with them on trips."

Analysis: The speaker is obviously attempting to make a careful placement of the John Madison family. He indicates, by Simple Assignment and Social-Class Configuration, as well as by Status Reputation and Real Interconnectedness, that the Madison family is at the top of the upper-middle class. This part of the interview shows clearly again that the personal characteristics of an individual, particularly of the head of the family, when translated into social terms and evaluated by his group, contribute greatly to his social status.

Page 14, lines 16-26 to Page 15, lines 1-4: "The next stratum starts with maybe the Madisons and the fringe and takes in certain other elements. This is what you'd better call the upper-middle class. This level is made up mainly of the women who dominate the Country Club, along with some other groups, especially the top and the fringe. The top dominates the Country Club; at least they are in it, but they're not active. They're the ones who, you might say, are behind the scenes and really control things. The fringe is pretty active, and this group of women are active, too. The women in this group just seem to split a gut to do things right. It's amusing as hell. We used to belong to the Country Club, but we don't any more. This Country Club is, of course, quite cosmopolitan. It's got a lot of people in it and diverse elements. Anybody who thinks he can afford to can get in and play golf, and so on. But it's this bunch of women who really dominate the club and keep the activities going, although I'm pretty damned sure they don't have as much say-so in it as they think they do."

Analysis: This context when related to "the fringe of society" context indicates that there are grades in the upper-middle class and that this stratum is a grade below the "fringe of society" but not a class below. This statement could not be made by use of the present interview alone. It was necessary to analyze other interviews and to see what families were listed by the present informant and compare them with the listings made of them by other informants.

Page 15, lines 5-26, to Page 16, lines 1-3: "Now, here are some illustrations of the people in this level. This is not all of them. There are a lot of gaps, but this is the type of people you find in here. Tim Rainey's family, Pete Belfield, Henry Bolton, well, you'd better put Everett Ball in there, too. That's by association. Boltons have the money, but Eleanor is Henry's daughter. Henry just kind of made a place for Everett; so he's in there by marriage and association rather than by money or family background. The Paul Littles are in here and the John Farmers. Mrs. Pearl Hooker, you'd better put her in there, too. The Phil Haskells and his sister, too, they're here. Then, there's George Harrison, although they have more or less dropped out of things the last few years. George's wife has really dropped out of everything lately. The Tilman Bascombs go in there, too. The Mathew Kingmans, well, both the Mathew Kingmans, Mathew Sr. and Mathew Jr., Martin Parishes, are in that group, too, and the Emmons Goodspeeds. Put Dick Thornton in there, too, and Michael

Spencer. Well, we've got to place this man Alton. I'll tell you, Alton's playing a very important role in this town. He's a great contrast to that man, Whiteford, who was in there before him. Alton is really up and coming. You just can't compare the church now with what it was when Whiteford was there. Alton isn't just exactly in this group, but he is on the edge of it and with some other people. But that's where Alton really belongs."

Analysis: Rather than deal with each of the above families separately, we will speak of them as a group. The technique of Social-Class Configuration is used, Real Interconnectedness, Status Reputation and, occasionally, Comparison. The only difference in the material here is that it applies to a grade below the "fringe of society" class and to a class below the material on the upper-class families.

Page 16, lines 4-8: The interviewer then asked, "Well, now, Brown, where are you going to put yourself?" He replied, "Hell, leave that out. Although we associate with this group most of the time, just leave me out of it. If you're putting me in, this [upper-middle-class clique] is where we belong. But just leave me out of it, and you can make up your mind where we belong."

Analysis: To place himself the speaker uses Real Interconnectedness (clique) and Simple Assignment ("that is where we belong").

Page 16, lines 9-26: "This next group is on the same level as the one I just gave you. Just a little different in age, that's all. It's not on a lower level. We will call it the Methodist Church group. At least they are the nucleus of it. There are a few others in the group, but they're practically all in the Methodist Church. It's not on a lower level. Now, the people in this group are the dominant people in the Methodist Church. Now, here's the ones that will be in this group: Wallace Newhouse, the John Harveys, the Howard Johnsons, Leon J. Dalton and his family, D. T. Addington's family, Fred McKinley's family. Now, that's a well-knit little group. They're all closely associated. They run around to one another's houses all the time. Now, there are two more families in that group, but I can't name them right now. These eight families have a bridge club, and they have dinner at one another's houses and are a group in themselves. Now, let me see here, we've left Agard out. Now, Agard's over in the Methodist Church. I don't want you to get me wrong; I don't want to be gossipy, but I've just got to tell you the truth. Now, what I'm going to tell you maybe I shouldn't, but I'm going to anyway.

"Agard and his wife are on the fringe of the M.E. group. They're on the fringe of the upper-middle group, too. They're social climbers, and that's all there is to it."

Analysis: The speaker structuralizes his placement by use of the church and cliques within the church. He also indicates how age plays a factor in determining clique memberships. Furthermore, he speaks of an association (a bridge club). The other techniques of Status Reputation, Simple Assignment, and Comparison are used.

SPECIAL READINGS

W. Lloyd Warner and Paul S. Lunt. *The Social Life of a Modern Community.* Vol. I, "Yankee City Series." New Haven: Yale University Press, 1941.

See pages 45-68 on how to interview; and pages 69-75 on how to analyze research data.

CHAPTER 7

Final Instructions for Using Evaluated Participation

THE use of each separate technique has been described and explained; and the process of analyzing the evidence of an interview to assign individuals and families to a particular class level also has been demonstrated. It is now necessary to complete our instructions for using the E.P. method by showing how the evidence resulting from the use of E.P. techniques just described is finally treated to stratify a community and to place any particular individual in the class hierarchy. We will first take up the problem of stratifying the community. Two procedures are possible; ordinarily they can be used together.

Soon after the researcher has established himself in the community and acquired a number of good informants with diversified social backgrounds, he should accumulate, by indirect interviewing, a number of Social-Class Configurations from his informants. He should compare the several levels identified by the various informants, see their similarities and differences, and, if no more interviewing is necessary for further classification, equate them. Since most or all of them will contain names of some of the same persons, he can further check the adequacy of his knowledge of the class levels established by the first process of the Matched Agreements technique.

The first charts of Matched Agreements will almost certainly establish the top and bottom levels and supply many of the names of people in these strata. Furthermore, they will tell much about the levels between the two extremes. The analyst should determine if there is a division between "old" and "new family" in the "upper class" and, should there be, find out whether the "old-family" group can enforce its superior status on the "new-family" group. The test of whether there is a "superior old family" or whether "old" and "new" families are co-ordinate can be made only by interviewing.

If there is a "superior old-family" group, the several techniques of Evaluated Participation will indicate it. For, if they are rated as "superior" and form a level of families which are exclusive and into which the "new" families wish to enter, it is certain that an upper-upper level exists. When charted, later additional configurations with more names test the earlier tentative conclusions and soon make it possible to determine what the class system is. The equation of the levels of several configurations demands internal consistency in each of them to indicate that the informants are reporting on a real social system, thereby insuring the researcher that his results are reliable. The cross checking of the placement of the same persons in the same class reduces the likelihood of error to a minimum and helps verify his conclusions.

Once a few hundred names have been placed by this procedure, evidence from other techniques on the class position of individuals mentioned in other interviews, not sufficient by itself, can be used and the names involved added to the list. For example, Symbolic Placement to indicate the class place of an individual may be used only in passing, while the informant spends the rest of the time discussing some other topic; or the informant may say as an aside that a particular individual is equivalent to certain people not previously placed. The class levels and the names in them supply a substantial body of supporting evidence permitting the use of the formerly unusable, fugitive references.

After several hundred names are given class placement, a further refinement is necessary to prepare for the employment of the I.S.C. method. For the I.S.C. to operate accurately, the placement of the individuals assigned to each level must be accurate. Therefore, any doubtful names about which evidence is insufficient should be thrown out; only those whose class position is securely established should be used. Once this is done, our research demonstrates that the four characteristics of the I.S.C. are closely correlated with the class levels established by the E.P., and the relatively inexpensive, time-saving I.S.C. can be safely substituted for determining the class position of the remaining members of the community.

Each of the people used to establish the class system of the community should be given a status personality card, and a card file should be set up for ease in studying them. On the left-hand vertical column of the card (see page 115 for illustration) are listed the techniques, and running along the top of the card are the five class positions. In the lower left-hand corner are listed the interviews from which the evidence has been abstracted. Each interview used for a particular card is numbered. The number assigned is then checked in the appropriate place for technique of placement and for class position. For example, Interview 81 (general number for the general research interview file) is Number 2 on John Doe's file. Interview 81, in reference John Doe, uses Symbolic Placement and Status Reputation, and places him as UM class. The number "2" is accordingly placed in the squares made by the UM vertical column and the Symbolic Placement and Status Reputation horizontal columns. The class-placement evidence from several informants about an individual is thus accumulated on one card. (For example, Interviews 1, 2, 3, and 4 on the sample card.) From this last procedure, class position is assigned.

The second method for stratifying a community, used in conjunction with the first during the earlier part of the research, is to establish an arbitrary status scale of from seven to ten points on which the relation and tentative positions of individuals can be placed until such time as it is known what the class levels are and where each of these individuals belongs. Furthermore, the first early references to class levels can also be assigned to these arbitrary points in the scale until their exact position is known. The ten-point scale, with many more levels on it than anticipated, can gradually be reduced until the arbitrary points correspond with the actual class levels. (In Jonesville it started at ten, was reduced to seven, and finally five.) [1]

Questions sometimes arise about disagreement among the informants on an individual's social place. Should this happen, two lines of procedure are possible. Either the card should be placed in a doubtful and "class unassigned" category because the information is unreliable or because two equally reliable and well-informed people disagree about a person's position; or when, after re-examining the evidence for the reliability of the informants, it is discovered that one of them is highly reliable and thoroughly conversant with the place of the person being studied and the other is less reliable and less well-informed, or if the meaning of one of the conflicting

[1] We wish to express our indebtedness to Mr. Arch Cooper for instituting this procedure in Jonesville.

references is not certain and the other one is clear and reliable, the uncertain evidence should be disregarded and the card kept.

Questions about the relative value of evidence from the several techniques should be raised. Institutional Membership is highly reliable for the placement of an individual when family and clique memberships are used, but less reliable when association and church memberships are the only ones available for placement. When it is found that a particular individual about to be stratified is a member of a particular family whose class has been determined, the chances are overwhelming that he belongs to the same class as his family because the members of most families belong to the same class. (See reservations on this statement made earlier.) This same procedure can be used for cliques with a little less reliability because cliques often spread over two classes. When Institutional Memberships for family, clique, association, and church are known, the Social Reputation of the individual is determined, and a competent informant rates the subject above, below, or equal to himself and others, the chances are overwhelming that the class analyst can place the individual in his correct status.

Simple Assignment and Comparison are also highly reliable techniques for placing individuals in the status hierarchy. Symbolic Placement is almost equally sure as a placement technique, but, unfortunately, Symbolic Placements are less often used for the lower-middle and upper-lower classes than for the top and bottom levels. Status Reputation by itself is often sharply accurate, but ordinarily the analyst needs to use one of the other techniques with it to be sure of exact placement. Status Reputation for a particular class is greatly strengthened by the informant's adding a list of names which can be used to validate what he says in much the same way that the names are used for Social-Class Configuration.

When some names have been previously established as being in a particular social class, the reliability of the Status Reputation is greatly increased. In the statement, "they are not in the top group [upper class] but they are good, substantial people," the informant first uses Simple Assignment ("they are not in the top group"), and then he adds, "but they are good, substantial people," indicating the people referred to are likely to be in a superior level. The inference for the analyst is that they are upper-middle because they appear to be immediately below the upper class and they are not

STATUS CARD

John Doe	Upper			UM			LM			UL			LL		
	++	+	−	++	+	−	++	+	−	++	+	−	++	+	−
Institutional Membership															
Family				1											
Clique				1											
Association				3											
Church															
Symbolic (Emblematic) Placement					2										
Status Reputation				4 3 1	2										
Comparison				1											
Simple Assignment															
Social-Class Configuration				1											

(1) Interview: 76, pp. 3–4
(2) " 81, p. 6
(3) " 120, p. 5
(4) " 376, pp. 9–10

Estimate of class position: upper-middle, probably UM ++

"common people." This inference is strengthened when the informant gives a list of names of several people who have been previously placed as upper-middle. The other names he uses that have not been previously placed are very likely to be of this same class.

The reader no doubt has noticed, while examining the sample status card, that each class position has been re-divided into three categories designated by the signs ++, +, and —. They indicate the grades within a class which were briefly discussed on page 97 and will be more fully dealt with in Chapter 11.

While placing the individuals who compose the sample to be used for the I.S.C., particular care should be exercised to be sure that mention of the characteristics of the I.S.C. are eliminated in order to guarantee that only Evaluated Participation is being considered. (This was done for a sizable sample of the Jonesville study.) A quick glance at the "sample interview" used to demonstrate the use of the several techniques shows that this is not difficult. It should be said that for all practical purposes in stratifying the community or finding the class position of an individual, such elaborate precautions are unnecessary.

In summary, the procedure for the use of Evaluated Participation includes the following steps:

1. Establish class levels by Social-Class Configuration from a number of interviews with several people.

2. Determine the names of a number of families and their class position on which there is general agreement among those interviewers who have used Social-Class Configuration.

3. Determine the Status Reputation, Symbolic Placement, and general ratings of the churches and a series of associations which have high, average, and low reputations.

4. Establish the class position of an added number of individuals by use of Comparison (or by other techniques) with individuals whose positions have previously been established by Simple Assignment and Social-Class Configuration.

5. Establish class position by membership in institutions whose class levels have been determined by Social-Class Configuration, Simple Assignment, or by their Status Reputation.

6. Establish class position of other individuals by Status Reputation and Symbolic Placement from previously established expressions for a given status.

7. And, finally, place each individual and his family in his social class on a status card.

When a sufficient sample for each class has been accumulated, the analyst can then determine the Index of Status Characteristics for each individual and the range for each class. When the last operation has been performed, the analyst has the necessary number of families and individuals socially placed as well as the several class levels established to be ready for the assignment of an I.S.C. to each of the individuals and their families.

SPECIAL READINGS

The readings for this chapter, the concluding one of instructions for the use of Evaluated Participation, should be extensions of readings from the publications listed for previous chapters to permit widening of the factual base and increasing knowledge about how class operates in

American communities. The readings might well include other publications mentioned in the last chapter.

Part Three

INSTRUCTIONS FOR USING THE INDEX OF STATUS CHARACTERISTICS

CHAPTER 8

Computing the Index of Status Characteristics

PRECEDING chapters have dealt with the various techniques for determining actual social-class participation by means of Evaluated Participation procedures. They constitute the basic procedures for this purpose. In many situations, however, it may be desirable to have a more simply applied technique for estimating social-class position when limitations of time, money, and personnel may make the more refined Evaluated Participation procedures impractical. It was to fill this need that the Index of Status Characteristics was developed.

There are three separate steps in obtaining an Index of Status Characteristics for any individual or family: [1]

(1) Making the primary ratings on the status characteristics which are to comprise the Index—usually occupation, source of income, house type, and dwelling area.

(2) Securing a weighted total of these ratings.

(3) Conversion of this weighted total into a form indicating social-class equivalence.

Each of these steps will be described briefly in this chapter, but the reasons for adopting these steps will not be given until later since they grow out of the research analysis described fully in ensuing chapters. The purpose of this chapter is to provide, in brief and simple form, an outline of instructions for any investigator who wishes to use the I.S.C. in connection with his own research work. For a description of the procedures by which the Index was developed, refined, and validated in one community study, the reader is referred to Chapters 9 through 13.

[1] The I.S.C. is determined for no one but the head of the family. All other members of the family who are unmarried and living in the same house are assigned the same social status. This recommendation is based on experience with this procedure in the Jonesville study, where it was found to be reasonably valid. See also W. Lloyd Warner and Paul S. Lunt, *The Status System of a Modern Community*, Vol. II, "Yankee City Series" (New Haven: Yale University Press, 1942).

MAKING THE PRIMARY RATINGS

The I.S.C. should normally be based upon ratings on occupation, source of income, house type, and dwelling area.[2] If the data for any one of these four ratings are lacking, the other three should be computed. If the data for two of the four are lacking, no Index should be attempted.

Each of the four status characteristics is rated on a seven-point scale which ranges from a rating of "1," very high status value, to "7," very low status value. These rating scales are presented in very brief form in Table 4. The scales are described in much more detail in Chapter 9; anyone planning to use the I.S.C. should certainly refer to the interpretations, qualifications, and definitions given in that chapter.

In the case of occupation and of house type, two alternate rating plans are available. It is probable that either of the alternate plans may be used with a reasonable expectation of good results. The most complete statistical validation is available for the form which was used in the main analysis of Jonesville, but for both occupation and house type later modifications were introduced which, in the judgment of the present investigators, offer some improvement over the original scales. In some cases, the nature of the data available may suggest a preference for some specific form of rating. It may well be, also, that further investigation will develop still further refinement and improvement of these rating scales, particularly as they are applied to new communities.

SECURING A WEIGHTED TOTAL OF THE RATINGS

The ratings on the separate status characteristics are combined into a single numerical index by assigning to each one a weight and securing a weighted total of the separate ratings. The weights are based on evidence from the Jonesville study and are designed to secure the maximum degree of social-class prediction.[3] When the

[2] See pp. 178-81 for suggestions as to the possible use of scales for amount of income and education as elements in the I.S.C. Before using these two characteristics, however, the reader should read the evidence presented in Chapter 11 as to the relative value of these characteristics for predicting social-class placement.

[3] See Chapter 11 for a description of the derivation of these weights.

data are available for all four of the ratings, the ratings should be multiplied by the following weights.

Occupation	4
Source of Income	3
House Type	3
Dwelling Area	2

TABLE 4

SCALES FOR MAKING PRIMARY RATINGS OF FOUR STATUS CHARACTERISTICS *

Status Characteristic and Rating	Definition
Occupation: Original Scale	
1.	Professionals and proprietors of large businesses
2.	Semi-professionals and smaller officials of large businesses
3.	Clerks and kindred workers
4.	Skilled workers
5.	Proprietors of small businesses
6.	Semi-skilled workers
7.	Unskilled workers
Occupation: Revised Scale	
(See Table 7 on page 140.)	
Source of Income	
1.	Inherited wealth
2.	Earned wealth
3.	Profits and fees
4.	Salary
5.	Wages
6.	Private relief
7.	Public relief and non-respectable income
House Type: Original Scale	
1.	Large houses in good condition
2.	Large houses in medium condition; medium-sized houses in good condition
3.	Large houses in bad condition
4.	Medium-sized houses in medium condition; apartments in regular apartment buildings
5.	Small houses in good condition; small houses in medium condition; dwellings over stores
6.	Medium-sized houses in bad condition; small houses in bad condition
7.	All houses in very bad condition; dwellings in structures not intended originally for homes
House Type: Revised Scale	
1.	Excellent houses
2.	Very good houses
3.	Good houses
4.	Average houses
5.	Fair houses
6.	Poor houses
7.	Very poor houses
Dwelling Area	
1.	Very high; Gold Coast, North Shore, etc.
2.	High; the better suburbs and apartment house areas, houses with spacious yards, etc.
3.	Above average; areas all residential, larger than average space around houses; apartment areas in good condition, etc.
4.	Average; residential neighborhoods, no deterioration in the area
5.	Below average; area not quite holding its own, beginning to deteriorate, business entering, etc.
6.	Low; considerably deteriorated, rundown and semi-slum
7.	Very low; slum

* The more extended description of these categories and qualifications as to their use contained in Chapter 9 should be read by anyone undertaking to make actual ratings of these characteristics.

The four products should then be added to secure a weighted total. For example, if the ratings for a given individual or family were 5, 5, 7 and 6, for occupation, source of income, house type, and dwelling area respectively, the weighted total would be secured as follows:

Characteristics	Rating		Weight	Product
Occupation	5	×	4	20
Source of Income	5	×	3	15
House Type	7	×	3	21
Dwelling Area	6	×	2	12
	Weighted Total			68

The weighted total may be any number from 12 to 84 inclusive. If the ratings for any individual were all 1's, he would get a 12 (the highest rating in the upper class). If they were all 7's, he would rate an 84 (the lowest in the lower class).

If the data for any of the four ratings are not available, the proper weights for the other three ratings may be obtained from Table 5. Thus, if the rating on occupation were missing, the other three ratings would be multiplied by 5, 4, and 3 respectively. The three products would then be totaled to secure a "weighted total" which would be comparable to that secured from four weighted products; this may also be any number from 12 to 84, inclusive.

TABLE 5

WEIGHTS FOR COMPUTATION OF I.S.C.

Status Characteristic	Weights to Be Used if All Ratings Available	Weights To Be Used if Ratings on One Characteristic Missing			
		Occupation Missing	Source of Income Missing	House Type Missing	Dwelling Area Missing
Occupation	4	–	5	5	5
Source of Income	3	5	–	4	4
House Type	3	4	4	–	3
Dwelling Area	2	3	3	3	–

If the investigator wishes only an index of socioeconomic status, he may use the Index in this numerical form, with small numerical values indicating high socioeconomic status and large numerical values indicating low socioeconomic status. If, however, he wishes to use the Index to estimate social-class position, a further step is necessary.

CONVERSION OF WEIGHTED TOTALS TO SOCIAL-CLASS FORM; OLD AMERICANS (NON-ETHNIC)

In converting the numerical index described in the preceding section to a form in which it indicates probable social-class position of the individual being rated, the investigator is faced with a rather difficult problem for which no simple mechanical answer can be provided. This arises from the fact that the relationship between social status, as measured by actual social participation and social reputation, and socioeconomic status, while doubtless fairly close in virtually all American communities,[4] probably varies somewhat from community to community in the exact nature of the relationship. If this is true, any formula for predicting social class from socioeconomic status developed from any data in one community cannot automatically be applied to another community if a high degree of accuracy for the placement of individual cases is required.

Three alternate suggestions are made as to how the procedures developed in connection with the I.S.C. for Jonesville may be adapted to the study of a new community. In describing these three methods of approach, it will be assumed for the moment that no important ethnic minority groups are being included in the study. The problem of adapting the procedures for differences due to the ethnic factor is a separate one which will be considered later.

[4] One exception to this general statement should be made. It is probably true that social participation and social reputation do not always vary directly with socioeconomic status at the very top of the scale. There is some evidence available to support the conclusion that in communities where there is a distinct upper-upper as well as lower-upper social class, the I.S.C. will not serve to distinguish between these two upper classes. In one community studied (not Jonesville, where there is no separation of the upper class), the upper-upper socioeconomic ratings fell below the ratings for lower-uppers. If this difference were encountered for any of the other classes, the value of the I.S.C. would be reduced, but since the upper-upper class rarely forms more than 3 per cent of the population, and more often than not much less, the problem encountered is small and inconsequential. Repeated tests show that two or three good informants can give the names of all the "old families" in a city, for such people are well known and highly visible in the social world of the community.

For most studies, however, which are not concerned with the establishment of the class levels themselves, the separation of the upper-upper and lower-upper classes is not sufficiently important to make it necessary to establish the division and the two upper classes can be lumped together. It seems probable that the I.S.C. is, for most practical purposes, a reliable method which may be expected to produce valid results in placing individuals in the several classes in any American community.

Under the first plan, a representative sample of the community, including families from all social levels, should be stratified on the basis of actual social participation and social reputation, using the various techniques for Evaluated Participation, as described in Chapters 3 to 7. When a sufficient number of families have been reliably placed in the community's social structure on this basis, I.S.C.'s should be computed for these same individuals. By studying the relationship between the social class as determined by E.P., on the one hand, and the I.S.C. ratings, on the other, the lines of class demarcation can be laid out.

It will be found that there is a certain range at the top of the I.S.C. scale which includes individuals who are almost always found to be upper class when stratified by means of the E.P. Below this there will be a range on the I.S.C. scale which includes individuals who are almost always upper-middle class. In between the two there may be a narrow indeterminate area where individuals are sometimes found to be upper-middle class and sometimes found to be upper class. This kind of determination can be carried on through the entire length of the I.S.C. scale, from upper class to lower-lower class.

After the scale for converting I.S.C. ratings into social-class equivalents has been thus established, it may then be used for predicting probable social-class equivalents for other individuals and families in the community. This is the procedure which was used in setting up the original I.S.C. for the Jonesville study. It is described more fully in Chapters 11, 12, and 13.

A second procedure, probably somewhat more efficient than the preceding one, involves the computation of the I.S.C. first for a sizable sample of individuals at various class levels, and then spot-checking by means of Evaluated Participation procedures to determine the location of the critical points on the I.S.C. scale which separate one social class from another. In following this method, after the I.S.C. is computed for a number of families in the community, the investigator selects families from certain specific I.S.C. ranges for more complete stratification by means of the E.P. method. In doing this the investigator has to make tentative judgments as to where the class dividing lines probably lie. In the absence of any other evidence, he might well select as a starting point the class dividing points found in Jonesville. These critical points can be determined from Table 6 which presents the conversion data developed for Jonesville.

TABLE 6

SOCIAL-CLASS EQUIVALENTS FOR I.S.C. RATINGS FOR OLD AMERICANS, JONESVILLE

Weighted Total of Ratings	Social-Class Equivalents
12–17	Upper Class
18–22	Upper Class probably, with some possibility of Upper-Middle Class
23–24	Indeterminate: either Upper or Upper-Middle Class
25–33	Upper-Middle Class
34–37	Indeterminate: either Upper-Middle or Lower-Middle Class
38–50	Lower-Middle Class
51–53	Indeterminate: either Lower-Middle or Upper-Lower Class
54–62	Upper-Lower Class
63–66	Indeterminate: either Upper-Lower or Lower-Lower Class
67–69	Lower-Lower Class probably, with some possibility of Upper-Lower Class
70–84	Lower-Lower Class

It will be seen from this table that Jonesville families who fall in the upper extreme of the I.S.C. range, from 12 to 17, are almost certainly upper class and that those who appear in the 18-22 range are somewhat less likely to be upper but still are predominantly so.

The families who fall in the narrow limits of 23 and 24 may be upper or upper-middle. For those two I.S.C. points, the class position is indeterminate, but anyone occupying such a position is either in between the two classes or is at the bottom of the upper class or the very top of the upper-middle class. Special study of Jonesville individuals at this point in the I.S.C. scale indicates that in most cases the position of the person placed is in neither one class nor the other and is truly indeterminate.

It will be noted that in Jonesville the range per class is comparatively great while the indeterminate range between classes is quite small. For example, the range for the upper class is 11 points, for the upper-middle, 9 points, and for lower-middle, 13 points. The range for upper-lower is 9 points, and for lower-lower, 18 points. The indeterminate part of the range between upper and upper-middle is but 2 points; between the next two classes, 4 points; between lower-middle and upper-lower, 3 points; and for the lowest two classes, 4 points.

In a new community, an investigator might well concentrate his first interviews and other E.P. techniques on individuals whose preliminary I.S.C.'s fall between 17 and 25, 33 and 38, 50 and 54, and 62 and 70, since the Jonesville data indicate that the dividing lines between the classes are likely to lie somewhere in those ranges. If further study indicates that the actual dividing lines in the new community are either above or below these ranges, additional interviewing and E.P. stratification would be necessary. This method has a rather obvious advantage over the first one suggested in that it concentrates the interviewing and stratification on those cases where knowledge of the correct social-class position of the individuals is most useful.

Both of the preceding methods involve use of E.P. procedures for stratifying some individuals on the basis of actual social participation and reputation, and checking of the I.S.C. against E.P. for selected cases. In studies where more or less exact social-class placements are required, it is strongly recommended that this be done. In cases where a close approximation is sufficient, however, and where some misplacement of a few individuals will not introduce serious error, it may be satisfactory to use the Jonesville conversion data presented in Table 6 without checking the class dividing lines for the new community.

CONVERSION OF WEIGHTED TOTAL TO SOCIAL CLASS FOR ETHNICS

A further problem in converting the Index of Status Characteristics into social-class equivalents arises from the fact that in any community where there are important ethnic minority groups the relationship between social class and socioeconomic status may vary from ethnic group to ethnic group, and the nature of this variation may itself vary somewhat from community to community. Whichever of the three procedures suggested in the preceding section is used, some consideration should be given to special treatment of individuals belonging to an ethnic group in the community if the most nearly exact social-class placements are desired.

If either of the first two procedures is used, the E.P. interviewing and stratification should include a sufficient number of both Old Americans and ethnics to make possible separate analyses of both groups. In some cases it may be found, as it was in Jonesville, that more accurate social-class prediction can be obtained by constructing separate conversion tables for Old Americans and for ethnic groups.

If limitations of time and personnel do not permit completely separate analyses for each ethnic group, it is probably true that no very serious error will be introduced by treating the ethnic individuals as Old Americans for the purpose of social-class prediction. The Jonesville data indicate, as will be shown more fully in Chapter 12, that the relationship between social class and status characteristics is not so different for ethnics (as compared with Old Americans) as might be supposed. For a more complete analysis of the effect of the ethnic factor on the status-characteristic relationship and for a suggested method of allowing for it, the reader is referred to Chapter 12.

SPECIAL READINGS

There is fundamental disagreement among theorists about how strongly social stratification is dependent upon the economic and technological base. Karl Marx and his followers insist our class system and ideology are phenomena of a capitalism base, and by changing the economic base, we could achieve a classless society. Other writers, admitting economic determinism, argue that class is a multi-factored phenomenon. The present writers belong to the second group. The following selections bearing on this dispute should be read:

Karl Marx. *Capital: A Critique of Political Economy.* Chicago: Charles H. Kerr & Co.

This reading gives the student the essentials of the Marxian position.

Max Weber. *The Protestant Ethic and the Spirit of Capitalism.* Translated by Talcott Parsons. London: Allen & Unwin, 1930.

Max Weber. *The Theory of Social and Economic Organization.* Edited by Talcott Parsons. 1st American ed. New York: Oxford University Press, 1947.

From Max Weber: Essays in Sociology. Translated, edited, and with an introduction by H. H. Gerth and C. Wright Mills. New York: Oxford University Press, 1946.

Alfred Winslow Jones. *Life, Liberty, and Property.* Philadelphia: Lippincott Co., 1941.

Discusses ideology and status.

Charles H. Cooley. *Social Organization.* New York: Scribner's Sons, 1929.

Walter R. Goldschmidt. *Small Business and the Community.* Report to the Senate Special Committee to study Problems of American Small Business. Senate Committee Print No. 13, 79th Congress, 2d session. Washington, D.C. U.S. Government Printing Office, 1946.

CHAPTER 9

The Status Characteristics and the Seven-Point Scales for Measuring Them

---

THE original Index of Status Characteristics, as first developed for the Jonesville study, was based upon six status characteristics—occupation, amount of income, source of income, education, house type, and dwelling area. In the process of testing and refining the Index in Jonesville, two of these characteristics—amount of income and education—were eliminated for reasons which will be given more fully in Chapter 11.

As a result of the Jonesville analysis the rating scales for certain of these status characteristics were revised, sometimes several times. The various stages of refinement of these scales, together with the final form of each rating scale, will be described in this chapter. This is done since some investigators may wish to use one of the earlier forms of the rating scales in preference to the one finally derived by the present analysts. The validation data presented in Chapters 10, 11, 12, and 13 are, of course, based upon the form of rating scale used in the initial Jonesville study. In each case, this original form is clearly indicated in the descriptions which follow.

Each of the four status characteristics had to be categorized and evaluated before an I.S.C. could be computed from them. This chapter describes these classifications, shows how they were constructed, and gives instructions for using them. In each case it was desired to recognize as many significant distinctions as possible and, at the same time, to have a system sufficiently standardized that a minimum of interpretation would be needed in applying it. The first step in each case was to determine the total range of each characteristic. When this had been done, it was possible to define the category at the top of the scale, the category at the bottom of the scale, and an average or middle category for each characteristic. Working from these three base points, additional categories were distinguished, two above average and two below average.

OCCUPATION: ORIGINAL SCALE

The classification of occupations prepared by Alba Edwards for the U. S. Bureau of the Census [1] was used as a starting point for a rating scale for occupations, although some important modifications were found to be necessary.

Edwards defines eleven occupational groups as follows:

V—Professional and semi-professional workers. This includes individuals who "perform advisory, administrative or research work which is based upon the established principles of a profession or science and which requires professional, scientific or technical training equivalent to that represented by graduation from a college or university of recognized standing."

O—Farmers and farm managers. This includes individuals who work their own farm or individuals who manage and supervise the running of farms for the owner.

1—Proprietors, managers and officials, except farm. A proprietor is an entrepreneur who owns and, alone or with assistance, operates his own business and is responsible for making and carrying out its policies. A manager is one who manages all or a part of the business of another person or agency; who has large responsibility in the making and carrying out of the policies of the business; and who, through assistants, is charged with planning and supervising the work of others. An official has large responsibilities in the making and carrying out of the policies of the concern.

2—Clerical, sales, and kindred workers. A clerical or kindred worker is one who, under supervision, performs one or more office activities, usually routine, such as preparing, transcribing, and filing written communications and records.

3—Craftsmen, foremen, and kindred workers. This includes individuals "engaged in a manual pursuit, usually not routine, for the pursuance of which a long period of training or an apprenticeship is usually necessary and which in its pursuance calls for a high degree of judgment or manual dexterity, and for ability to work with a minimum of supervision and to exercise responsibility for valuable production and equipment." These individuals may direct other workers under supervision.

[1] *Alphabetical Index of Occupations and Industries,* Prepared by Alba M. Edwards, Bureau of the Census, U. S. Department of Commerce (Washington, D.C.: U. S. Government Printing Office, 1940).

4–Operatives and kindred workers. This includes individuals "engaged in manual pursuit, usually routine, for the pursuance of which only a short period or no period of preliminary training is usually necessary and which in its pursuance usually calls for the exercise of only a moderate degree of judgment or of manual dexterity. Such jobs require only a moderate degree of muscular force."

5–Domestic service workers include those individuals performing personal services in private homes.

6–Protective service workers. A protective service worker is one engaged in protecting life or property.

7–Service workers, except domestic and protective, are those "engaged in cleaning and janitor services in buildings other than private homes, or performing services often of an individual character for other persons as a barber, cook, waitress, or practical nurse."

8–Farm laborers and foremen. A farm laborer is a hired worker or unpaid member of a farm operator's family who works on a farm. A farm foreman is one who directs farm laborers under the supervision of a farmer or farm manager.

9–Laborers, except farm, are those "engaged in a manual pursuit, usually routine, for the pursuance of which no special training, judgment or manual dexterity is usually necessary and in which the worker usually supplies mainly muscular strength for the performance of coarse, heavy work."

If there is difficulty in identifying a particular job or putting it in its correct general category, Edwards' splendid study should be used as a reference volume. Every variety and kind of job and position are listed and classified by him.

In order to adapt Edwards' classification to the requirements of the I.S.C. certain changes were necessary. On the one hand, it seemed advisable to subdivide some of the occupational groups in the Edwards' classification, and, on the other hand, it seemed desirable to combine certain of the categories. In making these changes the primary criteria were level of skill that a job required and prestige value attached to a job. On this basis a modified classification was constructed. As far as possible, each occupational group or category included jobs in other categories with respect to these two criteria. The classification used in the Jonesville analysis was as follows (the number preceding the category indicates the value or rating assigned to each occupational group):

1—Professionals and proprietors of large businesses (businesses valued at more than $5,000)

2—Semi-professionals and smaller officials of large businesses

3—Clerks and kindred workers (corresponding to Edwards' category 2)

4—Skilled workers (corresponding to Edwards' category 3)

5—Proprietors of small businesses (businesses valued at less than $5,000)

6—Semi-skilled workers (corresponding to Edwards' category 4 and also including protective workers and service workers categories 6 and 7)

7—Unskilled workers, including laborers and domestic servants (corresponding to Edwards' categories 5 and 9)

The question of farm managers and farm laborers was not considered as this classification was intended to apply only to an urban population.[2] There was no change in the classification of clerks and kindred workers; in both classifications they were in a category by themselves. The distinction between skilled, semi-skilled, and unskilled workers corresponded to Edwards' distinctions between craftsmen, operatives, and laborers. Protective workers and service workers were combined and equated with operatives, and domestic workers were combined with unskilled workers.

The greatest changes from the Edwards' classification occurred in the treatment of professionals and proprietors. On the one hand, some proprietors and professionals were equated, and, on the other hand, both professionals and proprietors were subdivided. Proprietors were divided into "large proprietors" and "small proprietors" on the basis of monetary value of business. Owners of businesses valued at $5,000 or more were called "large proprietors," and owners of businesses valued at less than $5,000 were called "small proprietors." Financial ratings of all businesses were obtained from a Dun and Bradstreet report for the community. This distinction between large and small proprietors was made since it was known that proprietors have different status and different prestige in the community, depending partially on the size of their business. This distinction avoided the dilemma, usually resulting from occupational classifica-

[2] For a consideration of how farm families are stratified, see Evon Z. Vogt, "Prairie Township: A Study of Social Stratification in the Rural Midwest" (Master's thesis, University of Chicago, December, 1946).

tions, of giving equal rating to the owner of the smallest neighborhood store and the owner of the largest factory.

Five thousand dollars was chosen as the dividing line after studying the range in size of businesses in the town and the distribution of businesses along this range. In addition, consideration was given to the way certain businesses had been ranked by individuals in the community. For example, it was generally said that X, with a business valued at $10,000, had a "very good business." Therefore, this had to be placed in the higher category. On the other hand, the store owned by Y, and valued at between $3,000 and $5,000, "didn't amount to much." Therefore, the line of separation was placed so it would go in the smaller category.

Small proprietors were given a rating of 5, between skilled workers and semi-skilled workers, after investigating the characteristics of a number of small proprietors. Since, for the most part, small proprietors had a lower status than skilled workers, had less education, and lived in poorer houses, it was judged that their occupation should rate below that of skilled workers. On the other hand, they rated higher in all these respects than semi-skilled workers and, therefore, were placed above this category.

The other important difference between the two classifications was in the treatment of professional people. While Edwards includes all ranks of professionals in one category, it was believed that some professions required more skill and had more prestige than others. Since professional men tended to rank in the community above office workers, they were placed directly above the latter category. Whether a professional man was given a rating of 1 or 2 on occupation depended primarily on the amount of training he needed for his particular profession.

While Edwards distinguishes between proprietors and professionals, it seemed that large proprietors and top professionals had about the same rating in the community. Either of these occupations was considered "acceptable" for members of the upper and upper-middle classes, and approximately equal status was derived from both. Therefore, it did not seem necessary to maintain this distinction.

There are a few particular cases to be considered. Widows who were not working were assigned the occupational status their husbands had had. Individuals who had retired were given an occupational rating equivalent to the jobs they had held when they were working. Soldiers were rated on the basis of the occupation they held in civilian life. Young men who had not worked before going into the army were rated according to their fathers' occupations. This procedure was also followed in the case of all adolescents. In general, when several people in the family were working, a rating was assigned on the basis of the occupation of the head of the family, usually the father.

OCCUPATION: REVISED SCALE

The occupational scale which has just been discussed is the one on which the analysis reported in Chapters 10, 11, 12, and 13 is based. That this classification was satisfactory is evident from the data in Chapter 10, which show a high correlation between occupational ratings and E.P. However, after the work on these data was completed, further modifications were made. Experience with this revised form of the occupational scale suggests that it is an improvement over the original form and that it should be used in future applications of the I.S.C. method.

The modified classification resulted when it was decided to treat occupation as a two-dimensional factor and to use the various occupational groups which had been defined by Edwards, modified as described in the preceding section, but to accept the fact that there were gradations within each of these groups with respect to degree of skill required for the job and the amount of prestige attached to the job. Because this form of classification was more fluid, the job of classification became easier and at the same time more accurate. Thus, any category of occupation was not limited to a single rating but could potentially be given a rating of from one to seven, depending upon the degree of skill required for a particular job rather than that associated with a general occupational group.

For example, while it had seemed a step forward to divide proprietors into two categories, the difference in value assigned to the two categories of proprietors was not always commensurate with the facts. The social evaluation which the community assigns to a proprietor is dependent upon the size of his business and the degree of success he has attained in his business. If other factors are equal, two individuals owning businesses only slightly different in size will differ only slightly in the social evaluation assigned them by the community. But by the classification of occupations which had been used, they might receive very different ratings on occupation. It seemed, therefore, that the ratings assigned to proprietors should take care of minor as well as major distinctions and that there should be not only two but several possible ratings for proprietors (see Table 7).

The second question to decide was how wide a range existed in the social evaluation assigned to proprietors. While owners of large businesses had the highest status in the community, the owner of even the smallest business, since he had invested some capital, ranked above the unskilled laborer. Therefore, it was possible to put a ceiling and a floor on the range of proprietors and to say in terms of prestige value that being a proprietor ranged from the highest category to the next to lowest. After investigating what size of business was most frequent, what size least frequent, and where there appeared to be breaks in distribution by size (see Table 7), the problem was faced of determining how specific businesses should be classified, what should be the range in size of businesses within each category, and where the distinction in monetary value should be made.

This line of reasoning was applied to all other types of occupations. A preliminary step in this direction had been made formerly by subdividing professionals. Now the process was carried one step further, and professionals were not necessarily limited to the two upper categories but in some cases received a lower rating. The rating assigned to a particular profession depended upon the amount of training and education needed in carrying out a particular job.

This method of treating the problem made the ratings of clerks and white collar workers more accurate. Previously, they had all received the same rating, although there was considerable variation in the level of skill and the prestige attached to a particular job. Since the present system is less rigid, it is possible to vary the rating. The same applies to service workers and protective workers. It is also a more satisfactory method of treating manual workers. Previously, because of the placement of small proprietors, there was a gap between skilled workers and semi-skilled workers and often, when there was little difference in the skill involved, there was a larger difference in the rating assigned to a particular job.

There has been no systematic attempt to classify farmers, but this method should make it possible to work out a classification. As the Jonesville study was concerned primarily with the urban population, the question was not pertinent. However, what little information was available indicated that farmers ranged along the total scale from very high to very low, with gentleman farmers, or those who did not work the land themselves, at the top of the scale and equivalent to professional men and proprietors in town, and transient farm laborers at the bottom of the scale.

Table 7 presents the revised occupational classification graphically and shows the classification which has been assigned to a series of occupations. A few explanations should be given on the method of arriving at the ratings. As already indicated, the primary factors considered in all cases were the degree of skill required for the job and the prestige value assigned to the job by the community. As the classification was set up with seven categories, there was an average or middle category, three categories below, and three above. Therefore, in assigning a rating to a job, there was an attempt to rate it from this point of view, to decide whether it was an average job, better than average, or below average, and assign it a comparable rating.[3]

The greatest difficulty is likely to arise in attempting to evaluate factory jobs, since it is sometimes difficult to know what the job consists of or how much skill is necessary to perform it. In Jonesville the ratings were finally based on the hourly wage paid for the job. In this community there was only one factory of any size; it employed about one-third of those gainfully employed in the community. The base pay rate for all jobs was secured, and from this the ratings were assigned. However, it will not always be possible to get this information. In such cases, it is recommended that the rating assigned by Edwards be used. From his alphabetical list of occupations, it is possible to determine whether any particular job is skilled, semi-skilled, or unskilled.

SOURCE OF INCOME

The second characteristic used in determining the I.S.C. is principal source of known income. While socioeconomic scales have

[3] The occupational scale designed by Mapheus Smith to measure social status or prestige of occupations was used to help evaluate some jobs. See Mapheus Smith, "An Empirical Scale of Prestige Status of Occupations," *American Sociological Review*, VIII, No. 2 (April, 1943), 185-92.

generally paid greater attention to the amount of income, the source of income is an equally good or better determinant of status.[4] In addition, it is generally easier to determine source of income than amount of income since it requires less detailed and exact information. People are not as reluctant in disclosing the source of their income as they are in a discussing the amount of income. Moreover, the source is generally known from the type of job; or, if the individual does not work, no more than a cursory examination is needed to discover how his income is obtained.

From interviews with various individuals in Jonesville, it was apparent that this was one of the criteria used in evaluating members of the community. There was a social stigma attached to the family that was on relief. On the other hand, it was a mark of prestige to say that a family possessed inherited wealth. Recognizing that these distinctions existed and that they were related to the general concept of social status made it possible to evaluate and classify the various possible sources on a seven-point scale.

Source of income was classified as follows:

1—Inherited wealth. Families were so classified who lived on money made by a previous generation. This includes money derived from savings and investments or business enterprises inherited from an earlier generation. Inherited wealth is frequently referred to as "old money" in contrast to "new money." This source of income has the highest prestige since it implies that there has been money in the family for several generations.

2—Earned wealth. Families or individuals were so classified if they lived on savings or investments earned by the present generation. This category implies considerable wealth, for the individual lives on interest from capital and has amassed sufficient money so that he does not need to work. This source of income applies most frequently to men who have made a large amount of money and are able to retire and live comfortably on their earnings. They differ from individuals who are retired because of old age and live on pensions, etc. (page 142). In the present case, it is not that they are too old to work, but that they no longer need to work. One gains prestige in American society by being a successful business man and

[4] See Chapter 10 for a discussion of the statistical correlation between these two factors and social status.

TABLE 7

REVISED SCALE FOR RATING OCCUPATION

Rating Assigned to Occupation	Professionals	Proprietors and Managers	Business Men	Clerks and Kindred Workers, Etc.	Manual Workers	Protective and Service Workers	Farmers
1	Lawyers, doctors, dentists, engineers, judges, high-school superintendents, veterinarians, ministers (graduated from divinity school), chemists, etc. with post-graduate training, architects	Businesses valued at $75,000 and over	Regional and divisional managers of large financial and industrial enterprises	Certified Public Accountants			Gentleman farmers
2	High-school teachers, trained nurses, chiropodists, chiropractors, undertakers, ministers (some training), newspaper editors, librarians (graduate)	Businesses valued at $20,000 to $75,000	Assistant managers and office and department managers of large businesses, assistants to executives, etc.	Accountants, salesmen of real estate, of insurance, postmasters			Large farm owners, farm owners
3	Social workers, grade-school teachers, optometrists, librarians (not graduate), undertaker's assist-	Businesses valued at $5,000 to $20,000	All minor officials of businesses	Auto salesmen, bank clerks and cashiers, postal clerks, secretaries to executives, supervisors of rail-	Contractors		

	$3,000		mail clerks, railroad ticket agents, sales people in dry goods store, etc.	plumbers, carpenters, watchmakers { business	railroad engineers and conductors	
5	**Businesses valued at $500 to $2,000**		Dime store clerks, hardware salesmen, beauty operators, telephone operators	Carpenters, plumbers, electricians (apprentice), timekeepers, linemen, telephone or telegraph, radio repairmen, medium-skill workers	Barbers, firemen, butcher's apprentices, practical nurses, policemen, seamstresses, cooks in restaurant, bartenders	Tenant farmers
6	**Businesses valued at less than $500**			Moulders, semi-skilled workers, assistants to carpenter, etc.	Baggage men, night policemen and watchmen, taxi and truck drivers, gas station attendants, waitresses in restaurant	Small tenant farmers
7				Heavy labor, migrant work, odd-job men, miners	Janitors, scrubwomen, newsboys	Migrant farm laborers

making a large fortune. Therefore, these individuals are given a higher rating than those who work for a living.

3—Profits and fees. This includes money which is paid to professional men for services and advice. It also includes money made by owners of businesses for sale of goods and royalties paid to writers, musicians, etc.

4—Salary. This is a regular income paid for services on a monthly, or yearly, basis. This category also includes the commission type of salary paid to salesmen.

5—Wages. This is distinguished from salary since the amount is determined by an hourly rate. It is usually paid on a daily or weekly basis.

6—Private Relief. This includes money paid by friends or relatives for the sake of friendship or because of family ties. It also includes money given by churches, associations, etc., when the agency does not reveal the names of those getting help. People receiving this form of income usually have no money themselves and only through this help are saved the shame of asking for public relief.

7—Public relief and non-respectable income. This includes money received from a government agency or from some semi-public charity organization which does not mind revealing the names of those getting help. A non-respectable income includes money made from illegal occupation as gambling, prostitution, and bootlegging (during prohibition).

People living on life insurance policies, social security benefits, or old age pensions were assigned the source of income on which they were dependent while they were working.

In general, if a person received income from more than one source, the chief source of income was used. However, there were some cases in which it was known that an individual's income was derived equally from two sources. In such cases it was possible to split the difference between the value assigned for two sources. This was done chiefly for members of the upper class who were working but were known to have inherited considerable wealth. It was also applied to business men who had a salary (4) and also had invested considerable money and derived part of their income from interest on earned wealth (2).

HOUSE TYPE: ORIGINAL SCALE

In the early phases of the total study, following the lead of the Yankee City study[5] and before the concept of the I.S.C. was developed, it was felt that house type was related to social status and that if the houses of the community were classified, this material might be used in conjunction with other information to indicate the general status of a family within the community.[6] The initial problem was to develop a simple but objective method of typing or ranking houses. Of all the factors which could be used, size and condition were most objective and easiest to judge. Therefore, they were used as basic criteria, though other factors were considered secondarily.

Houses were rated only on the basis of external appearance. The rating on condition included such factors as size and condition of the garden and lawn, extent to which the place was landscaped, placement of the house on the lot, and nearness to adjacent buildings. In addition, consideration was given to the degree of aesthetic appeal and architectural design. While judgment of such criteria is necessarily more subjective, it is undoubtedly a factor in the evaluation by the community and should, therefore, affect the field worker's rating of the house.

On the basis of these two criteria, a classification was constructed with five categories for size and five for condition. The five categories for size were represented by numbers 1 to 5, and the five categories for condition by letters A to E. Houses were classified as: Very large (1), Large (2), Medium (3), Small (4), and Very Small (5). Condition of the houses was described as Very Good (A), Good (B), Medium (C), Bad (D), and Very Bad (E). There are twenty-five possible combinations of these two criteria: 1A (very large houses in very good condition), 1B (very large houses in good condition), 1C (very large houses in medium condition), etc.[7]

[5] See Warner and Lunt, *The Social Life of a Modern Community.*

[6] This material was collected shortly before, and during the early years of, the war when the housing situation was less acute and families were still able to exercise some choice in acquiring a place to live. Despite a few glaring exceptions, surveys show that people still tend, more often than not, to rent and buy houses which fit their status.

[7] Only 24 types appeared in the Jonesville study. There were no very small houses in very good condition (5A); 3C houses (medium size in medium condition), which by definition were most nearly average in appearance, were also most numerous in the community.

Before a systematic classification of houses was undertaken, two field workers spent several days driving through different parts of the town to determine what was average housing for the community and also how great was the range in housing. When this had been done, a decision was reached on the characteristics which applied to each category or type of house. To determine to what extent the categories were distinguishable, several workers ranked houses independently and then compared their rankings. It was found that there was a high percentage of reliability; as the job of house typing continued, the disagreements which had appeared at first almost disappeared. It was found that of six different ratings on 30 dwellings (three people rating each dwelling twice), or 180 ratings, there were only two variations. To ensure the reliability of the ratings, houses were rechecked from time to time, and it was found that later ratings agreed with earlier ratings.

As a check on the way size was judged, a few owners were asked to give the number of rooms in their homes. This material compared favorably with the ratings assigned on external appearance. For example:

Rating	Number of Rooms
2C	10
2B	9
2C	9
2C	7
3C	7
3C	6
3D	6
3C	5
4A	5
4B	5
4D	5
4C	4

While there was some variation in the number of rooms within each size category, it was felt that some allowance could be made for possible variation in the size of the rooms. The ratings were also checked against evaluations placed on homes by the assessor's office and by real estate agents. However, this was not entirely satisfactory, for the evaluations depend not only on the house itself but also on its location in the town. A house in a good substantial area has a higher value than a comparable house in a poorer residential area.

This elaborate classification was useful for making a detailed study of housing and relating it to the concept of social status, but when the concept of the I.S.C. was introduced it was found to be better and easier to modify and condense this classification. The first step in simplification was to eliminate some of the least important distinctions made in the original classification. Distinctions between large and very large houses, between small and very small houses, and between good and very good houses were least important and could be eliminated. However, there was an important distinction between houses in bad and very bad condition and, therefore, this distinction was kept. (See below.) When these modifications were made there were twelve house types:

Large houses in good condition
Large houses in medium condition
Large houses in bad condition
Large houses in very bad condition
Medium houses in good condition
Medium houses in medium condition
Medium houses in bad condition
Medium houses in very bad condition
Small houses in good condition
Small houses in medium condition
Small houses in bad condition
Small houses in very bad condition.

The problem of ranking these house types was really a problem of determining how each type was evaluated by the community. In order to answer that question a sample of families was chosen whose class position had already been determined by participation and social reputation; the relationship between class position and house type was then examined.

Table 8 shows the results of this work. At the top of the chart are the various categories of houses. In the first column at the left are the five social classes in the community. The numbers in each square refer to the number of families of a particular class living in a particular house type. For example, of the 20 upper-class families in the sample, 16 live in large houses in good condition, 3 in large houses in medium condition, and 1 in a medium-sized house in good condition, etc. On the basis of this distribution, it was possible to rank these house types. However, it was also necessary to equate certain house types or give the same rating to different house types. This was done by determining which houses were socially equivalent or which house types had tenants of the same social status and presumably were similarly evaluated by the community. For example, medium-sized houses in bad condition and small houses in bad condition had about the same distribution. Therefore, these were given the same rating.

It will be noted that, according to these results, small houses in good condition ranked below small houses in medium or bad condition. It is believed that this was a function of area rather than house type. It so happens that, in Jonesville, small houses in good condition were concentrated in a new housing development which was considered to be an undesirable residential neighborhood. As the scale was intended to evaluate only housing and not dwelling area and since, if other conditions are equal, a house in good condition would be preferable to a house in bad condition, small houses in good condition were given a higher rating, i.e., 5, than would be justified on the basis of the data in Table 8, page 147.

It will also be seen that, with one exception, only members of the lower-lower class lived in houses in "very bad" condition. However, this category includes houses of all sizes. It appears, then, that when a house is greatly deteriorated, size is no longer important and evaluation depends on condition alone. However, results showed that this was not the case with houses in "bad" condition. Because of these facts the distinction between houses in "bad" and "very bad" condition was kept (though the distinction between houses in "good" and "very good" condition was eliminated), but houses in very bad condition were not distinguished on the basis of size. This decision was also validated by a remark made by a real estate agent who said he could not place an evaluation on houses of this type with any certainty because they were worth little more than the land they stood on.

So far, there has been no discussion of apartments. The town in which this survey was made had few regular apartment buildings, most of which were in good condition. The people living in them came entirely from the upper-middle or lower-middle classes. Because of these facts it was believed that apartments on the whole

TABLE 8

A PRELIMINARY DISTRIBUTION OF HOUSE TYPES

Class	House Types									
	Large houses in good condition	Large houses in medium condition	Medium houses in good condition	Large houses in bad condition	Medium houses in medium condition	Small houses in medium condition	Small houses in bad condition	Medium houses in bad condition	Small houses in good condition	All houses in very bad condition
Upper (20)	16	3	1							
Upper-Middle (26)	7	12	2	3	2					
Lower-Middle (39)	1	3	6	3	14	11	1			
Upper-Lower (57)					21	11	10	9	5	1
Lower-Lower (23)					1	3	5	4		10
Total (165)	24	18	9	6	38	25	16	13	5	11
Value Assigned	1	2	2	3	4	5	6	6	5	7

were considered to be at least average housing and, therefore, all apartments in regular apartment buildings were given a value of 4.

There were, however, some apartments or dwelling units over stores. While most of these were fairly modern, and therefore in reasonably good condition, interview material showed that this kind of dwelling was less desirable than a house in reasonably good condition. Therefore, all dwellings over stores were given a rating of 5.

More numerous than either of the dwelling types discussed above were apartments found in houses which had been converted into two or more dwelling units. If no other information was available, it was usually possible to determine this type of structure either by counting the number of mail boxes at the front door or observing whether there was a second outside stairway going to the second floor. It was impossible to give a single value to a dwelling of this type because the houses which had been converted varied greatly in size and condition. Therefore, it was decided that the whole structure should be rated as for single-family dwellings, but the dwelling unit in such a structure was rated one point below the evaluation assigned to the total structure. For example, a large house in good condition received a value of 2, but, if two or more families lived in this house, each dwelling unit received a value of 3.

All made-over stores and other structures not originally intended as dwelling units were given a rating of 7.

The complete classification used for house type and the value assigned to each is given below:

Rating	House Type
1	Large houses in good condition
2	Large houses in medium condition Medium-sized houses in good condition
3	Large houses in bad condition
4	Medium-sized houses in medium condition Apartments in regular apartment buildings
5	Small houses in good condition Small houses in medium condition Dwellings over stores
6	Medium-sized houses in bad condition Small houses in bad condition
7	All houses in very bad condition Dwellings in structures not intended originally for homes

All dwelling units in houses which had been converted into apartments received a value one point lower than that assigned to the total structure.

HOUSE TYPE: REVISED SCALE

The scale described in the preceding section was used for the analysis presented in Chapter 10, and results show that it was a satisfactory method of handling house type. However, as in the case of occupation, some modifications were introduced later, and, as it is believed that these modifications are an improvement, they are included here. The modifications were worked out in another community where it was known from the outset that the I.S.C. would be used, so the job of house typing was done specifically for that purpose.[8] It was decided to work out a system which required fewer operations and could be directly applied without the preliminary manipulations involved in the earlier scale.

Since houses ultimately were to be ranked on a seven-point scale, a classification was developed which defined seven grades of housing as follows: excellent, very good, good, average, fair, poor, and very poor. While the same general techniques for typing houses were used as had been used earlier in Jonesville, houses were not given a specific rating for size and condition but were classified on the basis of over-all appearance for size and condition and placed in one of the categories defined above.

As a point of departure in describing the seven categories of houses, three types were defined: Type 1, the best houses in the community; Type 4, the average house in the community; and Type 7, the very poor housing. The next step was to distinguish the ranks between 1 and 4, and 4 and 7, to distinguish the range for each and to get as equal steps as possible between each of these ranks. As a result, seven ranks were defined:

1–Excellent houses. This includes only houses which are very large single-family dwellings in good repair and surrounded by large lawns and yards which are landscaped and well cared for. These houses have an element of ostentation with respect to size, architectural style, and general condition of yards and lawns.

---

[8] Charles Warriner, of the Sociology Department of the University of Kansas, was primarily responsible for the development of this modification of the house-type scale.

2—Very good houses. Roughly, this includes all houses which do not quite measure up to the first category. The primary difference is one of size. They are slightly smaller, but still larger than utility demands for the average family.

3—Good houses. In many cases they are only slightly larger than utility demands. They are more conventional and less ostentatious than the two higher categories.

4—Average houses. One-and-a-half to two-story wood-frame and brick single-family dwellings. Conventional style, with lawns well cared for but not landscaped.

5—Fair houses. In general, this includes houses whose condition is not quite as good as those houses given a 4 rating. It also includes smaller houses in excellent condition.

6—Poor houses. In this, and the category below, size is less important than condition in determining evaluation. Houses in this category are badly run-down but have not deteriorated sufficiently that they cannot be repaired. They suffer from lack of care but do not have the profusion of debris which surrounds houses in the lowest category.

7—Very poor houses. All houses which have deteriorated so far that they cannot be repaired. They are considered unhealthy and unsafe to live in. All buildings not originally intended for dwellings, shacks, and over-crowded buildings. The halls and yards are littered with junk, and many have an extremely bad odor.

Using this classification, houses intended for one family but converted into multiple-family dwellings were handled as they had been in the first case; each dwelling unit was given a rating one point lower than the rating arrived at on the basis of the total structure. Apartments in regular apartment buildings were not limited to one rating but ranged from good housing to bad housing. It should be emphasized that in ranking apartments the total size of the structure is less important than the condition and the way the building is kept up, for the single fact that an apartment building is large does not make it a desirable place to live; a small apartment building may be considered a very good place to live. The best way to rank apartments seemed to be on the basis of the size of living unit per individual family and the building's exterior condition.

DWELLING AREA

The fourth characteristic used in the revised I.S.C. was dwelling area. This takes cognizance of the fact that most towns are divided into a series of ecological areas which are considered to have unequal prestige and unequal value, both socially and economically. Various types of information point to the fact that certain parts of town are more desirable as residential areas than other parts of town. There are wide variations in property evaluation; as already said, the value of a particular house is dependent not only on the house itself, but also on its location in the community. The variations are apparent to one who notes the changes in appearance between different sections of the community. It was found that individuals with the same social status tend to concentrate in the same areas, and members of the different classes had different geographical distributions in the community. The members of the community are, themselves, consciously aware of these distinctions and are able to verbalize about these distinctions in the community. For example, an upper-middle-class man said:

> The several social strata in town are segregated into definite ecological areas, and in each area you generally find a class distinction. This particular area is in transition. Right here used to be the best section in town, but this has shifted to the west side. The axis of the town north and south is Division Street. East of Division and south of the railroad tracks is the lower- and middle-class area. West of Division and south of the tracks is the top and upper-middle-class section. The top stratum lives over on Main Street, Calhoun Street, Jefferson Street, and in there. The lowest classes live along the canal and north of the tracks and east of Division. This latter area is where the first generation Poles live. The second generation Poles are building that new section north of Benton and east of Pine. Most of it is north and west of the northwestern boundary. The poorest American class have rented flats along the canal from the state in perpetuity for from one dollar to ten dollars per year. They have erected their own houses. The poorest section in town is south of the canal and behind the old tannery. Sometime, a fire will clean all that section out. Most of the upper-class people will not admit that that section exists, especially the women.
>
> When we first came here, this layout of the town wasn't very apparent to us, but we were told when we started to look for a house not to rent a house north of the railroad tracks and to try and get something west of Division; we should get in close to Division on the east side, say

a block or two away. We were told that if we got over on the east side down close to the Mill and the canal that we would be talked about and looked down upon. Now that is about the way that the town is divided into ecological and social strata. If you put the two together you have the social structure in outline.

The line of demarcation between adjacent areas is sometimes clearly defined by the community; in other cases it is vague, and the extent and the limits of each area had to be determined by the field workers. In the latter cases, primary importance was given to the general appearance of the neighborhood. A superior area has an air of orderliness and cleanliness with wide streets and many trees. An inferior area is littered with paper, dirt, and debris, and has an air of barrenness caused by the lack of trees, grass, or flowers. Attention was paid to the general appearance of the houses of the neighborhood, for while housing was judged as a separate factor, it is related to the reputation and appearance of a neighborhood.

Further evidence is offered by noting where the members of the various classes live. The distribution of the members of the various social classes was plotted on a map. It was found that members of the same class tended to live in the same part of town; certain sections had a high concentration of lower-class families. Moreover, as the class position of the residents changed from one area to another, the areas themselves changed in general appearance and community evaluation.

On the basis of these criteria, sixteen dwelling areas were defined, each one with a sufficient number of distinguishing characteristics that it could be separated from adjacent areas. While the job of defining so many areas was tedious and time-consuming, it was felt that the results, when applied to the study of social class, were rewarding. By subdividing the town to such an extent, the major as well as the minor distinctions were recognized, and each area was more homogeneous than would have been possible otherwise. However, such an extensive survey may not be necessary in every case. Subsequent research in Chicago has shown that fairly accurate ratings on the areas of a town can be obtained from a few interviews with people who know the town and are interested in status areas.

The criteria used for defining these areas were also used for ranking them. They were classified as good through average to very bad, and ranked on a scale according to their desirability as a place to live. In the process of ranking them, it became apparent that some of these areas, though separated geographically, were socially equivalent as judged by general reputation and social status of individuals living there. For example, most of the areas on the periphery of Jonesville were lower-class neighborhoods, and while they were separately defined, they had similar characteristics and similar evaluations. As is to be expected, the areas at the two extremes of the scale are most clearly defined and easiest to rank. Most of the areas defined fall in a general category of average or slightly below. A description of the levels and each category is given below:

1—Very high. In Jonesville, as in most towns and small cities, this includes but one area. Residents, aware that this area has a high status reputation, remark that "no one can live here unless his family has lived in the community for at least three generations." The best houses in town are located in such an area. The streets are wide and clean and have many trees.

2—High. Dwelling areas felt to be superior and well above average but a little below the top. There are fewer mansions and pretentious houses in such districts than in the first. However, the chief difference is one of reputation.

3—Above average. A little above average in social reputation and to the eye of the scientific observer. This is an area of nice but not pretentious houses. The streets are kept clean and the houses are well cared for. It is known as a "nice place to live" but "society doesn't live here."

4—Average. These are areas of workingmen's homes which are small and unpretentious but neat in appearance. In these areas live "the respectable people in town who don't amount to much but never give anybody any trouble."

5—Below average. All the areas in this group are undesirable because they are close to factories, or because they include the business section of town, or are close to the railroad. There are more run-down houses here because there are people living in these areas who "don't know how to take care of things." They are more congested and heterogeneous than those above. It is said that "all kinds of people live here, and you don't know who your neighbors will be."

6—Low. These areas are run-down and semi-slums. The houses are set close together. The streets and yards are often filled with debris, and in some of the smaller towns, like Jonesville, some of the streets are not paved.

7—Very low. Slum districts, the areas with the poorest reputation in town, not only because of unpleasant and unhealthy geographical positions—for example, being near a garbage dump or a swamp—but also because of the social stigma attached to those who live there. The houses are little better than shacks. The people are referred to by such terms as "squatters along the canal," and are said to be lazy, shiftless, ignorant, and immoral. This general reputation is assigned to most people living in such sections regardless of their abilities or accomplishments.

It might be stated here, for use by the reader in checking our computation of I.S.C.'s in Chapter 14, that the following areas in Jonesville were ranked as follows: Main Street, 1; West Side, 2; Northern Main and Southeast, 3; Chicken Hatchery, West Newtown, Mill, and East Benton, 4; Northwest, Business Area, and East Newtown, 5; West End, Old Town, East Washington, and Polish Area, 6; and Towpath, 7.

EDUCATION AND AMOUNT OF INCOME

In the original I.S.C. amount of income and education were used in addition to the four factors already discussed. In the revision of the I.S.C., these factors proved unnecessary (see Chapter 10) and, as this information was more difficult to obtain, they were eliminated. However, in certain cases they may prove useful. In one study now underway, it has been found easier to get information on education than on dwelling area and, therefore, this factor is being substituted. Since the work has already been done, the classifications originally used are included here.

The following classification was used for education:

1. Professional or graduate school
2. College education (1 to 4 years)
3. High school graduate
4. One to three years of high school
5. Grammar school graduate (finished 8th grade)
6. Four to seven years of school
7. Zero to three years of school

This classification was set up for the Jonesville community. No distinction was made between those who had graduated from college and those who had gone to college for part of the four-year period because so few people in the community had had any college education. On the other hand, as a large part of the population had had grammar school education or less, a larger number of distinctions were made at the lower end of the scale. A break was made between three and four years of schooling because it was found, on comparing education, occupation, and housing, that there were more significant distinctions here than at any other point. No one with a third-grade education or less had more than a semi-skilled job, while several individuals with a fourth-grade education had skilled jobs. Comparable differences were also found in housing. In another community where the educational level was higher, the classification might be more useful if a distinction were made between some college and graduation from college, and no distinction made between one and seven years of grammar school.

The classification used for income was as follows:

1. Very high ($6000 and above)
2. High ($3000–5999)
3. Above average ($1800–2999)
4. Average ($1200–1799)
5. Below average ($900–1199)
6. Low ($600–899)
7. Very low (below $600)

These figures were based on the known incomes (circa 1941) of a sample of the population and individuals' attitudes towards money and estimates of what makes a large, average, or small income. For example, various members of the upper-middle class were known to have incomes between $3500 and $6000 and, though not "very high," were said to have "a good income" or "doing better than most." While members of the upper and upper-middle classes thought that a job paying $1500 did not amount to much, the lower classes considered this sum a good income and hoped to have a job some day that would pay as well. Most clerical jobs, for which salaries were known, paid between $100 and $150 a month. Some jobs in the largest factory paid up to $2000 a year ($1.05 an hour), but the average was about $1400 (70 cents an hour) and some went as low as $900 (45 cents an hour).

THE ETHNIC FACTOR

In addition to the characteristics which have already been discussed, it is clear that the factor of ethnicity must be dealt with. However, the fact of belonging or not belonging to an ethnic group is a different kind of characteristic from those that have been discussed here and must be treated differently (see Chapter 12).

SUMMARY

While the four characteristics—occupation, source of income, house type, and dwelling area—are needed to derive an I.S.C., often it is necessary to know only two facts about an individual: his occupation and his address. The first gives occupation itself and also source of income. Ordinarily, a man working in a factory receives a wage, a man working in an office receives a salary, and a man who runs his own business receives profits. The address tells where he lives, and, consequently, when the houses have been classified and the dwelling areas defined, the other two characteristics, house type and dwelling area, are known.

It is necessary to have a fairly complete description of the occupation. Lists such as city directories can be used in some cases. This is a simple way of getting information on professional men and proprietors in the community. It gives sufficient information on jobs such as stenographers and beauty operators where the function of a particular job is well known. In other cases, the information may not be sufficiently specific; directories frequently give place of work but not the particular job. In these cases it is necessary to get additional information from the man himself, or from his employer, or from an acquaintance. In Jonesville, the work was greatly facilitated by getting a list of all employees of the large factory. The list specified the kind of job and the pay rate for such a job. Consequently, it was comparatively easy to classify the job according to the level of skill. For purposes of deriving an I.S.C., it is recommended that lists of employees be obtained, wherever possible, from all concerns hiring any sizable number of people.

The address can be obtained from any accurate list such as the city directory or telephone book (though the latter generally includes only the middle and upper income brackets). In Jonesville, two additional sources were used: the list of registered voters and their addresses and the records of the rationing board. The latter source was believed to be the most complete and most accurate. The present address is preferred in all cases, but, if this is difficult to obtain, a former address will usually be satisfactory; for though families move from house to house there is generally not a great change in house type—except in critical times like the present when families are forced to take any housing which is available. To test the validity of this assumption, several addresses were secured for families which had moved a great deal. It was found that, while the particular house type might change, the general level of housing and dwelling area rarely varied more than one point.

When the necessary information is collected for any family or individual (occupation, source of income, house type, and dwelling area), each of the four characteristics is given a numerical rating from 1 to 7 depending upon its relative position in the classification. The figure 1 refers to the top category of each characteristic, 2 is next highest, etc. Therefore, persons of high status tend to have low numerical scores, as indicated by the I.S.C., and persons of low status tend to have high numerical scores. As the systems of weighting applied to the various characteristics and the method of measuring the factor of ethnicity are taken up separately, the final steps in obtaining an I.S.C. will be discussed in another section.

Here are three examples showing how the ratings on which an I.S.C. is based are obtained:

Mr. X is a doctor who lives at 200 More Street. A doctor is a professional man with a rating of 1 on occupation. From this occupation he receives fees for services rendered which gives him a rating of 3 on source of income. In addition, it is known that he has inherited considerable money from his family; inherited wealth receives a rating of 1. The difference is split: $\frac{1+3}{2} = 2$; and he receives a rating of 2 on source of income. The house at 200 More Street has been described as a large house in medium condition and receives a rating of 2. This is in the best area of town and, therefore, he receives a rating of 1 on dwelling area.

Mr. Y owns a market, valued at $4,000, and lives in an apartment over his store. As a proprietor, he receives a rating of 4, on the basis of the size of his business. He makes his living from profits gained from the sale of goods; he receives a rating of 3 on source of income. Living over a store, he receives a rating of 5 on house type, and, since he lives in the business area which has been given a rating of 5, he receives a rating of 5 on dwelling area.

Mrs. Z is a widow living on an old age pension at 100 Withington Street. When her husband was alive he had a skilled job at the factory. Therefore she is assigned the occupational rating of 4 that her husband would have were he alive. He was paid a wage when he was working and, therefore, she receives a rating of 5 on source of income. The house at 100 Withington Street has been classified as an average-sized house in average condition with a rating of 4. However, it is known that this house has been remodelled and now consists of two apartments, one on the first floor and one on the second floor. Therefore, her rating on housing is moved down one point, to 5. This house is located in an average area, and she receives a rating of 4 on dwelling area.

The specific classifications used here were designed for a particular community; certain modifications might be necessary in other communities. A possible change in the educational classification has already been suggested. In a large city, with a number of large business concerns, a different monetary value might be assigned to each category of proprietors. There may be a change in the status and, consequently, in the rating assigned to a mayor, high school principal, etc., depending on the size of the community. However, while there might be a change in the range allowed within any category, the general method of classification and the framework developed here will have general use and can be applied to all communities.

SPECIAL READINGS

This chapter provides instructions for the basic field procedure in obtaining the range of I.S.C.'s for a community or an I.S.C. for a family or individual. The readings and problems listed are related to all the remaining chapters, with the exception of Chapter 15. Further reading will be given only where necessary special instructions are given for particular points in each chapter.

Prepared by Alba M. Edwards. *Alphabetical Index of Occupations and Industries.* Bureau of the Census, U.S. Department of Commerce. Washington, D.C.: U.S. Government Printing Office, 1940.

The reader should acquaint himself with this basic work on American occupations. He should not try to read all of it but familiarize himself with it sufficiently to know what is in it and how he might use it.

F. W. Taussig and C. S. Joslyn. *American Business Leaders.* New York: Macmillan Co., 1932.

A valuable book showing how Americans move from low to high levels in our occupational hierarchy.

Percy E. Davidson and H. Dewey Anderson, *Occupational Mobility in an American Community.* Stanford University, Calif.: Stanford University Press, 1937.

W. Lloyd Warner and J. O. Low. *The Social System of the Modern Factory.* Vol. IV, "Yankee City Series." New Haven: Yale University Press, 1947.

See pages 54-90 and pages 108-196 to understand what is happening to job hierarchies.

Part Four

RELATIONSHIP BETWEEN EVALUATED PARTICIPATION AND THE INDEX OF STATUS CHARACTERISTICS: A FIELD STUDY

CHAPTER 10

Analysis of the Status Characteristics and Social-Class Placement

CHAPTERS 8 and 9 have described in some detail the method of using the I.S.C. as it is now recommended for use in other communities and by other investigators. It is the purpose of this chapter, and the three which succeed it, to present a description of the process by which the I.S.C. was developed and its validity tested in Jonesville, so that prospective users may have some measure of the degree of confidence which they may place in results obtained from it.

It was originally thought that the I.S.C. might serve three useful purposes. First, it could serve as one means of checking the assumption that social-class participation and certain socioeconomic characteristics are in large part mutually determined factors. Further information on the closeness of this relationship would give greater insight into the nature of social-class structures and of the forces which determine and accompany them. Second, if a substantial degree of relationship were found to exist between the two indices (I.S.C. and E.P.), it would be possible to predict or estimate with some degree of accuracy, on the basis of the I.S.C. alone, in what social class a given individual or family would participate. This would be of real, practical importance, especially in further aspects of the Jonesville study, since it would make possible the social-class placement of a number of individuals and families whose occupation, income, education, and other status-characteristics data were known or could be easily obtained, but for whom interview, association, clique, and other direct-participation evidence were either lacking or insufficient for definite class placement. Third, it might be possible to use the I.S.C. in simplifying the problem of making a social-class analysis in other communities.

The original Index of Status Characteristics, as first developed for the Jonesville study, was based upon seven-point ratings on occupation, amount of income, source of income, education, house type, and dwelling area. The Index was a simple arithmetical average of the six seven-point ratings and ranged from 1.0 to 7.0. The method of computing this Index, and its form, were modified during the course of the analysis to be described in this report. For simplicity of reference, the Index in its original form, as described in this paragraph, will be hereafter referred to simply as the original I.S.C., the Index in its modified form, as described later, will be referred to as the I.S.C.

At the time the analysis and refinement of the Index of Status Characteristics were begun, several problems with respect to the Index then being developed and used were identified. Among these were the following:

1. How closely does the rating of individuals by each one of the six status characteristics (and by the Index combining them) conform to the rating of those same individuals by Evaluated Participation?
2. Which of the six status characteristics are most useful and which least useful in estimating social participation, and how may they best be combined into an index for this purpose?
   a. Can any of the six be eliminated, thus simplifying the computation of the Index, without seriously impairing the power of the Index to predict social-class participation?
   b. Should any of the characteristics be given special weighting to improve the accuracy of estimating social-class participation, and, if so, what weighting?
3. What special adjustment can be made for the fact that it is difficult to get reliable data on two of the traits (amount of income and education) and that these data are lacking entirely for a substantial proportion of any random group of individuals?
4. How may the fact of ethnicity, which is not easily reducible to a rating scale, but which is presumably important in determining social-class participation, be best included with the other six traits for estimating social-class participation?

In order to analyze the relationship existing between the I.S.C. and the E.P., it was necessary, of course, to have a group of individuals or families for whom both indices were available. Furthermore, it was desirable that the group to be studied be limited to those for whom the E.P. was determinable with a relatively high degree of certainty. When Jonesville families for whom both these conditions were met were segregated from the others, the group comprised 303 families.

Most of the principal analysis of the relationship between status characteristics and social participation was carried through on the basis of the Old American group, which comprised more than two-thirds of the families available for analysis, with subsequent supplementary analyses for the ethnic groups. This seemed desirable both because of the predominantly Old American make-up of the community and because it seemed reasonable to suppose that the relationships could be studied somewhat more satisfactorily in those cases where the complicating ethnic factor was not present to confuse the pattern. It was thought that, if major relationships were established for this simpler group, it would then be possible to determine what adjustments might be necessary for the various ethnic groups.

RELATIONSHIPS BETWEEN THE STATUS CHARACTERISTICS AND SOCIAL-CLASS PLACEMENT (SIMPLE CORRELATIONS)

The relationship which existed between ratings on occupational level, the first of the six status characteristics to be considered, and social-class placement as measured by the E.P. scale, is indicated in a preliminary way in Table 9.

TABLE 9

RATINGS ON OCCUPATION, BY SOCIAL-CLASS PLACEMENT, FOR OLD AMERICANS

Social Class (E.P.)	Ratings on Occupation							Totals
	1	2	3	4	5	6	7	
Upper Class............	44							44
Upper-Middle Class.....	29	7	11	1	2			50
Lower-Middle Class.....	3	3	12	18	5	3		44
Upper-Lower Class......		1		7	1	15	4	28
Lower-Lower Class......					1	13	28	42
Totals...........	76	11	23	26	9	31	32	208

Even a superficial inspection of this table shows that there was a very definite degree of correspondence between the ratings on occupation and the social class to which the various individuals belonged. The table indicates clearly, for instance, that no individual with an occupational rating of less than 1 appeared in the upper class; that no individual with an occupational rating of 1, 2, 3, or 4 appeared in the lowest social class; and that, in general, high occupational ratings tended to indicate high social-class placement, and low occupational ratings, low social-class placement. That the correspondence was not exact is also evident. It was impossible, for instance, to estimate with any degree of accuracy the social-class placement of individuals with an occupational rating of 5, since such individuals were found in four out of the five social-class groups. Further evidence of lack of complete correspondence may be seen in the fact that one individual with a rating of 2 on occupation was in the upper-lower class, while two other individuals with a rating of 5 on occupation were in the upper-middle class. Despite these exceptional cases, however, the general tendency was definitely toward agreement.

Tables were constructed similar to Table 9 presenting data tabulated according to this pattern for all six status characteristics—occupation, amount of income, source of income, education, house type, and dwelling area. In general, the relationships exhibited were similar to those indicated in Table 9.[1] No matter which one of the six characteristics was analyzed, it was evident that there was a strong and definite relationship between that characteristic and social-class placement; and it was likewise evident that there was enough variation to preclude an accurate estimate of social-class placement on the basis of any one of the characteristics taken singly.

Actually, of course, there never was any real expectation that it would be possible to estimate social-class placement from any one of the six status characteristics taken singly. It was hoped, however, that some index combining several of them might be used for this purpose. The original Index of Status Characteristics, as first tried out tentatively in Jonesville, consisted of a simple average of ratings on the six status characteristics (or on four or five of them if data were lacking on one or two) for any given individual or family. Since the division involved in the averaging was always carried to one decimal place, the resulting average ranged through a 61-point scale, from 1.0 to 7.0. The extent to which this index was related to the social-class placement of Old Americans is indicated in a general way in Table 10.

[1] Anyone interested in examining these original data may do so by writing to the senior author at the University of Chicago.

TABLE 10

RATINGS ON THE ORIGINAL I.S.C., BY SOCIAL-CLASS PLACEMENT, FOR OLD AMERICANS

SOCIAL CLASS (E.P.)	RATINGS ON ORIGINAL I.S.C.							TOTALS
	1.0–1.9	2.0–2.9	3.0–3.9	4.0–4.9	5.0–5.9	6.0–6.9	7.0	
Upper Class	37	7						44
Upper-Middle Class	3	38	9					50
Lower-Middle Class		3	33	8				44
Upper-Lower Class				19	9			28
Lower-Lower Class				1	26	14	2	43
Totals	40	48	42	28	35	14	2	209

Since it has already been indicated that there was a fairly close relationship between each of the six status characteristics and social-class placement, it is scarcely surprising to find that Table 10 indicates a marked degree of relationship between the Index combining all six characteristics and social-class placement. But in Table 10 it is also clear that social-class placement could not be completely predicted from this Index. The fact that there were three lower-middle-class individuals with index ratings between 2.0 and 2.9 and nine upper-middle-class persons with lower indices (3.0 to 3.9) will illustrate the overlapping and indeterminancy which existed.

The degree of correspondence between ratings on the six characteristics (or on the Index combining them) and social-class placement may be described somewhat more precisely by means of the statistical concept of correlation. The appropriate correlation coefficients are presented in Table 11.

These correlations, and all later ones, were computed by treating the E.P. scale in its expanded form, including ++'s, +'s, and —'s, as a 15-point scale. The correlations were also computed using only the 5-point scale and disregarding all placement within the social classes. In no case did the resulting coefficients differ from those given in Table 11 by more than one point in the second place. This is to be expected, since the correlation of E.P. ratings on the 5-point scale with those on the 15-point scale was itself .988.

While the correlations reported in Table 11 are relatively high, it is clear that no one of the six status characteristics provided a satisfactory basis for predicting social class within narrow degrees of accuracy, even though any one of them could be used to estimate the most likely social class. If social class were to be predicted on the basis of one status characteristic, the most accurate prediction would be obtained by basing it upon occupation and the least accurate by basing the prediction on education.

That the Index of Status Characteristics, combining the six separate characteristics, was a better base for predicting social-class placement than was any single characteristic, is indicated by its standard error, which is almost half that of any of the single characteristics. If social class were to be predicted on the basis of this Index, there would be a two-out-of-three chance that the prediction would not be in error by more than one point on the 15-point scale. Before determining whether this prediction could in any way be made more accurate, it was necessary to examine in some detail the

TABLE 11

CORRELATION COEFFICIENTS OF SIX STATUS CHARACTERISTICS, AND THE ORIGINAL I.S.C. COMBINING THEM, AND SOCIAL-CLASS PLACEMENT, FOR OLD AMERICANS

Status Characteristic	Number of Cases	Correlation with E.P.	Standard Errors of Estimate*
Occupation	208	.91	1.8
Amount of Income	108	.89	2.0
Source of Income	209	.85	2.3
House Type	204	.85	2.3
Dwelling Area	205	.82	2.5
Education	97	.78	2.7
Original I.S.C.	209	.97	1.1

* The standard errors of estimate are given in terms of the 15-point scale described in the accompanying text. Thus a standard error of 1 is the distance from a 3+ (Lower-Middle Class, ordinary) to a 3++ (Lower-Middle Class, strong). The reader who is familiar with the statistical concept of the standard error will recall that it is a measure of the degree of accuracy with which one can expect to predict one variable (in this case E.P. social-class placement) from another variable (in this case, the status characteristics). One may say that, if social class is predicted from the status characteristics, the chances are two out of three that the deviation between the predicted class position and the true class position, if it were known, is not greater than the standard error. By extending the range of error to three times the standard error, one includes the maximum deviation between predicted and true class positions which is likely to occur in 99.7 per cent of the cases. Thus if the standard error is two points (as it is for prediction on the basis of amount of income alone) one can say that the true social-class position is almost certainly somewhere within six points of that predicted from the Index. Since a six-point error in prediction might mean an error of two whole social classes, it is clear that amount of income alone is not a very satisfactory basis for predicting social class.

relationships which existed among the six status characteristics themselves.

RELATIONSHIPS AMONG THE STATUS CHARACTERISTICS (INTERCORRELATIONS)

The previous section has reported the analysis of the degree of relationship existing between each one of the six status characteristics and social-class placement. It was shown that an individual's most likely social-class placement could be estimated on the basis of any one of the six characteristics, though with a fairly wide margin of error. It was shown also that social-class placement could be estimated on the basis of the original Index combining the six characteristics with a much smaller error than when the estimate was based on any single characteristic alone.

In order to refine the Index and determine which of the characteristics had the greatest relative importance, and whether any were sufficiently unimportant to justify their elimination from the Index, it was necessary to know the degree of relationship existing between any combination of status characteristics, on the one hand, and social-class placement, on the other. What would be the margin of error in estimating social class if, for example, the estimate were based on both occupation and amount of income rather than on either one alone? Or what would be the margin of error if the estimate were based upon a combination of three, four, or five of the six characteristics?

In order to answer questions such as these, it was necessary to analyze not only the degree to which each characteristic was related to social-class participation but the degree to which the characteristics were related to each other. This is a common statistical conception, the reason for which is not hard to demonstrate. The correlation coefficients and standard errors of estimate indicated that, if a man's occupation were known, some definite indication of his most likely social class was already at hand. They also indicated that, if the amount of a man's income were known, some definite indication of his most likely social class was available. The fact that the two correlations were of approximately equal size indicated that the degree of definiteness of this indication of social class was about the same, whether based upon occupation or amount of income.

It does *not* follow, however, that by knowing *both* occupation and amount of income, a prediction of social class could be made with twice as great a degree of definiteness. An extreme example will illustrate the reason for this. If complete correspondence were found to exist between occupation and amount of income—if every 1 on occupation were always accompanied by a 1 on amount of income, every 2 by a corresponding 2, etc.—then, knowing a person's rating on amount of income would add absolutely no knowledge not already included within the occupational rating. To the extent that one rating tends to correspond more or less closely with another, the second rating is useless as a basis for improved prediction. Prediction on the basis of two or more characteristics is better, i.e., more accurate, than prediction based on one alone only if it can be shown that the additional characteristics are not mere repetitions of the one already used but actually contribute some new knowledge about the individual.

It is evident that the best possible index for predicting social class would be made up of a number of status characteristics, each one as highly related as possible to social-class placement, but each one as little related as possible to each of the other status characteristics included in the Index. It is the purpose of this section to report evidence as a basis for determining whether any of the six status characteristics used in Jonesville were so highly related to the others that they contributed little that was new and might, therefore, be properly eliminated from a revised Index.

A glance at the nature of the six status characteristics—occupation, amount of income, source of income, education, house type, and dwelling area—suggested that there was probably a high degree of relationship among the six. All were measures, more or less, of a socioeconomic standard of living; and a person rated high on one was likely to be rated high on the others. The fact that this anticipated relationship actually existed for two of the characteristics, at least, is indicated clearly in Table 12 which shows the correspondence between ratings on occupation and amount of income for those individuals for whom both ratings were available.

The close relationship between occupation and amount of income is evident. It was especially marked at the upper and lower extremes of the income scale where the rating on income made it possible to predict almost exactly the occupational rating. The relationship is less completely determined in the middle of the scale

TABLE 12

Ratings on Occupation and Amount of Income, for Old Americans

Ratings on Amount of Income	Ratings on Occupation							Totals
	1	2	3	4	5	6	7	
1	21							21
2	19		1					20
3	7	6	5	8				26
4	2			5		10	2	19
5				1			5	6
6							6	7
7					1	2	6	9
Totals	49	6	6	14	1	12	19	108

where, for instance, a rating of 4 on amount of income could be associated with almost any occupational rating.

Similar tables, showing the relationship between the ratings on each one of the six status characteristics and each of the other five, were constructed. In general, the relationships which they exhibited were similar in pattern to those shown in Table 12.[2] The degrees of relationships between these different sets of ratings may be expressed most conveniently as correlation coefficients. The coefficients for the fifteen different possible combinations of the six status characteristics are given in Table 13.

It will be seen from Table 13 that the two characteristics showing the highest degree of correspondence were occupation and amount of income; i.e., those individuals who had high occupational ratings also tended to a considerable degree to have high ratings on amount of income. The reasonableness of this correspondence is evident. In Table 13 it may be noticed that the four pairs of characteristics which had the highest correlation all involved the amount-of-income rating. Evidence will be presented later to show definitely that it was not necessary to include the amount-of-income rating in the Index since the Index would predict social-class participation almost as accurately without including amount of income as with it in. The data of Table 13 suggest that the principal reason for this may well be that the factor of amount of income was largely taken into account already when occupation, source of income, house type, and dwelling area were included.

[2] Anyone interested in examining these original data may do so by writing to the senior author at the University of Chicago.

TABLE 13

INTER-CORRELATIONS AMONG RATINGS ON THE SIX STATUS CHARACTERISTICS, FOR OLD AMERICANS

Pairs of Status Characteristics	Number of Cases	Correlation Coefficient
Occupation—Amount of Income	108	.87
Amount of Income—Source of Income	108	.82
Amount of Income—House Type	103	.81
Amount of Income—Dwelling Area	104	.81
Occupation—Education	97	.77
Occupation—Source of Income	208	.76
House Type—Dwelling Area	201	.74
Source of Income—House Type	204	.71
Occupation—House Type	203	.71
Education—House Type	96	.70
Occupation—Dwelling Area	204	.70
Source of Income—Dwelling Area	205	.69
Education—Dwelling Area	94	.65
Source of Income—Education	97	.64
Amount of Income—Education	66	.59

RELATIONSHIPS BETWEEN THE STATUS CHARACTERISTICS, IN VARIOUS COMBINATIONS, AND SOCIAL-CLASS PLACEMENT (MULTIPLE CORRELATIONS)

The data regarding the degree of relationship existing between each of the six status characteristics and social-class placement, presented in Table 11, on page 168, and the data regarding the degree of relationship existing among the status characteristics themselves, presented in Table 13, were combined to produce an indication of the degree of relationship existing between any two or more of the status characteristics, on the one hand, and social-class placement, on the other. In other words, it was now possible to determine the extent of relationship between (a) occupation *and* amount of income and (b) social-class placement. This, in turn, would indicate the degree of accuracy with which social-class placement could be predicted on the basis of both occupation and amount of income taken together, and would provide the basis for the first steps in revising the Index.

Correlation coefficients and standards of estimate for the fifteen possible pairs of status characteristics are given in Table 14. These data are exactly comparable to those given for individual characteristics in Table 11, on page 168, and may be interpreted in the same way.

A comparison of the coefficients in Table 14 with those of Table 11 indicates that the coefficients based upon pairs of status characteristics were, as would be expected, larger than those based upon single characteristics, and that the standard errors of estimate were correspondingly smaller. It should be noted, however, that the five poorest of the coefficients in Table 14 are smaller than the best one in Table 11. This means that, as far as prediction of social class is concerned, a better prediction could be made on the basis of occupation alone than on the basis of any of the five bottom pairs of characteristics in Table 14.

On the other hand, the best of the combinations indicated in Table 14 were considerably better as bases for prediction than any single characteristic indicated in Table 11. If, for example, social class were to be predicted from a combination of occupation and house-type—the best combination of two characteristics—the prediction would almost certainly fall within four points of the true social-class placement (three times the standard error), whereas a prediction from occupation alone (see Table 11) was almost certain to fall within a range of five and a half points.

TABLE 14

MULTIPLE CORRELATION COEFFICIENTS AND STANDARD ERRORS OF ESTIMATE, FOR PAIRS OF STATUS CHARACTERISTICS AND SOCIAL-CLASS PLACEMENT, FOR OLD AMERICANS

Pairs of Status Characteristics	Multiple Correlation with E.P.	Standard Error of Estimate
Occupation and House Type	.953	1.31
Occupation and Dwelling Area	.946	1.41
Amount of Income and Education	.946	1.41
Occupation and Source of Income	.943	1.45
Occupation and Amount of Income	.934	1.66
Source of Income and House Type	.918	1.73
Amount of Income and House Type	.917	1.74
Occupation and Education	.916	1.74
Amount of Income and Source of Income	.916	1.74
Source of Income and Dwelling Area	.911	1.80
Amount of Income and Dwelling Area	.908	1.82
Source of Income and Education	.903	1.87
House Type and Dwelling Area	.894	1.95
Education and House Type	.885	2.03
Education and Dwelling Area	.880	2.06

It seemed reasonable to suppose that inclusion of more than two status characteristics in the Index would give a still better prediction. Some data regarding certain groupings of three, four, five, and six characteristics are given in Table 15.[3]

Each of these sets of characteristics yielded relatively high correlations and relatively small standard errors, as would be expected.

TABLE 15

MULTIPLE CORRELATION COEFFICIENTS AND STANDARD ERRORS OF ESTIMATE FOR CERTAIN SETS OF THREE OR MORE STATUS CHARACTERISTICS, FOR OLD AMERICANS

Set of Status Characteristics	Multiple Correlation with E.P.	Standard Error of Estimate
Six Characteristics. Occupation, Amount of Income, Source of Income, Education, House Type, Dwelling Area	.974	.98
Five Characteristics. Occupation, Amount of Income, Source of Income, House Type, Dwelling Area	.973	1.00
Four Characteristics. Occupation, Source of Income, House Type, Dwelling Area	.972	1.02
Three Characteristics:		
Occupation, Source of Income, House Type	.966	1.13
Occupation, House Type, Dwelling Area	.964	1.16
Occupation, Source of Income, Dwelling Area	.961	1.20
Source of Income, House Type, Dwelling Area	.935	1.54

It should be noticed, however, that the last combination of characteristics in the table (source of income, house type, and dwelling area), though including three characteristics, is a less satisfactory basis for estimating social class than four of the sets of two characteristics in Table 14. This is probably due to the fact that this combination is the only one in Table 15 which does not include the

[3] This table does not include all possible combinations of three, four, five, and six characteristics. The work of computing all of these would have been tremendous and would not have yielded results commensurate with the effort. Those given in Table 15 are the ones which the process of refinement of the Index of Status Characteristics, described in the next chapter, indicated would be most useful.

occupational rating which, it will be recalled, is the best single characteristic for predictive purposes.[4]

SPECIAL READINGS

W. Lloyd Warner and Paul S. Lunt. *The Social Life of a Modern Community.* Vol. I, "Yankee City Series." New Haven: Yale University Press, 1941.

See pages 239-251 for house type.

F. S. Chapin. *Contemporary American Institutions.* New York: Harper & Bros., 1935.

Sinclair Lewis. *Babbitt.* New York: Harcourt, Brace & Co., 1922.

Christopher LaFarge. *The Wilsons.* New York: Coward-McCann, 1941.

Booth Tarkington. *The Magnificent Ambersons.* Garden City, N. Y.: Doubleday, Page & Co., 1919.

Read these novels for descriptions of the houses of upper and middle-class people.

[4] There is a slight discrepancy between the standard error of estimate for all six characteristics combined, at the top of the table, and that given earlier for the original Index of Status Characteristics (which was based on all six) in Table 11. This is due primarily to the fact that the statistical formula used in computing the correlation coefficients and standard errors of estimate for the combinations of characteristics in Table 15 assumes that the component characteristics are combined with optimum weights, that is, with weights that produce the highest possible degree of correlation with the social-class placement (and, therefore, the smallest possible error of prediction). Since the original Index of Status Characteristics was based upon the six characteristics weighted equally, its error would naturally be somewhat greater than that for the optimum combination which is assumed in Table 15. The difference in the standard errors is an approximate indication of the extent to which the Index might be improved by simply improving the weighting of the six characteristics.

CHAPTER 11

Refinement of the Index of Status Characteristics

IN the preceding chapter, four specific questions were raised as to the possibility of refining the original Index:

1. Should any of the characteristics be given special weighting to improve the accuracy of estimating social-class participation, and, if so, what weighting?
2. Can any of the six status characteristics be eliminated, thus simplifying the computation of the Index, without seriously impairing the power of the Index to predict social-class participation?
3. What special adjustment can be made for the fact that it is difficult to get reliable data on two of the traits (amount of income and education) and that these data are lacking entirely for a substantial proportion of any random group of individuals?
4. How may the fact of ethnicity, which is not easily reducible to a rating scale, but which is presumably very important in determining social-class participation, be best included with the other six traits for estimating social-class participation?

The basic data needed for answering the first three of these four questions have been presented; the refinement of the Index in terms of them will be described in this chapter. The problem of ethnicity will be dealt with in the next chapter.

It will be noticed that the first two questions above are somewhat contradictory, the first one dealing with any possible improvement in the predictive power of the Index, and the second dealing with simplifying the Index, even at the expense of a small loss in predictive power. Actually, these two purposes, though to a degree contradictory, are related in that each depends upon determining the relative importance of each status characteristic in the prediction of social class. The original Index, by simply averaging the ratings on the six characteristics, assumed each to be of equal importance in predicting social-class participation. If it could be shown that certain of the characteristics were more important than others for predictive purposes, then the more important factors could be given heavier weighting in the computation of a revised Index; the results would be an index with a higher predictive value than the original, unweighted one. If, in this determination of the relative importance of the various factors, it should be discovered that certain ones are relatively unimportant (i.e., that they would have relatively small weights), then these relatively unimportant ones might be eliminated entirely from the revised Index without seriously decreasing its value for estimating social-class placements.

Thus, both problems reduce, basically, to one, i.e., the determination of the best possible weights to be attached to the six ratings on status characteristics. Once such optimum weights are determined, it is easy to improve the Index to its maximum predictive power, or to determine whether certain characteristics can be eliminated without seriously impairing the predictive power of the Index—or to do a combination of these two things.

By means of the much-used statistical formula known as a regression equation, it is possible to determine what optimum weights will provide the most accurate prediction possible. In the case of predicting social-class placement on the basis of all six status characteristics, the optimum weights were found to be those given in Table 16. If the most accurate possible prediction of social class is wanted, the ratings on the six characteristics should not be simply totaled and divided by six, but should, first, be multiplied by the respective weights indicated in Table 16, and then added. Since two of the weights have negative signs, those ratings, after being multiplied by their weights, should be *subtracted* from the total to arrive at the best index. If these troublesome negative weights be disregarded for a moment, it will be seen, on the basis of the weights in Table 16, that occupation would be twice as important as dwelling area, with source of income and house type falling in between.

The statistical meaning of the two negative weights is definite enough.[1] Unreasonable as it may seem at first glance, the most ac-

[1] For those interested in the partial correlations, they were as follows:

	Zero Order	Partial
Social Class and Occupation	.91	.64
Social Class and Amount of Income	.89	—.28
Social Class and Source of Income	.85	.54
Social Class and Education	.78	—.20
Social Class and House Type	.85	.55
Social Class and Dwelling Area	.82	.49

TABLE 16

OPTIMUM WEIGHTS FOR I.S.C. BASED ON ALL SIX CHARACTERISTICS, FOR OLD AMERICANS

Status Characteristic	Weight *
Occupation	12
Amount of Income	— 7
Source of Income	8
Education	— 3
House Type	8
Dwelling Area	6

curate possible prediction of social class would be obtained by adding up the weighted ratings on the four characteristics with positive weights and then *subtracting* the weighted ratings on amount of income and on education. The resulting figure would be an Index more closely related to social-class placement than any other single figure that could be computed from the data available. This should not, however, be interpreted to mean that amount of income and education are negative characteristics in the sense that a low rating on amount of income and on education is typically associated with high social-class placement. That this is not the case is clearly indicated by the data in Table 11 on page 168. It does mean that amount of income and education, taken in combination with the other four characteristics, are negative characteristics. In the case of amount of income, at least, this is probably due to its close relation to the other four factors (see Table 13 on page 172). There it is shown that amount of income correlated highly with occupation, source of income, house type, and dwelling area. It may well be that, since amount of income was reflected in major part in those four ratings, to include it also as a separate rating would give amount of income more weight in the final total than was justified. The negative weight for amount of income could be interpreted, then, as a correction for over-weighting. Although there is nothing in the statistical data to prove that this is a correct interpretation, it seems reasonable. It might also be argued that these data indicate that income alone is not significantly related to social participation, that it is so related

* The actual regression equation was

$$Y = 1.17\,X_1 - .70\,X_2 + .82\,X_3 - .31\,X_4 + .77\,X_5 + .63\,X_6 - 1.13$$

where Y is social-class placement on a 15-point scale, and X_1, X_2, X_3, X_4, X_5, and X_6 were ratings on occupation, amount of income, source of income, education, house type, and dwelling area, respectively, each on a 7-point scale.

only when that income is reflected in house type, dwelling area, and the other symbols of social-class participation.

A somewhat analogous explanation might be given for the negative weight for education, though here the explanation is not so evident, since in Table 13, on page 172, education has relatively low correlations with the other characteristics. It should be remembered, however, that Table 11, on page 168, shows that education has the lowest correlation with social-class placement of any of the other characteristics. It may be that the inter-correlations of education with the other characteristics, though low as compared with other inter-correlations, are high compared with the predictive value of education as a separate factor.

Whatever the explanation, the statistical fact cannot be questioned. If the sole criterion for the construction of the Index of Status Characteristics were to be the highest possible predictive value, then the weights just given should be used.

The weights given in Table 16 supplied the basis for a possible simplification of the Index since each weight corresponded to the relative importance of its particular characteristic in the determination of social class (relative importance, when taken in conjunction with the other five, and not necessarily when taken in a different combination of characteristics). The smallest weight, disregarding entirely the question of positive and negative weights, was that assigned to education. In other words, in the best possible Index (best in the sense of most accurate prediction of social class) the rating for education would contribute less than any other of the five ratings. If any one of the six characteristics were to be eliminated, the education rating could be eliminated with the least loss in the predictive value of the Index.

The second line of Table 15 indicates that an Index based on five characteristics (with education eliminated) would be nearly as accurate as one based on all six. The correlation coefficient for an Index based on five is necessarily smaller than that based upon six, but the difference is so slight that it appeared only when the correlations were carried out to three decimal places. For all practical purposes, it could be disregarded. This small difference in the correlation coefficients is reflected in a slightly larger standard error of estimate, but the increase is very small.

While the elimination of the education rating from the Index could be justified on the purely statistical grounds that its retention did not increase the predictive value of the Index enough to warrant the additional effort of including it in the computation, there were at least two other reasons which contributed to the decision to eliminate it. One was the difficulty of finding a completely satisfactory interpretation of the negative weight which would otherwise have to be applied to the education rating; the other was the difficulty of securing accurate information on education. It will be recalled that one of the questions posed at the beginning of this study dealt with the necessity of making some special adjustment because of the frequent lack of satisfactory data on education.

After it was determined to eliminate education from the Index, new weights were computed for the five remaining characteristics. These weights are given in Table 17.

Although the size of the weights changed somewhat when education was eliminated, the general pattern remained the same. Amount of income still had a negative weight, and occupation was

TABLE 17

OPTIMUM WEIGHTS FOR I.S.C., BASED ON FIVE CHARACTERISTICS (EXCLUDING EDUCATION), FOR OLD AMERICANS

Status Characteristic	Weight *
Occupation	9
Amount of Income	—3
Source of Income	7
House Type	6
Dwelling Area	5

* The actual regression equation was

$$Y = .95\,X_1 - .34\,X_2 + .73\,X_3 + .63\,X_5 + .51\,X_6 - 1.25$$

where Y was social-class placement on a 15-point scale, and X_1, X_2, X_3, X_5, and X_6 were ratings on occupation, amount of income, source of income, house type, and dwelling area, respectively, each on a 7-point scale.

still weighted nearly double that of the dwelling area, with source of income and house type falling in between. If the Index were to be further simplified by the elimination of still another characteristic, Table 17 indicates that the least contribution to the total predictive power of the Index was made by the amount-of-income characteristic. As in the previous elimination of education, consideration was given to the nature of the negative weight if amount of income were kept and to the difficulty of securing accurate information with regard to amount of income in many cases.

The third line of Table 15, on page 174, indicates that an Index based on four characteristics, with both amount of income and education eliminated, would be almost as accurate for prediction as the ideal six-characteristic Index, the correlation remaining .97, and the standard error of estimate only slightly higher than for the indices based on either five or six characteristics. It, therefore, seemed clear that both education and amount of income should be eliminated, since data were lacking on one or both of them for approximately half the cases, and since, even when present, they added very little to the predictive value of the Index. As a matter of fact, comparison of the correlation coefficients and standard errors of estimate for the original Index of Status Characteristics based upon six characteristics, as reported in Table 11, on page 168, with comparable data for the new Index based upon four characteristics, as reported in Table 15, on page 174, indicates that the new Index had a slightly higher predictive power than the original one. This means, simply, that the slight loss occasioned by eliminating education and amount of income as components of the Index was more than offset by the improvement in the Index brought about by better weighting of the remaining elements.

After both education and amount of income were eliminated from the Index, new weights were computed for the remaining four characteristics. They are given in Table 18.

TABLE 18

OPTIMUM WEIGHTS FOR I.S.C., BASED ON FOUR CHARACTERISTICS (EXCLUDING AMOUNT OF INCOME AND EDUCATION), FOR OLD AMERICANS

Status Characteristic	Weight *
Occupation	4
Source of Income	3
House Type	3
Dwelling Area	2

* The actual regression equation was

$$Y = .84\,X_1 + .64\,X_3 + .56\,X_5 + .43\,X_6 - 1.14$$

where Y was social-class placement on a 15-point scale, and X_1, X_3, X_5, and X_6 were ratings on occupation, source of income, house type, and dwelling area, respectively, each on a 7-point scale.

In this revised form all of the weights were positive, with occupation being weighted twice as much as dwelling area, and source of income and house type halfway between the other two.

Some consideration was given to the possibility of simplifying the Index one step further by eliminating one other characteristic. From Table 18 it is evident that the characteristic contributing the least to the total Index was now the dwelling area. An examination of the fourth line in Table 15, on page 174, however, reveals that there would be a greater increase of the standard error of estimate if dwelling area were eliminated than was the case with previous eliminations. While the increase in error still would not be large, there seemed to be no special reason for introducing the larger error, data on dwelling area being relatively easy to secure for all individuals in the community. Since no great simplification of the Index would be achieved, and a relatively sizable increase in the error of prediction would occur, it was decided to keep the Index based on four characteristics—eliminating only amount of income and education—and to use the weights indicated in Table 18.

The original Index of Status Characteristics was a simple arithmetical average of the six ratings (or of four or five when necessary). The Index thus ranged from 1.0 to 7.0. If it had seemed desirable to have the revised Index in a similar form, this could have been easily accomplished by dividing, not by the number of ratings, but by the sum of the weights. Thus, the rating for occupation would be multiplied by 4, for source of income by 3, for house type by 3, and dwelling area by 2. These products would then be totaled and divided by 12 (the sum of the weights). The resulting Index would be a simple weighted average and would range from 1.0 to 7.0

Since the chief purpose of the Index of Status Characteristics, however, was the prediction of social-class placement for individuals, it seemed more desirable to have the Index in a form which would make its use for that purpose most convenient and which, at the same time, would make the interpretation of its significance as simple as possible. In order to accomplish this, it was determined to express the Index, not in terms of the weighted average just referred to, but in terms of the most likely social-class placement as indicated by the Index. Thus, it would be more immediately meaningful to be able to say that John Jones had an Index which indicated he was probably in the upper-middle class, than to say that John Jones had an Index of 2.4. The latter would be useful only if a table of equivalent values were always at hand to convert the otherwise meaningless figure into a social-class designation.

In order to accomplish this, a table of equivalent social-class predictions was prepared, based upon the regression equation which gave the most likely social-class placement for any given combination of status-characteristic ratings.[2] This is reproduced as Table 19.

The social classes predicted by the Index were designated by the letters A, B, C, D, and E, in order to avoid any confusion with

TABLE 19

PREDICTED SOCIAL-CLASS PLACEMENTS FOR VARIOUS WEIGHTED TOTALS OF FOUR STATUS CHARACTERISTICS, FOR OLD AMERICANS

Weighted Total of Four Status Characteristics	Revised I.S.C.—Predicted Social-Class Placement		Equivalent E.P. Ratings
12	A++		1++
13–17	A+	Upper Class	1+
18–22	A−		1−
23–27	B++		2++
28–32	B+	Upper-Middle Class	2+
33–37	B−		2−
38–41	C++		3++
42–46	C+	Lower-Middle Class	3+
47–51	C−		3−
52–56	D++		4++
57–61	D+	Upper-Lower Class	4+
62–66	D−		4−
67–71	E++		5++
72–75	E+	Lower-Lower Class	5+
76–84	E−		5−

the 1, 2, 3, 4, and 5 designation which had been used to label the class level on the E.P. scale. To make comparisons easy, ++'s, +'s, and —'s were used on the two scales in an exactly analogous manner.

[2] Because of the approximations involved in rounding off the weights and because the weights were taken, for ease of calculation, as one-half of the coefficients in the multiple regression equation given in the footnote to Table 18, on page 181, the multiple regression equation as reported in the footnote on page 181 was not used as the basis for the table of equivalents in Table 19. Instead, the weighted totals were obtained for each of the Old American families, by applying the 4, 3, 3, 2 weights to the ratings on occupation, source of income, house type, and dwelling area. The correlation between these weighted totals and social-class placement was then found to be .970. The regression equation based on these weighted totals ($Y = .21 X - 1.12$, where Y was social-class placement on the 15-point scale and X was the weighted total computed as described) was then used as the basis for the social-class predictions included in Table 19.

Thus a B ++ designated a person whose Index of Status Characteristics indicated that his most likely social-class placement was in the upper-middle class and that he was most likely near the top of that class, on the borderline of being in the upper class. It was exactly analogous to a 2 ++ on the E.P. scale, except that the 2 ++ was a social-class placement based upon interviews, association data, clique material, and other direct evidence, while the B ++ was a social-class prediction based upon the four status characteristics (occupation, source of income, house type, and dwelling area).

By means of Table 19, the social class of any Old American in Jonesville could be predicted very simply and, in most cases, with a considerable degree of accuracy. All that was necessary was to (a) rate the individual in question on the four status characteristics according to the rating scales already described; (b) multiply these four ratings by their respective weights, 4, 3, 3, and 2; (c) total the four weighted ratings; and (d) read the predicted social class directly from Table 19. Hereafter, this predicted social class will itself be referred to as the Index of Status Characteristics. Data will be presented in Chapter 13 to indicate in some detail the accuracy of this prediction.

The data already presented provided the basis for making a fairly satisfactory adjustment for those individuals for whom data on any of the four status characteristics might be lacking. The last four lines of Table 15, on page 174, indicate that an Index based upon any three of the four characteristics, while not quite as satisfactory as one based upon all four characteristics, was still a fairly good one. By calculating regression equations for each of the four possible sets of three characteristics, it was possible to determine the optimum weights for an Index based upon three characteristics alone. These yield an Index which, while not quite as accurate as the one based upon four characteristics, is still the most satisfactory one which could be derived on the basis of three. These optimum weights for cases of incomplete data are indicated in Table 20.

This table means that if occupation, for example, were missing for a given individual, the best prediction of social-class placement could be obtained by weighting the individual's ratings on source of income, house type, and dwelling area, with the weights 5, 4, and 3 respectively. Since the total of each of these sets of weights is the same as the total of the weights used in the revised Index, approximate social-class placement could be read directly from Table 19 without further adjustment.

TABLE 20

OPTIMUM WEIGHTS FOR I.S.C., BASED ON THREE CHARACTERISTICS, FOR OLD AMERICANS, TO BE USED WHEN DATA ARE MISSING ON ONE CHARACTERISTIC

Status Characteristics to Be Used in Index	Weights to Be Used if Ratings on One Characteristic Missing*			
	Occupation Missing	Source of Income Missing	House Type Missing	Dwelling Area Missing
Occupation	–	5	5	5
Source of Income	5	–	4	4
House Type	4	4	–	3
Dwelling Area	3	3	3	–

* The actual regression equations upon which these weights were based were

$$Y = 1.22\,X_3 + .80\,X_5 + .67\,X_6 - 2.07$$
$$Y = 1.02\,X_1 + .69\,X_5 + .53\,X_6 - .10$$
$$Y = .95\,X_1 + .82\,X_5 + .67\,X_6 - 1.14$$
$$Y = .93\,X_1 + .75\,X_3 + .74\,X_5 - .93$$

where Y was social-class placement on a 15-point scale, and X_1, X_3, X_5, and X_6 were ratings on occupation, source of income, house type, and dwelling area, respectively, each on a 7-point scale.

SPECIAL READINGS

W. Lloyd Warner and Paul S. Lunt. *The Social Life of a Modern Community*. Vol. I, "Yankee City Series." New Haven: Yale University Press, 1941.

See pages 239-251 for Dwelling Area.

For descriptions of the dwelling areas of upper and middle-class people, refer to the three novels mentioned at the end of Chapter 10: *Babbitt,* by Sinclair Lewis; *The Wilsons,* by Christopher LaFarge; and *The Magnificent Ambersons,* by Booth Tarkington.

CHAPTER 12

Further Refinement of the Index of Status Characteristics for Ethnics

THE material in this chapter is presented as a report on how an adaptation of the I.S.C. was made for the factor of ethnicity in the study of Jonesville. It is hoped that the method of approach will be useful in other communities, although the specific figures reported here would probably not be directly applicable, since it can probably not be assumed that the effect of ethnicity on social class is uniform from city to city and from one ethnic group to another.

It is well known that ethnicity has a definite effect—usually a limiting one—on social participation in the community. It was assumed, therefore, that some special adjustment on the I.S.C. would have to be made to allow for the effect of ethnicity on social-class participation. The method of adjustment for ethnicity necessarily depended upon certain assumptions concerning the nature of the relation between ethnicity and social-class participation. If it were assumed that being an ethnic always pulled a person "down" in the sense that he would be found participating at a social level lower than he would be if the same individual were an Old American, an adjustment of the Index, by merely subtracting some factor which would result in lowering the Index for the ethnic individual, might be indicated. The size of the factor to be subtracted could vary according to the seriousness of the downward-pull operating for each different ethnic group. On the other hand, if the fact of ethnicity tended to pull down only those individuals who would otherwise be well above the average participation of the ethnic group and did not pull down still further those individuals whose characteristics were such that they participated at or below the ethnic group level anyway, the adjustment would have to be somewhat more complicated. Or, if the fact of ethnicity served to pull down those above the average level of the ethnic group and to pull up those below that level, then a still different type of adjustment would have to be made. As a still further possibility, if it should be found that ethnicity pulled down the level of social participation and also pulled down the level of status characteristics to the same degree, no adjustment for ethnicity would be needed. As a matter of fact, some evidence was found, as will be reported later, to support, in part, all of the foregoing suppositions.

The simplest way to secure at least a preliminary indication of the nature of this relationship for the various ethnic groups seemed to be to predict their most likely social class on the basis of the Index of Status Characteristics developed for Old Americans. It was thought that an analysis of the nature of the discrepancies between the social class predicted by treating the ethnics as Old Americans and their actual social class as determined by the E.P. scale might reveal the nature of the effect of ethnicity on social-class participation.

The 93 ethnic families, for whom both status characteristics and E.P. social-class placement were available, were first divided into four groups, as follows:

Ethnic Group	Number of Families
Scandinavians	60
Poles	4
Southern Mountain Whites	9
Other Ethnics	20
	93

The Poles were kept as a separate group, despite the very small number of them in the sample, because of the importance and number of the Polish group in the community. The "Other Ethnic" group included five Irish families, five English, four German, three Italian, one Scotch, one Bohemian, and one Jewish; none of the groups in this classification constituted large or important elements in the total population of Jonesville.

For each of the individuals in these ethnic groups, an Index of Status Characteristics was computed, treating each individual as an Old American. These indexes were then compared, for each individual, with the actual social-class placement as determined by the E.P. to determine whether there were any marked discrepancies. Even for Old Americans, of course, some discrepancies between predicted and actual social-class placement would have been expected and, presumably, any higher degree of discrepancy found for ethnics would be due to the fact of ethnicity. A summary of these data is presented in Table 21, which gives, for comparative purposes, data on the amount of discrepancy existing for Old Americans.

TABLE 21

ACCURACY IN PREDICTION OF SOCIAL CLASS ON THE BASIS OF THE I.S.C. WHEN NO ALLOWANCE IS MADE FOR ETHNICITY, FOR VARIOUS ETHNIC GROUPS

Group	Total Number of Families	Accuracy in Placement		
		Correct Class Placement and Correct Position Within Class*	Correct Class Placement but Incorrect Position Within Class*	Incorrect Class Placement*
Old Americans	208	41.8%	42.3%	15.9%
Scandinavians	60	23.4	51.6	25.0
Poles	4	0.0	75.0	25.0
Southern Mountain Whites	9	33.3	11.1	55.6
Other Ethnics	20	15.0	45.0	40.0

* "Correct" class placement means agreement with the social-class placement indicated by the E.P. but not necessarily with the three-fold grade or position within each class. Correct placement within a class means agreement not only as to the social class but also as to the position within it (++, +, and −).

It will be seen at once that prediction of social class for any of the groups of ethnics, without allowing for ethnicity, would introduce a sizable error. Whereas 42 per cent of the Old Americans were placed not only in the correct class but also in the correct position within the class by means of the I.S.C., less than one-fourth of the Scandinavians would be placed with that degree of accuracy. Whereas less than 16 per cent of Old Americans were placed in the wrong social class altogether by means of the I.S.C., from 25 to 56 per cent of the ethnic groups would be incorrectly predicted. Thus it was apparent that some adjustment was necessary to allow for ethnicity if the accuracy of prediction for the ethnic groups were to approximate that for Old Americans.

It seemed natural to suppose that predicting social class for ethnic families without making any allowance for their ethnicity would "over-predict" them, i.e., would result, in general, in assigning to them social-class predictions higher than the positions the families really occupied. In order to check the assumption that the errors of predictions were likely to be predominantly in one direction, the errors were tallied for each ethnic group according to whether the predicted social-class position was higher or lower than the actual position as determined by the E.P. The results are shown in Table 22.

TABLE 22

ERRORS OF PREDICTING SOCIAL CLASS ON THE BASIS OF REVISED I.S.C. WHEN NO ALLOWANCE IS MADE FOR ETHNICITY, BY DIRECTION OF ERROR, FOR VARIOUS ETHNIC GROUPS

Group	Total Number of Families	Errors in Placement (Including Both Errors within a Social Class and between Social Classes)		
		Total Number of Errors	Per Cent Predicted Too High	Per Cent Predicted Too Low
Old Americans	208	121	53.7%	46.3%
Scandinavians	60	46	69.6	30.4
Poles	4	4	50.0	50.0
Southern Whites	9	6	100.0	0.0
Other Ethnics	20	17	70.6	29.4

Several interesting facts are indicated by the data in this table, though conclusions must be drawn very tentatively because of the very small numbers involved in at least two of the ethnic groups. It is apparent that for Scandinavians, Other Ethnics, and even more markedly for Southern Mountain Whites, there was the expected tendency for the prediction of social class to be too high when the individual was treated as an Old American. In the case of the Scandinavians, for example, there were more than twice as many cases of predictions which were too high as there were of predictions which were too low; in the case of the Southern Whites, every single case of error (albeit there were only six of them!) was a case of over-prediction. It should likewise be noticed, however, that while the majority of the cases of errors were over-predictions, there was a significant number of under-predictions as well. Some explanation of this will be given later.

Despite these discrepancies in individual cases, the *average* social-class position for each of the ethnic groups, as predicted from the Old American I.S.C., and the *average* social-class position, as determined by the E.P., were surprisingly similar, with the single exception of the Southern Whites. This is indicated in graphic form in Chart VII. It will be noticed in this chart that, as expected, each of the ethnic groups participated, on the average, at a level distinctly lower than the Old American group, with the Polish and Southern White groups being the farthest below the Old American level of participation. Whereas the "typical" or average Old American was to be found in the lower-middle class, the "typical" or average Southern White or Pole, in Jonesville, was apparently to be found on the border line between the upper-lower and the lower-lower classes. The typical Scandinavian was in between, at the border line of the lower-middle and upper-lower classes.

CHART VII

AVERAGE I.S.C. (COMPUTED ON OLD-AMERICAN BASIS) AND AVERAGE E.P., FOR VARIOUS ETHNIC GROUPS

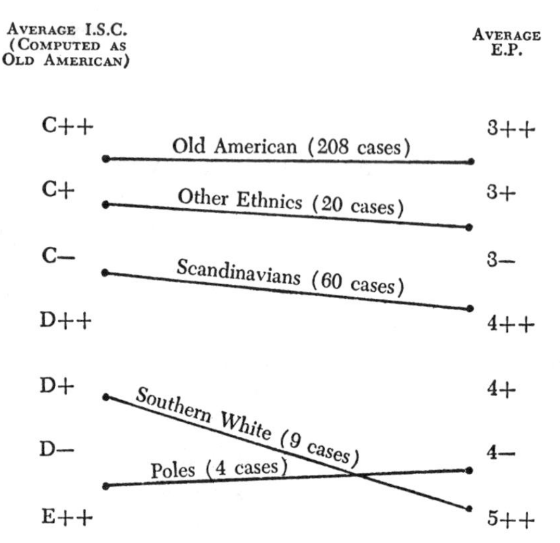

Most important, however, from the point of view of possible readjustment of the Index to allow for ethnicity is the fact that, with the exception of Southern Whites, there was very little discrepancy between the average social-class placement of the same group when predicted by the I.S.C.—even though that I.S.C. was standardized for Old Americans and made no allowance for ethnicity. It might seem at first glance as though no adjustment for ethnicity were necessary, except in the case of the Southern Whites, and that the Old American Index would work satisfactorily for the ethnic individuals without modification.

It should be pointed out that, even if this were so, it could not be assumed that ethnicity was not an important factor in determining, or limiting, social-class participation. It is possible that being a member of a particular ethnic group might determine to some degree one's status characteristics as well as his level of social-class participation. It is evident from the average E.P. for Scandinavians in Chart VII, for example, that the Scandinavians, taken as a whole, participated on a somewhat lower level than Old Americans, presumably due to the fact of their ethnicity. On the other hand, it is also evident from the average I.S.C. for this group, that their status characteristics were generally below the average for Old Americans. The fact that the line for Scandinavians in Chart VII is below that for Old Americans, but that it is relatively level rather than inclined, may be interpreted to mean that status characteristics of Scandinavians tended to be somewhat lower than those for Old Americans, and that their social-class participation was lower, *but that their social-class participation was not, on the average, much lower than their lower status characteristics would lead one to expect.* Apparently the fact of ethnicity limited the status characteristics which a Scandinavian was likely to acquire and limited the level of his social participation, but it did not, on the average, lower his social participation below that which would be indicated by his status characteristics.

The same kind of interpretation can be made for the "Other Ethnic" group and, subject to the limitation of the small number of cases, for the Polish group. The Southern Whites seem to present a somewhat different relationship. If the nine Southern Whites available for this analysis were typical, it would seem that the social-class situation in Jonesville was such that, for this group, the fact of their ethnicity severely limited their status characteristics (averaging at a D+ as compared with a C+ or C++ for Old Americans) and that it pressed down their social-class participation still further, even below that which would be expected on the basis of their low status characteristic. Thus, they were found to participate at a 5++ level, on the average, whereas their Index of Status Characteristics would lead one to expect participation at a 4+ level.

It should be remembered that the above deals with averages only. It is true that for Scandinavians, Poles, and Other Ethnics, the *average* social participation was about what would be expected on the basis of their Index of Status Characteristics. It does not follow, however, that this was true for all the individuals. The data already presented in Tables 21 and 22, on pages 188 and 189, suggest that considerable inaccuracy of individual prediction was introduced by using the Old American Index in unadjusted form for ethnic families. One explanation for this apparent contradiction was given by inspection of the individual cases of error in prediction. In general, there was a tendency for the Old American Index to over-rate individuals at the upper reaches of the scale and to under-rate them toward the lower end. This was especially true for Scandinavians and for the few Poles. That is, an ethnic individual, who, on the basis of the Old American Index would be expected to be in the upper-middle class, was likely to be in the lower-middle class, while an individual whose Index indicated lower-lower class participation might be in the lower portion of the upper-lower class instead. The "pull-up" effect at the bottom was less pronounced than the "pull-down" effect at the top, but both were evident. These two compensatory tendencies apparently accounted in large part for the fact that the average of the ethnic groups was not seriously in error despite significant errors in individual cases.

The procedures by which adjustments were made to allow for the factor of ethnicity, and thus to increase the accuracy of predicting social class for ethnic groups in Jonesville, will be described below for each ethnic group.

SCANDINAVIANS

From the standpoint of rigorous statistical theory the most desirable procedure would have been to subject the 60 Scandinavians to precisely the same analysis as was originally undertaken for the group of 208 Old Americans. Correlations could have been computed to show the degree of relationship between each of the six status characteristics and social-class placement, the degree of relationship among the characteristics themselves, and the degree of relationship between different sets of characteristics and social-class placement. The best combination of characteristics could then have been selected, and the optimum weights could then have been determined.

This complete repetition of the process applied to the Old Americans would have been desirable theoretically because of the impossibility of being sure that the same relationships found to exist for Old Americans were applicable for Scandinavians. It might have been found, for instance, that the relative importance of the six characteristics in the determination of social-class placement was somewhat different for Scandinavians. Perhaps occupation would have required a higher—or a lower—relative weighting for this group; or it might have been found that education and amount of income were more important in determining the social class of Scandinavians than for Old Americans, and that these characteristics should not be eliminated from the Index for this group. By carrying through the entire process *de novo,* on a basis exactly comparable to that described in the preceding chapter for Old Americans, a new Index might have been developed—an Index which would have been the best possible method of predicting social-class placement for Scandinavians on the basis of the data available.

There are several reasons why this was not done. First, the smaller number of classes of Scandinavians would have made any such detailed analysis less reliable than in the case of the larger group of Old Americans; second, the fact that the Index of Social Characteristics, as devised for Old Americans, served fairly well for predicting social-class placement even for Scandinavians indicated that, at best, not a great deal of improvement in the Index could be expected from a complete re-analysis; and, third, the increased complexity of the final I.S.C. which would be inherent in a differing set of weights for the four characteristics—or possibly even the selection of different characteristics for inclusion in the Index for Scandinavians—would probably more than offset any slight increase in the predictive power of the Index.

It was decided, therefore, in the interest of simplicity, to accept the same selection of four characteristics—excluding amount of income and education—and to accept the same weighting for the four characteristics, but, at the same time, by means of a new regression equation, develop a new table of equivalences comparable to that presented for Old Americans in Table 19 on page 183 but based upon the relationships found to exist for Scandinavians. These new equivalences are given in Table 23.[1]

TABLE 23

PREDICTED SOCIAL-CLASS PLACEMENTS FOR VARIOUS WEIGHTED TOTALS OF FOUR STATUS CHARACTERISTICS, FOR SCANDINAVIANS

Weighted Total of Four Status Characteristics	Revised I.S.C.—Predicted Social-Class Placement	
18–23	B+	Upper-Middle Class
24–30	B−	
31–36	C++	
37–43	C+	Lower-Middle Class
44–49	C−	
50–56	D++	
57–63	D+	Upper-Lower Class
64–68	D−	
69–75	E++	
76–82	E+	Lower-Lower Class
83–84	E−	

A comparison of Table 23 with Table 19 on page 183 will reveal the important differences. The "pull-down" effect at the top of the scale is illustrated by the example of an individual whose ratings on the four status characteristics were such that his weighted total was 19; if he were an Old American he would probably be in the upper class (A−, in Table 19); but, if he were a Scandinavian, with precisely the same status characteristics, he would most likely be in the upper-middle class (B+, in Table 23). The "pull-up" effect is observable at the low end of the scale, where the Scandinavian's most likely social-class placement was slightly higher than for an Old American. Thus an individual with status characteristics yield-

[1] The correlation between the weighted totals and the E.P. scale was found to be .86 for the Scandinavians, as compared with .97 for Old Americans. This indicates that the social-class placement for Scandinavians was not as closely related to status characteristics, even when including ethnicity as a factor, as was social-class placement for Old Americans. It is possible, of course, that a complete re-analysis of the Scandinavians might have yielded somewhat different weights for the four characteristics and so have increased the correlation slightly, but it is not likely that the correlation could possibly have been raised to the .97 shown for Old Americans. The regression equation upon which Table 23 is based is as follows: $Y = .15\ X + 1.85$, where Y was social-class placement on the 15-point E.P. scale, and X was the weighted total of the status-characteristic ratings, each on a 7-point scale.

ing a weighted total of 76 or 77 would be an E— if he were an Old American but an E+ if a Scandinavian. There is a central range, about 57-61 on the weighted total, where there were no differences between the two groups. Individuals with characteristics at this level would be D+'s (center of the upper-lower class) whether they were Old Americans or Scandinavians.

Table 23 was used for deriving an I.S.C. for Scandinavians just as Table 19, on page 183, was used for deriving an I.S.C. for Old Americans.

POLES

The fact that only four Poles were included in the original cases to be analyzed for this study made it impossible to draw any conclusions about the factors which determine Polish class status, or to make any very satisfactory adjustment of the Index of Status Characteristics for this group. Yet the size and importance of the Polish group in Jonesville seemed to justify some further attention to this problem. Since no satisfactory analysis could be carried out on the basis of four cases, an attempt was made to secure some additional Polish families for whom the necessary data were available or could be obtained relatively easily. Thirty-eight additional Polish families were located for whom the desired four status characteristics were available and for whom the E.P. social-class placement had been determined. It is probable that in some of these cases the placement had not been made as definitely as in the original cases studied in the main analysis. Also, for more than three-fourths of these additional cases, social-class position had been determined only for the five main classes, not for the fifteen positions within classes; that is, many were classified simply as upper-lower class or lower-lower class without any ++, +, or — designation.[2]

On the basis of the 42 available Poles—four original ones and the 38 additional cases—a supplementary analysis was made exactly comparable to that just described for Scandinavians. Weighted totals were computed for the status characteristics of each Pole, and a table of equivalent social-class predictions constructed, based

[2] For the purpose of the correlation analysis, it was necessary to assign these cases to some position within the class. It seemed most reasonable to treat them as +'s, i.e., at the center of the class. While this is not entirely justifiable, it seemed the most reasonable assumption to make under the circumstances.

upon a regression equation for the 42 Polish families.[3] The table of equivalents for Poles is given as Table 24 which is comparable in form and interpretation to Table 19, on page 183, for Old Americans and Table 23, on page 194, for Scandinavians.

TABLE 24

PREDICTED SOCIAL-CLASS PLACEMENTS FOR VARIOUS WEIGHTED TOTALS OF FOUR STATUS CHARACTERISTICS, FOR POLES

Weighted Total of Four Status Characteristics	Revised I.S.C.—Predicted Social-Class Placement	
39–53	D++	
54–68	D+	Upper-Lower Class
69–82	D−	

It will be seen at once that the social-class range for Poles was relatively narrow and that there was a strong "pull-down" effect at the upper end of the scale. Individuals with characteristics such that as Old Americans (Table 19, on page 183) they would be at the top of the lower-middle class (C++) were, as Poles, found at the top of the upper-lower class (D++) instead. On the other hand, there was a "pull-up" effect at the bottom of the scale. Poles with status characteristics such that their weighted totals were below 68 were found to be at the bottom of the upper-lower class (D−), whereas if they were Old American their most likely social-class placement would have been in the lower-lower class (E++, E+, and E−).

SOUTHERN MOUNTAIN WHITES

The Southern Mountain Whites could not be analyzed by using the same techniques used for Scandinavians and Poles. It was discovered that the nine cases used in the sample could not readily be

[3] The correlation between the weighted totals and the E.P. social-class scale was found to be .51, as compared with .86 for the Scandinavians and .97 for Old Americans. This indicates a much less definite relationship between the status characteristics and social-class placement for Poles than for the other groups. This was probably due in part to the serious lack of variability among the Poles available for analysis. (Of the 42 cases, all but 7 were in the upper-lower class.) If a more widely scattered sample of Poles had been available for study, probably a higher degree of correlation could have been found. At any rate, the regression equation ($Y = .07X + 6.9$) yields the best estimate that could be made of Polish social class based upon these data. The accuracy of prediction could not be as high as for other ethnic groups, however.

augmented and that whatever adjustments were to be made would have to be made on the basis of these cases. Therefore, no correlation analysis or regression equation could be attempted. Yet the data summarized in Chart VII, on page 190, made it apparent that serious errors would be introduced into the prediction of social class for Southern Whites if the fact of their ethnicity were disregarded.

By comparing the average of the social-class predictions based on the Old American Index of Status Characteristics and the average of the social-class placements on the E.P. scale, it was discovered that, by adding eight points to the weighted total of the characteristic ratings, the two averages could be made practically to coincide. While this adjustment still did not bring about an exact prediction of all the nine Southern Whites, at least, by over-predicting some individuals a little and under-predicting others a little, it placed the Southern White group where it belonged. This also changed the nature of the errors of prediction from large errors, all in one direction (predicted too high), to smaller errors, some in one direction and some in the other.

Accordingly, an approximate Index of Status Characteristics for Southern Whites was arrived at by computing the weighted total just as for Old Americans, adding eight points to this weighted total, and then using the regular Old American table of social-class equivalents as given in Table 19, on page 183. These steps have been consolidated in Table 25, from which a Southern White's most likely social-class placement may be read directly, the eight-point adjustment having already been taken care of in the construction of the table. Only those ranges of social class in which the nine Southern Whites actually occurred are shown, since there is no way of knowing whether the same relationship would hold in other parts of the scale.

OTHER ETHNICS

The group of 20 "Other Ethnic" families was not large enough, homogeneous enough, or important enough to justify correlation and regression-equation analysis. Since it was shown in Chart VII, on page 190, that the group was, on the average, placed correctly by the use of the Old American Index, no adjustment of the type made for Southern Whites could be made or was needed. While inspection of the individual cases indicated that there were a few cases

TABLE 25

PREDICTED SOCIAL-CLASS PLACEMENTS FOR VARIOUS WEIGHTED TOTALS OF FOUR STATUS CHARACTERISTICS, FOR SOUTHERN WHITES

Weighted Total of Four Status Characteristics	Revised I.S.C.—Predicted Social-Class Placement	
44–48	D++	
49–53	D+	Upper-Lower Class
54–58	D–	
59–63	E++	
64–67	E+	Lower-Lower Class
68–84	E–	

of rather wide error in prediction—both over-predictions and under-predictions—if they were treated simply as Old Americans, there seemed to be no feasible way to make any adjustment which would not introduce as many new errors as it corrected. Since the group was not an important one in the total Jonesville population, it seemed best to make no adjustment but to predict social-class participation for this group, when necessary, by treating them simply as Old Americans.

SPECIAL READINGS

W. Lloyd Warner and Leo Srole. *The Social Systems of American Ethnic Groups.* Vol. III, "Yankee City Series." New Haven: Yale University Press, 1945.

Refer to pages 67-103 to see how ethnics rise.

Louis Wirth. *The Ghetto.* Chicago: University of Chicago Press, 1928.

A study of ethnic adjustment in a metropolitan setting. Refer especially to pages 282-91.

Allison Davis, Burleigh B. Gardner, and Mary R. Gardner. *Deep South.* Chicago: University of Chicago Press, 1941.

Refer to pages 1-58 for a contrast of race and color-caste with ethnic groups.

St. Clair Drake and Horace R. Cayton. *Black Metropolis.* New York: Harcourt, Brace & Co., 1945.

Read pages 769-782 for a comparison of color-caste in the Deep South with the urban North; also pages 710-715 for the Negro class system.

CHAPTER 13

Accuracy of Estimating Social-Class Placement by Means of the Revised Index of Status Characteristics

ONE of the chief values of the Index of Status Characteristics—and one of the main purposes for which it was developed—is as an aid in the estimation of the social-class position of an individual or family for whom the social-class position would otherwise be unknown. Preceding chapters have described the process by which the Index was first developed and then revised in order to increase its efficiency. It is the purpose of this chapter to present certain evidence on the degree of accuracy of prediction achieved, so that any user of the Index will have some basis for determining its reliability under varying conditions.

The test of the accuracy of the Index was accomplished by re-examining the 303 Jonesville families upon which the study, reported in Chapters 10, 11, and 12, was based. Since an Index of Status Characteristics was available for all but two of these, it was possible to "predict" social-class placement for them just as if their correct social-class placement had not been known.[1] Then, since there was also available an E. P. rating, giving their probable social-class placement, it was possible to compare the predicted with the actual social-class placements and to secure measures of the accuracy of the prediction.

Within reasonable limits these measures of accuracy of prediction should be applicable for similar families or individuals to whom the Index of Status Characteristics might be applied. It should be pointed out, of course, that in applying the Index to new cases, particularly in a new community, the accuracy of prediction would be

[1] In two cases data were available for status-characteristic ratings on only two of the four characteristics, and no Index was computed. The 38 additional Poles referred to on p. 195 were not included in the analysis of this chapter, both because of the probable lower reliability of their social-class placement on the E.P. scale and because of the lack of the ++, +, and — designations for most of them.

somewhat less than when applied to the same cases that were used as a basis for its refinement and validation. Two studies using the I.S.C. have been conducted in segments of the Chicago population. Preliminary analyses make it clear that the I.S.C. will determine class differences in this metropolitan area, but it is not yet clear what the class limits of the range are or how far the indeterminate areas extend.

NUMBER AND SIZE OF ERRORS

Perhaps the simplest way to make a preliminary analysis of the error of prediction is to study the number and size of the errors occurring when social class is actually predicted—an "error" being defined for the present as a discrepancy between the social class predicted from the I.S.C. and the social-class placement as determined by E.P. It must be understood that a discrepancy in position within a social class is here considered an error as well as a discrepancy between two social classes.

In order to make more clear this meaning of the term "error," two sets of symbols are illustrated in Table 26, one designating social-class participation as determined by the E.P., the other designating social-class prediction from the I.S.C.

TABLE 26

SYMBOLS FOR DESIGNATING E.P. AND I.S.C. SOCIAL-CLASS PLACEMENTS

Social Class	Grade Within Social Class	E.P. Designation	I.S.C. Designation
Upper	Strong	1++	A++
	Solid	1+	A+
	Weak	1−	A−
Upper-Middle	Strong	2++	B++
	Solid	2+	B+
	Weak	2−	B−
Lower-Middle	Strong	3++	C++
	Solid	3+	C+
	Weak	3−	C−
Upper-Lower	Strong	4++	D++
	Solid	4+	D+
	Weak	4−	D−
Lower-Lower	Strong	5++	E++
	Solid	5+	E+
	Weak	5−	E−

It will be readily seen that an "error" defined in this way does not necessarily mean an error in designation of the main social class. An "error" of either one or two points (as between an E.P. placement of 2++ and an I.S.C. prediction of B—) may still place the prediction in the correct social class. An error of only one point (as between 2++ and A—) *may*, however, result in a wrong designation of the social-class in a borderline case. This problem will be taken up in more detail a few paragraphs further on.

The number of errors of different size, as defined above, is given for Old Americans and for ethnics separately in Table 27.

It will be seen at once from Table 27 that the Index cannot be relied upon to indicate, with any great degree of accuracy, the exact

TABLE 27

NUMBER AND SIZE OF ERRORS IN PREDICTING SOCIAL-CLASS PARTICIPATION ON THE BASIS OF THE I.S.C.

Size of Error in Prediction of Social Class	Old Americans			Ethnics		
	Number of Cases	Per Cent of Total	Cumulative Percentage	Number of Cases	Per Cent of Total	Cumulative Percentage
No error (correct placement)	87	41.8%	41.8%	23	24.7%	24.7%
Error of 1 position	89	42.8	84.6	45	48.4	73.1
Error of 2 positions	32	15.4	100.0	18	19.4	92.5
Error of 3 positions	—	—	—	6	6.4	98.9
Error of 4 positions	—	—	—	1	1.1	100.0
Totals	208	100.0%	—	93	100.0%	—

position of any individual or family on what may be thought of as the 15-point E.P. scale (including the three positions in each of five social classes). For less than half of the Old Americans and for less than one-quarter of the ethnics in the Jonesville group did the Index give a prediction which was exactly correct. While such exact prediction is not possible on the basis of this Index, it is possible to be fairly certain that, for Old Americans at least, the predicted social-class position will not be off more than one point, and to be almost completely certain that it will not be wrong by more than two points. Thus, Table 27 shows that, while only 42 per cent were placed with exact accuracy, an additional 43 per cent were off by only one point, i.e., were predicted for positions immediately adjacent to those in which the E.P. indicated they were actually participating—giving a total of 85 per cent either correctly placed or off only one point. All of the additional 15 per cent were found to be actually participating within two points of the place predicted for them. One may conclude, then, that if the Index is applied to Old Americans and under conditions similar to those prevailing when the present group was rated, one may expect that in approximately 85 per cent of the cases the actual social-class position, if it were known, would not vary more than 1 point from that predicted and that in no case would it be likely to be more than 2 points different.

That one cannot use the Index with the same degree of assurance when predicting social class for ethnics is evident. In the case of Jonesville ethnics (Scandinavians, Poles, Southern Whites, and Other Ethnics taken together), approximately a quarter of the group could be predicted with exact accuracy and another 50 per cent with an error of only one point; but it was likely that in approximately 25 per cent of the cases the error would be two points or more, occasionally reaching up to four points. This lesser degree of accuracy for the ethnic predictions may be due to either of two factors, or perhaps to a combination of these factors: first, because of the small number of cases involved, especially for the non-Scandinavian ethnics, the entire process of adjusting the Index to allow for ethnicity may not have been as accurate and complete as would have been desirable; second, it may be that social-class participation for ethnic peoples is actually less rigorously related to status characteristics—at least, to those here considered—and that other factors (such as degree of language accent, perhaps, or length of time in this country) may be of greater relative importance.

Whatever the explanation, Table 27 indicates that, while the Index does have definite value for predicting social class for ethnic individuals within certain margins of error, those margins of error must be larger for ethnics than for Old Americans. When the accuracy of prediction for ethnics was considered for the various ethnic groups separately, no marked variations were found among the groups.

As pointed out earlier, an error in placement of either one or two points may or may not result in an error in social-class designation. If, for example, an individual is actually at the bottom of the upper-middle class (2—) and his Index of Characteristics is a

B++, there is an "error" of two points, yet the correct social class has been predicted; on the other hand, if the Index had been C++, the "error" would have been only one point, yet the Index would indicate lower-middle class instead of upper-middle. In most cases, an error in the main class designation is more serious, and more to be avoided if possible, than an error in placement within a social class, even if the actual size of the latter error should be greater.

Table 28, presenting data on accuracy of prediction, distinguishes between those errors of placement which do not affect the main social-class designation and errors which involve a mistake in the social class itself. These data are presented in graphic form in Chart VIII. It is clear that, while less than half of the Old Americans were predicted in exactly the right position, the great bulk of the errors of prediction did not affect the social-class designation itself. In 84 per cent of the cases, the social class predicted by the Index of Status Characteristics was found to be the correct one as determined by the E.P. For ethnics, the proportion was somewhat smaller, the comparable figure being 72 per cent.

TABLE 28

ACCURACY IN PREDICTION OF SOCIAL-CLASS PARTICIPATION ON THE BASIS OF THE REVISED I.S.C., BY TYPE OF ERROR

PLACEMENT	OLD AMERICANS			ETHNICS		
	Number of Cases	Per Cent of Total	Cumulative Percentage	Number of Cases	Per Cent of Total	Cumulative Percentage
Correct Class Placement and Correct Position within Class	87	41.8%	41.8%	23	24.7%	24.7%
Correct Class Placement but Incorrect Position within Class	88	42.3	84.1	44	47.3	72.0
Incorrect Class Placement	33	15.9	100.0	26	28.0	100.0
Totals*	208	100.0%	—	93	100.0%	—

* In all cases in which an error in the social class itself was made, the class predicted was always one immediately adjacent to the actual class. In no case, either Old American or ethnic, did the prediction differ from the actual placement by more than one social class.

CHART VIII

ACCURACY OF PREDICTION OF SOCIAL CLASS (E.P.) ON THE BASIS OF THE I.S.C., BY IMPORTANCE OF ERROR

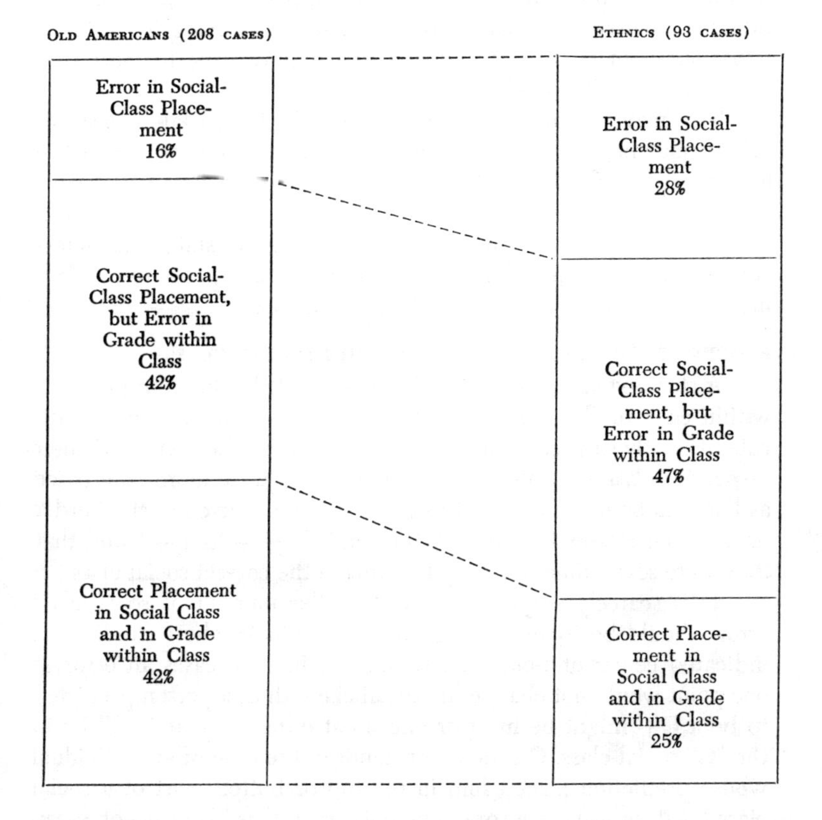

This leaves 16 per cent of the cases for Old Americans and 28 per cent for ethnics whose social class was wrongly predicted by the Index of Status Characteristics. The remainder of this chapter will present data which seek to identify the conditions under which these errors were most likely to occur and under which they were most likely to be absent; consideration will also be given to the possibility of further refinement of the Index with a view to lowering this margin of error.

ERRORS ANALYZED BY SOCIAL-CLASS LEVEL

An examination of the errors in social-class prediction by the different social-class levels indicated that the percentage of errors for individuals predicted as being in the upper-lower class was considerably higher than that for those predicted as being in the class either above or below the upper-lower. This was true for both Old Americans and Ethnics.[2]

This may be due in part to the nature of the social-class structure. It may be that this is evidence that the upper-lower class is the least sharply defined and the least rigorously related to status characteristics. It probably indicates also that the lower-middle and lower-lower classes are the most closely related to status characteristics—less than 10 per cent of the Jonesville cases predicted as falling in each of these two classes failed to do so.

ERRORS ANALYZED BY POSITION WITHIN SOCIAL CLASS

A startling variation in the size of error at the different positions within each of the social classes is shown in Table 29 which indicates that those predictions which occurred at the center of their respective classes (those with the symbol +) were more than twice as likely to be exactly correct as those which occurred at the border lines of the classes (those with the symbols ++ and —) and that they were seven times as likely to indicate the correct social class.

It is scarcely surprising that a smaller number of social-class errors should be found among those individuals whose predictions indicated center-of-a-class position, since in such cases an error of one point would not change the social class; thus, a person predicted to be a C+ might be in error one point either way and still be in the "C" social class. On the other hand, in the case of an individual whose prediction placed him in the top or bottom part of a social class (++ or —), an error of one point might, as likely as not, mean a misclassification for the main social class. This might explain, at least in large part, the substantial difference in errors in social-class placement indicated in the last line of Table 29. Whereas 22 per cent of the Old Americans whose prediction included a ++ or — were predicted in the wrong social class, only 3 per cent of those with a + belonged in some other class. The same relationship held for the ethnics, though not in so striking a degree.

---

[2] The detailed statistical data upon which these statements are based are not presented here but may be examined by writing to the authors.

TABLE 29

ACCURACY IN PREDICTION OF SOCIAL-CLASS PARTICIPATION ON THE BASIS OF THE REVISED I.S.C., BY POSITION WITHIN THE SOCIAL CLASSES

PLACEMENT	OLD AMERICANS				ETHNICS			
	Top (++) (60)	Bottom (−) (82)	Middle (+) (66)	Top and Bottom (++, −) (142)	Top (++) (31)	Bottom (−) (36)	Middle (+) (26)	Top and Bottom (++, −) (67)
Correct Class Placement and Correct Position within Class.........	31.7%	29.3%	66.7%	30.3%	22.6%	16.7%	38.5%	19.4%
Correct Class Placement but Incorrect Position within Class.........	53.3	43.9	30.3	47.9	48.4	44.4	50.0	46.3
Incorrect Class Placement.....	15.0	26.8	3.0	21.8	29.0	38.9	11.5	34.3
Totals....	100.0%	100.0%	100.0%	100.0%	100.0%	100.0%	100.0%	100.0%

The preceding paragraph does not explain, however, the fact that individuals (either Old American or ethnic) who were predicted as being in the + portion of their social class (see Table 29) not only were more likely than the others to be in the correct social class, but were twice as likely to be correctly placed within the class as well. Thus, whereas only 30 per cent of the ++'s and —'s among the Old Americans were placed exactly (position within class, as well as correct class), 67 per cent of the +'s were exactly placed. In the ethnic group, while the amount of error is greater, the proportion is still two-to-one in favor of those designated as +'s.

The only reasonable interpretation of this greater accuracy of prediction toward the center of the classes seems to be that the +'s, presumably, the "typical" members of the social class, are more fixed in their positions, less likely to be socially mobile, and more likely to conform to the status-characteristic pattern typical of their class. In this same line of reasoning, the ++'s and —'s, on the other hand, are apparently not only located near the border lines of the classes (so that a slight error may result in incorrect placement) but are also inherently less stable, in the sense that their social-class participation is not so closely related to their status characteristics. In many cases, they are probably individuals or families who are either upward or downward mobile and for whom there may be a time lag between the movement of the status characteristics and the social participation.

The relationship may be seen more clearly in Chart IX, which indicates that the tendency for those predicted as + actually to be + on the E.P. scale was much greater than for those predicted at the other two positions.

CHART IX

ACCURACY OF PREDICTION OF SOCIAL CLASS (E.P.) ON THE BASIS OF THE I.S.C., BY GRADE WITHIN THE SOCIAL CLASS, FOR OLD AMERICANS

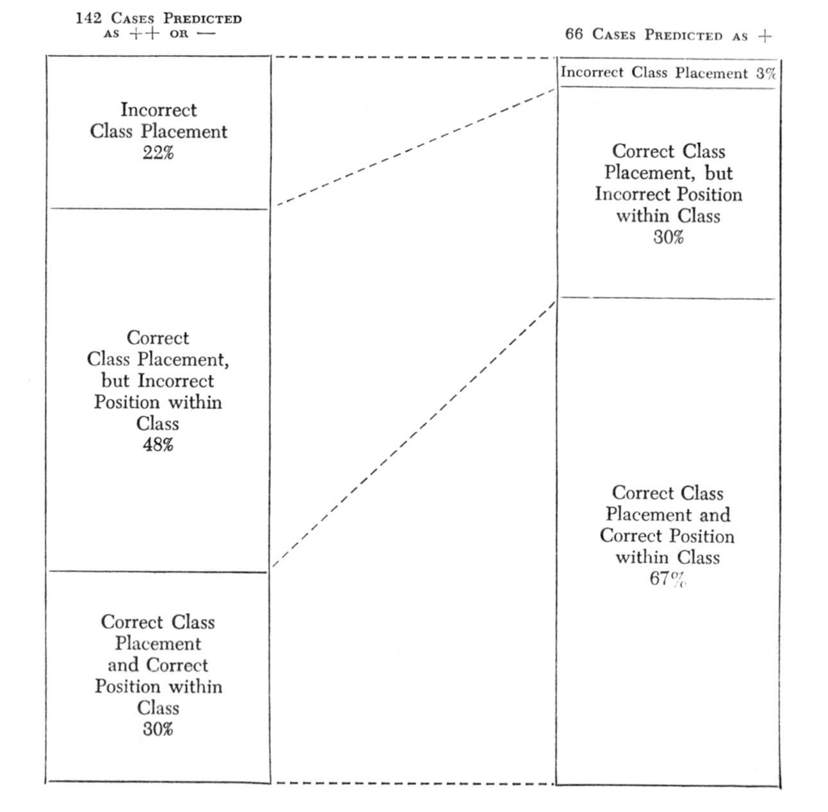

POSSIBLE IMPROVEMENT OF THE ACCURACY OF PREDICTION

While the degree of accuracy which has been reported is considerably higher than that usually found for predicting anything as uncertain and variant as human behavior on the basis of presumably "determining" characteristics, it was desired to increase the accuracy still further if in any way possible.

The regression equation used as the basis for the prediction method in computing the I.S.C. automatically provided the "best" prediction of social participation on the basis of the status characteristics, subject to the assumption that the relationship between the E.P. and the I.S.C. and its underlying ratings on characteristics, was a linear one, i.e., that the amount of change in the E.P. which was associated with a given amount of change in the I.S.C. was constant, or nearly so, at all points on the scale. While the statistical test for linearity was not computed for all relationships, inspection of the scatter-diagrams made it clearly evident that the relationships were all substantially linear. This was borne out by the size of the correlation coefficients (e.g., .97 for I.S.C. and E.P. for Old Americans), since lack of linearity always lowers the correlation coefficient.

On purely statistical grounds, it seems safe to conclude that the Index as described in this report is about as accurate a means of prediction as can be derived from the given status-characteristic data. Nevertheless, the individual cases of error in social-class prediction were inspected carefully to see whether some common type of pattern-of-ratings might be observed which would make possible further refinement of the Index. There were 33 such errors in social-class prediction among the 200 Old Americans.[3]

In the case of 16 of the 33 errors in social-class prediction, other individuals with precisely the same pattern of characteristic-ratings were found to be correctly predicted. Thus, the first error listed was an individual whose pattern of ratings was 1-2-2-1 (Occupation 1, Source of Income 2, House Type 2, and Dwelling Area 1) and whose Index of Status Characteristics indicated he should be in the upper class, but who was actually found to be in the upper-middle class. Three other individuals, however, with precisely the same pattern of ratings (1-2-2-1) were found to be actually in the upper class,

[3] Eight families whose I.S.C.'s were based on only three status characteristics were excluded from this analysis.

just as predicted. It is evident that no improvement of the Index of Status Characteristics could take care of this kind of error, since any change which would place the 1-2-2-1 pattern of ratings in the upper-middle class would correct one error and create three more! Half of the errors in social-class prediction were found to be of this type, where it was clear that the error must be due to some idiosyncrasy of personal behavior or some factor other than the four included in the I.S.C. It was obviously impossible, on the basis of the four characteristics included in the I.S.C., to distinguish social class more accurately in such cases.

Inspection of the remaining 17 errors of prediction did not reveal any consistent type of pattern which seemed to result in error; it was, therefore, concluded that these cases, too, could not be predicted more accurately on the basis of the characteristics included in the Index.

The following are suggested as four explanations which might well be expected to produce some discrepancies between social class predicted from the I.S.C. and social class as measured by the E.P.

1. *Effect of personal idiosyncrasies of behavior.* Insofar as social class is based upon social reputation, it is, of course, influenced to some degree by such matters of personal behavior as drunkenness, presence or lack of social ambition, handicaps due to extreme ill health, qualities of personality, etc. To the degree that these are largely individual matters, they cannot be readily included in any Index of Status Characteristics, and occasional discrepancies in prediction must be expected because of them.

2. *Possibility of some general characteristic not included in present I.S.C.* It might be that there is some general status characteristic not now included in the I.S.C. which would help to account for a few of the discrepancies in prediction and thereby improve the predictive power of the Index. Some characteristic such as type of clothing and neatness of personal appearance might be found, for example, which would provide the additional information needed to classify the errors more accurately.

3. *Possible effect of social mobility.* No account has been taken in the present analysis of the fact that some individuals are more or less static in the social scale whereas others are in the process of moving upward or downward on the scale. It may be that in the case of the mobile ones the status characteristics, as measured by

the I.S.C., do not move simultaneously with the actual social-class participation as measured by the E.P. An individual who has recently moved up the occupational scale from an office clerk to an executive position, for example, will show an increased I.S.C. at once, since the occupation rating will be higher, but it is likely that the individual's social-class participation would go up more slowly. In the meantime there would be a lag which might explain some of the "errors" of prediction. The Index, in such cases, would be predicting the social-class in which the individual will ultimately participate whereas the E.P. would indicate the one in which he is participating now.

On the other hand, an individual whose income is falling and whose status characteristics are falling accordingly may hang on to his social reputation and his social-class participation for a time, even though it will probably eventually fall to conform to his new status-characteristic level. During this time there would be a natural discrepancy between the I.S.C. and the E.P.

4. *Possibility of error in original social-class placement by means of the E.P.* This entire analysis has assumed, of necessity, that the E.P. indicated the "correct" social-class placement of each individual or family studied. This was necessary, since the E.P. was, at least presumably, the *best* indication available of the actual social class of each family. The process of determining the E.P. is basically clinical, however, and in some cases errors may have been made in this placement. Such errors might be the result of insufficient information about a given family or might be due to misinterpretation of the significance of such information. Any error in E.P. placement would, of course, be represented by an unexplained error in prediction on the basis of the I.S.C.

In order to test the extent to which explanations like the preceding, and especially 1, 2, and 3 above, might account for the 33 errors in social-class placement (Old Americans only), the cards, representing the families for which errors of prediction had been made, were given to one of the status analysts who was familiar with many of the Jonesville families. She was asked to indicate any special circumstances which were known regarding their personal behavior, mobility, etc. The analyst was not told of the nature of the discrepancy for which an explanation was being sought. While no attempt was made to secure a complete analysis of each case, it was thought that even an informal examination of some of these cases might yield information which would be suggestive as to possible reasons for misprediction. The results are indicated in Table 30.

The 23 cases in the upper portion of the table are families for whom the predicted social class was higher than the actual one. It will be noticed that 6 of these were accounted for as being up-

TABLE 30

SPECIAL EXPLANATIONS FOR CASES IN WHICH SOCIAL CLASS INCORRECTLY PREDICTED, FOR OLD AMERICANS

Social Class		Explanation Given by Analyst				
Predicted (I.S.C.)	Actual (E.P.)	Number of Families	Upward Mobile	Downward Mobile	Special Circum-stances	No Explana-tion
Upper	Upper-Middle	8	4	2	4*	1
Upper-Middle	Lower-Middle	7		1	2	4
Lower-Middle	Upper-Lower	2			1	1
Upper-Lower	Lower-Lower	6	2			4
Upper-Middle	Upper	4		1	2	1
Lower-Middle	Upper-Middle	1		1		
Upper-Lower	Lower-Middle	3				3
Lower-Lower	Upper-Lower	2				2

* Includes two cases also classified as upward mobile and one case which is also classified as downward mobile.

ward mobile. The 3 cases listed as downward mobile are less easy to account for, since no obvious explanation for the downward movement of social-class participation and the lag in status characteristics seems to present itself. The "special circumstances," in the next to the last column of the table, varied considerably, frequently being based upon a mixed marriage in which the man was thought by the community to have married "beneath" his class, with consequent detriment to his social-class participation, even though there is no indication of this in the four status characteristics. The cases of "no explanation" do not necessarily mean that no explanation exists; no systematic attempt was made to investigate each of these families carefully, and it may well be that these are merely cases with which the analyst happened to be less familiar.

The 10 cases in the bottom portion of Table 30 are those for whom the predicted social class was lower than the actual one. Two of these 10 were accounted for as being downward mobile; 2 by special circumstances; and 6 are at present unaccounted for.

FINAL MODIFICATION OF THE INDEX

The data presented in this chapter, particularly those included in Table 29, on page 207, indicate that the Index of Status Characteristics is a much more satisfactory predictor of social class than of position within social class, though it possesses some merit for the latter purpose, too. Inasmuch as the interest in social-class analysis is primarily in the determination of the correct social class, and only secondarily in the determination of relative position within the class, it is suggested that the Index be used only for social-class prediction unless position within the class is specifically wanted. In the latter case, the lesser reliability of the Index predictions should be kept in mind.

One further modification of the Index was made to insure more definite statements about the accuracy of any given prediction. This modification involved the determination of the specific ranges within which the correct social class could be predicted with (a) almost perfect accuracy, (b) only moderate accuracy, and (c) virtually no accuracy at all. In general, of course, those cases which could be predicted with almost perfect accuracy were those whose prediction placed them near the middle of a social class, and those which could not be predicted accurately at all were those whose prediction placed them on or near the border line between two classes, in an area where their exact social-class placement was largely indeterminate. The cases which could be predicted with moderate accuracy were found in between these two groups, at points on the scale where the social-class position could not be determined with real certainty, but where some definite indication could be given as to the most likely position.

These ranges were determined by inspection of the distribution of weighted totals on the I.S.C. in relation to the actual E.P. social-class placement. Table 19, on page 183, for example, indicates that those individuals whose weighted totals ranged from 12 to 22 were predicted, on the basis of the regression equation, to be in the upper class. An examination of the original data indicated that all of those from 12 to 17 actually were in the upper class, while of those from 18 to 22, 21 cases were in the upper class and 8 cases in the upper-middle class. It seemed reasonable to assume, therefore, that other Jonesville individuals with weighted totals ranging from 12 to 17 would almost certainly be upper-class, while those from 18 to 22, while most likely upper-class, might not necessarily be so. Similar examination of the data for all Old Americans and for each of the ethnic groups separately revealed that all individuals or families could be classified fairly satisfactorily into three groups on the basis of the certainty of the correctness of the prediction which could be made for them.

The data derived in this manner are presented in Table 31 in which three types of symbols are used to indicate three types of certainty of prediction:[4]

A, B, C, D, E	Families whose social class is almost certainly (96 chances out of 100) the one indicated by the Index.
A_b, B_a, B_c, C_b, etc.	Families whose social class is most likely (69 chances out of 100) the one indicated by the capital letter, but which may (31 times out of 100) be as indicated by the small letter instead.
A or B, B or C, etc.	Families whose social class is almost certainly one of the two indicated, but for whom it is just about as likely to be one as the other.

The above interpretations of these symbols may be used for Old Americans and for ethnics alike, since the greater unpredictability of ethnics has been taken care of in the wider bands of indeterminancy and uncertainty in Table 31 for ethnics.

When the data in Table 31 were used for predicting the social class of the 339 families upon which this study is based (including the 38 Poles obtained for the supplementary analysis), it was found that the distribution of predictions among the three groups was as indicated in Table 32.

This table indicates that in almost two-thirds (64 per cent) of the cases one could be almost certain (96 per cent certainty) that the social class was as indicated by the I.S.C.; that in about half of

[4] Table 31 is based both on inspection of the original scatter-diagrams and on data from the regression equations. The social class predicted for any family from Table 31 will always be the same social class that would have been predicted from the regression equations except for those borderline cases which in Table 31 are listed as indeterminate (A or B, B or C, etc.) and which in the earlier tables were assigned to a single social class on the basis of the regression equations. The dividing lines between cases of near certainty, moderate certainty, and indeterminancy are, however, based solely on subjective inspection of the scatter diagrams.

TABLE 31

CONVERSION TABLE FOR I.S.C. FOR ETHNIC GROUPS (FOR PREDICTING SOCIAL CLASS ONLY, WITHOUT POSITION WITHIN SOCIAL CLASS)

<table>
<tr><th rowspan="2">Weighted Total</th><th colspan="3">Index of Status Characteristics</th></tr>
<tr><th>Old American</th><th>Scandinavian</th><th>Polish</th></tr>
<tr><td>12–17</td><td>A</td><td></td><td rowspan="7"></td></tr>
<tr><td>18–22</td><td>A_b</td><td rowspan="3">B</td></tr>
<tr><td>23–24</td><td>A or B</td></tr>
<tr><td>25–30</td><td rowspan="2">D</td></tr>
<tr><td>31–32</td><td>B or C</td></tr>
<tr><td>33</td><td rowspan="2">B or C</td><td rowspan="4">C</td></tr>
<tr><td>34–37</td></tr>
<tr><td>38</td><td rowspan="4">C</td><td rowspan="5">C or D</td></tr>
<tr><td>39–41</td></tr>
<tr><td>42–49</td><td>C_d</td></tr>
<tr><td>50</td><td>C or D</td></tr>
<tr><td>51–53</td><td>C or D</td><td>D_c</td></tr>
<tr><td>54</td><td rowspan="2">D</td><td rowspan="3">D</td><td rowspan="4">D</td></tr>
<tr><td>55–62</td></tr>
<tr><td>63–66</td><td>D or E</td></tr>
<tr><td>67–69</td><td>E_d</td><td>D or E</td></tr>
<tr><td>70</td><td rowspan="3">E</td><td rowspan="3">E</td><td rowspan="2">D or E</td></tr>
<tr><td>71–79</td></tr>
<tr><td>80–84</td><td></td></tr>
</table>

the remainder (17 per cent) one could be moderately certain (69 per cent certainty) of the accuracy of the prediction; and that in the remainder (19 per cent) of the cases the correct social class could

TABLE 32

DISTRIBUTION OF CASES AND ACCURACY OF PREDICTION, FOR MODIFIED I.S.C., FOR ALL GROUPS (OLD AMERICANS AND ETHNICS COMBINED)

Accuracy of Prediction	Number of Cases	Per Cent of Total Cases	Per Cent Predicted Correctly
Almost-certain predictions (A, B, C, D, E)	217	64%	96%
Moderately-certain predictions (A_b, C_c, D_c, E_d)	59	17	69
Indeterminant predictions (A or B, B or C, C or D, D or E)	63	19	—
Totals	339	100%	—

not be determined with any satisfactory degree of certainty at all (other than that it was one of the *two* classes indicated).

Corresponding figures for each of the ethnic groups considered separately do not differ substantially from those reported in Table 32 for the total.

These last several chapters have given precise and detailed instructions on the use of the I.S.C. and shown what the evidence is for its reliability as a measurement of social class and how it might be used as a supplement to or substitute for Evaluated Participation. The next chapter tells in simple, practical terms how to get an I.S.C. rating on anyone you are interested in—no doubt many will be interested in trying it out on themselves.

SPECIAL READINGS

Select appropriate publications from the last chapter.

CHAPTER 14

Practical Instructions for Finding an Individual's I.S.C.

LEARNING what must be done to derive an I.S.C. for any particular individual is not difficult, but learning how to do it accurately takes time, patience, and considerable experience. The quickest way to begin learning how is to work out a few cases under our instruction. We have now had the preliminary instructions on how to perform several operations and have arrived at the time in our training when each person can (under the writers' supervision) work through the operations on a few cases as preparation for doing others by himself. The present training will be divided into three steps, each a little harder than the preceding one. The analyst during this introductory practice will learn that the most commonplace facts can often be translated into an Index of Status Characteristics that is a reliable statement of almost anyone's socioeconomic position and an accurate indicator for the great majority of Americans of their social-class position. When social-class values and behavior are known, that knowledge will reveal a tremendous amount about the social background, the aspirations, abilities, and social equipment of each person for whom we have an I.S.C. and provide a reliable estimate of his capacities and previous experience. The chapter following this one is designed to instruct the reader in acquiring a full understanding of class values and behavior.

To begin the first of the three steps, short vignettes describing six Jonesville high school children are presented. Each, for purposes of instruction, has been oversimplified, but each one is a real case taken from the Jonesville research. Each description consists of no more than two sentences containing four basic facts about the social life of each child; the facts about them are ordinarily on the records of, or known by, most high school teachers, or by the personnel offices of the businesses and industries which employ them. We will select descriptions of two of them and analyze them step by step until we have translated the four facts into four ratings out of which we will derive an I.S.C. for each child.

To give practice to those learning to be class analysts, the second step will be to study the four remaining cases and without help derive I.S.C.'s for them. Once they are found, the analyst can look at Chart X, on page 221, to find what index we gave them and, by turning to the Appendix, find all the steps and reasoning used to arrive at each Index. He can thereby learn, first, by acting on his own and, later, by checking his operations and results with ours.

For the third step, four more cases are presented; but we do not give our own analysis of these, other than to tell their I.S.C. and social-class positions in the Appendix. Our results are not to be looked at until the student has completed the I.S.C.'s for all four individuals. When we reach this point, final instructions will be given in this chapter to tell the class analyst how to go out on his own and find I.S.C.'s for other individuals or, when necessary, how to stratify an adequate sample of any town or city.

Here are the descriptions of the six high school children:

Billy Brown leaves his house, an old, run-down, jerry-built structure that is beyond repair, and walks from the center of Towpath across The Canal each day to go to school. His family has often been on relief, and the relief check and wages from his father's low-skilled jobs are the principal source of the family's income.

Anna Carlson lives in a medium-sized house, in moderate repair, over in Milltown. Her father is a semi-skilled worker in The Mill and his wages are the family's principal source of income.

Evelyn, daughter of P. S. Patrick, who is a clerk out at The Mill, lives with her parents in an average house on a fairly nice street in the Southeast region.

Jane Dalton lives in Southeast. Her house is one of the larger and better cared for in town, and her father, considered one of the most successful large businessmen in town, bought it from profits made in his business.

Jim Stevens' father inherited from his father the old Stevens mansion, with its beautifully cared-for gardens, and the Stevens fortune. The home, on Main Street, was part of the estate Jim's grandfather had accumulated, and Jim's father now spends his time as manager of the larger estate.

Mary Stanlicki, from one of the Polish families over in Northwest, lives in a small and not so well cared-for house which is indistinguishable from most of the other dwellings which line the narrow streets of that region. The source of her father's income is rather dubious, but he is ranked as a semi-skilled worker.

We have said no more knowledge than that contained in the two sentences is necessary to assign each child to a tentative class position in Jonesville. And, generally speaking, the reader will soon discover that, with this same amount of information, he can place his friends or enemies, or anyone in his own town. This can be done by personnel offices, by school administrators, market researchers, advertisers of products with a possible class difference in their customers, or by class analysts themselves.

The reader should reread the cases several times until he knows all the facts included in them about the life of each of these children. Once the facts are precisely lodged in his memory, he can place these data in the larger pattern of the social life of Jonesville and, by discovering their larger significance, quickly derive several basic insights into why these children act and speak as they do and make the critical decisions which irrevocably assign them to their place in the world of Jonesville.

Let us anticipate our conclusions by saying that, after examining the facts in the two sentences about each of these children, the class analyst trained in the use of the I.S.C. can make a quick estimate and say that Anna Carlson is likely to be upper-lower class, that Mary Stanlicki and Billy Brown are almost certainly lower-lower class, Evelyn is slightly above them, probably in the lower-middle class, while Jim Stevens is certain to be upper, and Jane Dalton, upper-middle class.

The question arises immediately—how is it possible to know, and to prove that you know, that each child belongs to the particular class assigned to him? Let us use the information given and answer these questions while working out the I.S.C. of these children. Once a class analyst is confident of his knowledge and use of the I.S.C. techniques, he is ready to derive similar indices for people he knows or for anyone else about whose status he needs exact knowledge.

A re-examination of the few facts we have on the family of each child tells us that we know the occupation of the father, his source of income, the kind of house the family lives in, and the part of town in which the family resides. These four facts are sufficient to place each of them, for in the research on Jonesville, all the houses, the dwelling areas, occupations, and sources of income were typed and ranked to find the relative place and range of type for each characteristic. Hence, it will not be necessary in rating these six cases for the reader to go through this long process of calculations again. Instead, he should refer to the scales in Chapters 8 and 9 to find the rankings.

We learned by statistical method to determine how heavily each of the four characteristics should weigh in assigning class placement to a family. Occupation received a weight of 4, Source of Income, a 3, House Type, a 3, and Dwelling Area, a 2. By multiplying the score of each characteristic by its weight, we discover the amount of influence it exercised, and by adding the results, we determine the Index of Status Characteristics.

Jim's house is a 1, for it belongs to the best category of house in Jonesville. We know this because it is large—a mansion—and has well cared-for gardens and grounds. On the other hand, Billy's house is a 7, the poorest category of house in town; it is a shack and in a condition beyond repair. Billy's father has been on relief most of the time, which gives him a rating of 7 for his principal known source of income. Even when the father does work, he is employed at unskilled tasks, and this level of occupation is also at the end of the scale, a 7. Jim's father inherited his income and therefore gets a 1 for source of income; he manages the large farms of the estate and so rates a 1 for occupation. Billy's family lives in Towpath, across The Canal, a rating of 7 on dwelling area. Jim lives in the nicest section of the city, where the 400 live, a 1 area. These two extreme cases, deliberately chosen, are all 1's or 7's.

The computations for Billy and for Jim illustrate how the facts of their brief personal sketches are translated into an I.S.C.

	Billy	Jim
Occupation	$7 \times 4 = 28$	$1 \times 4 = 4$
Source of Income	$7 \times 3 = 21$	$1 \times 3 = 3$
House Type	$7 \times 3 = 21$	$1 \times 3 = 3$
Dwelling Area	$7 \times 2 = 14$	$1 \times 2 = 2$
	84	12

The four 1's for Jim, when multiplied by their weights and added, produce the sum of 12; the four 7's for Billy, 84. The small number, it will be recalled, indicates highest status; the large number indicates lowest status. These numbers become indices of the relative places of the two boys in the status hierarchy of Jonesville. Between the two are all the other status positions found in the town.

At this point the reader should analyze the remaining four cases and make his rating of them. The steps and reasoning used in working out the I.S.C. for each of them are given on pages 263-64. Now we should look at Chart X to satisfy ourselves that we have placed each family correctly and with due objectivity. In its far left-hand column are the names of the six individuals; at the top of the chart, the four characteristics. Numbers in parentheses at the top of each column are the weights for the four characteristics. The rating for each characteristic for each individual is given, and on the extreme left is his I.S.C. and probable social class.

CHART X

SOCIAL CHARACTERISTICS OF SIX INDIVIDUALS

	Occupation (4)	Source of Income (3)	House Type (3)	Dwelling Area (2)	I.S.C. and Class
Jim Stevens........	1	1	1	1	12 Upper
Jane Dalton.......	1	3	2	3	25 Upper-Middle
Evelyn Patrick.....	3	4	4	3	42 Lower-Middle
Anna Carlson......	6	5	4	4	59 Upper-Lower
Mary Stanlicki.....	6	6	6	5	70 Probably Lower-Lower
Billy Brown.......	7	7	7	7	84 Lower-Lower

It should be clear by now to even the most skeptical that the Index of Status Characteristics provides us with fairly close approximations of the relative place of a family or individual in Jonesville. It appears highly probable that Jim Stevens is higher than anyone else, that Billy Brown is lowest, and that the others fall in the serial order assigned them.

Skeptical critics might ask, "How do you know that Jim Stevens is upper-class and that Jane Dalton is upper-middle, or that Evelyn Patrick is lower-middle rather than being in the class above or the one below? Since the score for each characteristic and the indices of characteristics ascend and descend in a continuing series, how do the writers know, and how can the readers find out, where upper-middle begins and upper class ends, or where any two other classes begin and end?" The answers to these questions have been given by the statistical analysis showing that there is a very strong relation between the I.S.C. range and the class order, and that the former will either tell quite reliably for most people what the actual class position is or indicate that the status position of a person is indeterminate, meaning, more often than not, that it is in between the two classes or on the edge of one or the other.

The next step in our discussion should clear up most of the remaining questions. We should recall that the range of I.S.C.'s, running from a perfect 12 to a perfect 84, were fitted into the social class of several hundred test people who range from the top upper class through all the other classes down to lower-lower. By statistical methods we found which part of the range of indices securely located people who were in the upper, middle, and lower classes. We also learned where the range was indeterminate for class and when it located people who were in between two classes because their social characteristics belonged to two levels. The combination of I.S.C. and E.P. methods demonstrated that, while the classes in the status system of Jonesville blended into each other, they, nevertheless, had an existence and place of their own.

Now the reader can go on to the four additional practice exercises. Each one should be worked out as were the six cases just analyzed. On page 264 we give our rating and the class position for these four people as a check on the accuracy of the reader's placement.

Arthur Milette lives over near The Mill where he is employed as a semi-skilled laborer. His house is rather small, but he has kept it in good condition.

Roy Banyard's father is hired by one of the large farm owners as a farm laborer. The income from this job, supplemented by odd jobs that he is able to get in the neighborhood, has kept him off relief. His house, quite inadequate for his wife and six children, is a ramshackle structure located in Towpath.

James Hamilton lives on Main Street with his parents in one of the nicest houses in Jonesville. He will finish medical school in a year or two and is planning to become a doctor like his father, who has been one of the outstanding physicians in the town for over twenty years.

Eugene Pickett wasn't able to go on to college like some of the boys he had known in high school. But, then, their fathers had better jobs; his father was only a watchman. They dressed better than he and lived in nicer homes. He had always been a little ashamed of his small, not too well-kept house, which was in poor condition. And even more, he didn't like living in Oldtown.

We are now ready for instructions for finding the I.S.C. of individuals or for stratifying a community. We will adjust our method to two kinds of problems by giving two sets of instructions. In the first set we will tell how to get an approximation of an I.S.C. rating which will not always be absolutely exact but for many purposes will be sufficient; this method is not adequate for those who need to have a very exact and precise placement. For the latter contingency, another set of instructions will be given.

Since the first is easier to learn and can well serve as a step to the second, we will discuss it first. It should be said that for those who know their city well, and have an intimate knowledge of the details of the four characteristics for their town, these operations may be almost as accurate and reliable as the more painstaking second set of operations.

To begin with, a practicing analyst should choose as his subject for class placement someone he knows fairly well. Let us assume that the status analyst's first subject is socially adult, that he no longer is in school or college, that he lives in his own house, has an occupation, and his own source of income. If he is not adult, then the analyst should work out the father's Index of Status Characteristics and use it for the subject's. If the subject is a woman, he should remember that a married woman ordinarily occupies the same social position as her husband and should be ranked by the husband's I.S.C.; an unmarried woman living at home, by her father's.

Start by placing the subject with his occupation. The list of occupations and their rank in Chapter 9 will guide your efforts. After you have ranked occupation, examine the ranking of this person's principal source of known income. (If he has two sources of income that are approximately equal, add and divide, and use the average. For example, if he receives part of his income from fees and an approximately equal amount from bonds he has inherited, his source-of-income rating would be a 2 [3 + 1 ÷ 2]).

Now come the two difficult characteristics: house type and dwelling area. For dwelling area, first look at Chapter 9 and ascertain the approximate rating of the area should it have been in Jonesville. To do this, start with the two extremes. In other words, see if it is a 7 or a 1. If not, see if it is a 2 or a 6 or 5. When you have located approximately the rating of the neighborhood of the person you are attempting to rate, score it accordingly. Now, return to your own city or home town and run over its dwelling areas in your own mind and determine what the range is. Again start with the two extremes and work towards the average. Be sure you put all the neighborhoods into the seven-point scale.

When you turn to house-typing, you will find it difficult unless surveys have been previously conducted in your community. However, the status analyst can arrive at a close approximation by the following procedure. Look in Chapter 9 and see what kind of house the person you are rating would occupy in terms of its size and condition. After you have rated his house for Jonesville, return to your community and in your mind's eye examine the range of houses in his town. After you have categorized and rated them, place his house in the scale.

The rest is a matter of giving the proper weight to each of the four traits and adding them to get the Index. This procedure should be followed for a number of people, using the guide we have given above in the cases of the several children who were rated by us. This practice should provide the necessary rough skill to give an approximate class rating to people you know. At least, when you conclude your efforts, you will have a socioeconomic index of your subjects' approximate place in the social stratification of the community. When you have compared the I.S.C.'s with the Evaluated

Participation of Jonesville, you will have a fairly close estimate of their social-class positions. Needless to say, the range from community to community will shift somewhat but the differences are not great. Our own preliminary investigations have shown that the differences appear to be small. However, the reader should be warned that this problem has not been sufficiently investigated to make sure that all cities and towns will show the same kind of relation between Evaluated Participation and range of I.S.C.'s.

Most readers will probably find themselves and their friends in the range which coincides with the levels above the Common Man. We know this from previous studies of American reading habits.[1]

The more exacting procedure necessary when the class placement must be precise does not demand different operations after the data are collected, but it does take more time and care during the collection of the evidence which precedes the analysis. Furthermore, the kind of evidence collected will vary in accordance with the kind of problem faced by the class analyst. If he is dealing with a subtle psychological problem which concerns one or a very few individuals where even the nuances of the subject's status problem may be of decisive importance in understanding the case, evidence for the I.S.C. should be gathered carefully and it should be accompanied by careful interviewing of the subject and those around him to permit the analyst to relate the subject's attitudes about social mobility to the interview material and his feeling about social class to the I.S.C. Ordinarily, such elaborate preparation for placement is not necessary.

Another situation in which the more exact procedure is necessary occurs if the class analyst has the task of stratifying a large number of individuals, such as those who pass through the personnel offices of business or industry or through the registry of public and private schools in a city. In these circumstances the E.P. is impossible to get, but a precisely worked-out I.S.C. can serve just as well.

The procedures necessary in securing an exact and precise I.S.C. can be found in the answers to two questions. The questions are: What does one do to gather the necessary evidence for each of the four characteristics? And how are these operations modified in

[1] See Warner and Lunt, *The Social Life of a Modern Community*, pp. 366-78.

towns and cities of different sizes? Let us answer these questions together.

The principles of evaluation underlying all four characteristics vary only slightly from city to city and from town to town, but the objects (characteristics) to which they are applied may vary considerably. For example, generally speaking, in all American cities large houses in good condition—the mansions of Nob Hill—are given a higher ranking than the pretty little bungalows of Suburbia, which, in turn, are felt to be superior to the broken-down shacks of the slums. The social principles of size and condition for houses operate everywhere. But what is a very large house in excellent condition in one community may be no more than a large house in fair condition in another, for the obvious reason that in the latter city there are houses which are still bigger and the standards of care are higher and probably more rigorously applied. Most of the people of the United States identify themselves with their community, and the vast majority, if not all, of our communities supply us with the values and beliefs about which characteristics are high, average, or low, which social levels are in upper, middle, or lower class, and which people are in these classes. The principles of evaluation are nationwide; their application varies from community to community. However, the variation is not very great because these basic essentials do not change radically from community to community.[2]

Occupational and source-of-income scales which hold for Boston or Chicago are equally valid for San Francisco and Dallas. Salaries outrank wages whether one lives in New Orleans or Seattle. Except in rare instances, there will be no need to modify the scales presented in Chapter 9. If the analyst will use the Alba Edwards lists and our method of scaling them, he will get an exact rating of an individual's (or his father's) occupational position. Knowing the

[2] Work is continuing on the I.S.C. as a measurement of social class. Studies are now being made of its effectiveness in placing the social classes of Negroes. The factor of color-caste in some communities seems to indicate that other characteristics, such as education and skin color, should be substituted for house type and dwelling area. Research is being done on racial stratification. More work needs to be done on the ethnic group's influence on class, and the present conclusions on the Polish and Scandinavian groups, that it pulls the top people down and tends to build up those at the bottom, should be tried on other cultural groups and in other communities. These studies should include dark-skinned people such as Orientals, Mexicans, and other Spanish-Americans.

occupation, more often than not the analyst will know the principal source of known income, for he will know whether a particular job yields a wage, a salary, a profit, or a fee. A few questions on the sources of income will tell him finally if the job is the principal source of livelihood.

When the class analyst has the ratings for occupation and source of income, he has a solid base and can proceed to acquire the evidence for rating the other two characteristics and for getting an exactly placed I.S.C.

This is true because he will have seven-twelfths of the necessary information (occupation weighing 4 and source of income 3, house and area, 3 and 2 respectively). He also knows that, while there is variation between the ratings for the several characteristics, they ordinarily fit into a pattern; hence, he knows that, more often than not, the house and area ratings will vary only so much above or below the weighted occupation and source-of-income index. For example, if a man's occupational rating is 5 and his source of income a 4, their weighted total is 20 plus 12, or 32. Normally, his house and neighborhood are not likely to be 1's or 7's; the range of probability lies from 2 to 6, with the chances high that the neighborhood scores will be no higher than 3 or lower than 5.

But the importance of these differences must be stressed; if the man and his family are striving to improve their lot and "to go around with a nicer class of people," a larger proportion of their income may be spent in "getting a nice house in a nice neighborhood." Under these circumstances, they might very well have a 3 house in a 2 area, thereby pulling them up to a 47 instead of a 54 or 55 if they spend their money without adjusting to the demands of status.

Most class analysts confronted with a large sample, where a whole town or city must be stratified, would do well to use the following procedure:

1. Select a sample of several hundred heads of families by:
   a. obtaining cases from the top to the bottom along the occupational scale. (City directories are excellent sources for this preliminary information.)
   b. checking them to make sure they are well distributed throughout the city and that the occupations indicate

their principal sources of income and cover all types of income source.

2. Translate the occupation and probable principal source of income into a rating for each head of a household.

3. By previous knowledge or interview, establish the major social areas and their relative ranking. Remember that several areas may have approximately the same value. Make a map of the areas and indicate the value of each area by putting its rating after its name on the map. Sub-areas of higher and lower ranking should be delineated and ranked. People living in the larger area know the differences.

4. Drive through the residential areas and examine the size and condition of the houses. Apartment houses and hotels should be treated separately and after the house scale has been established. Drive from the best part of town to the worst and back again. Do this several times until the grades of houses in size and condition have been established. Always remember that the scale, while being established, starts from two extremes, the best and worst, and moves towards the middle. Whenever possible, have several people do this separately and then match their results until agreement is reached on the scale. A few discreet inquiries at real estate offices and the tax assessor's on number of rooms in a house will help check on its size.

The outside appearance of an apartment can be used for its condition, but not its over-all size. The apartment unit itself, the number of rooms a family has, must be known for establishing size. Inquiry at real estate offices will quickly establish the size range for apartments in a city. When related to condition, the types of apartments may then be equated to their proper place in the scale for house type.

Hotels tend to have reputations as total units for being good, poor, or indifferent places to live. They should be treated accordingly, ranked and related to the scale for house types. If this proves too difficult or expensive, remove the house-type characteristic and depend, with the modified weights, on the other three for getting the Index.

If the city has a reliable directory, the name, address, and occupation will provide much of the basic information for working out at least a preliminary range of I.S.C.'s running from the upper class 12 to the 84 of the lower-lower. The establishment of this (continuous) range assures the analyst he is likely to have a sample of all strata.[3]

Once the I.S.C. range is established for the limited sample, it should first be compared with what we have given here about the relation of the several parts of the range to the several classes. When necessary, this will help the analyst take the next step. Since the I.S.C. range is likely to vary a little from community to community, but only a little, the careful investigator should use the individual cases that fall on, or nearly on, each side of the peak, particularly those in the "indeterminate areas," and find out, by interviewing those who know or by observations, what their class position is. This last procedure will provide an I.S.C. that indicates class position with the utmost certainty, but it is not necessary for all researches.

This range of I.S.C.'s, including all social strata and all socio-economic groups, running from 12 to 84, can henceforth be used for each individual case that appears. The school principal or teacher, or the personnel man, by getting the occupation and address of an individual, in a few minutes can first translate them into ratings for the I.S.C. and then, by comparing the individual's I.S.C. with the range, establish his status and social background. Furthermore, a comparison between the scores of occupation and source of income with those of house and area often gives very valuable information about the social values of the family. In many cases it tells whether the family is striving to improve the social standing of its members,

[3] Other characteristics can be added to or substituted for those now being used. Some of these, which are fairly certain to be good indices of class, are education, amount of rent, furniture, and a combination of certain social and secular ideologies. Education, the use of which is described in this volume, sometimes may not be hard to get, but, ordinarily, reliable information about it is not easily obtained. Our present research on household furniture, particularly for the living room, shows that such combinations as window treatment (curtains, drapes, etc.), seating arrangements, and floor decorations can be used as a simple index of status (see Chapter 15 for Chapin's earlier studies).

The principal criteria for new characteristics to be added to the present ones are: that they reflect class differences equally along the whole range and that every family in the community has the characteristic and can be measured by it. For purposes of measurement alone, the characteristics' importance in the daily lives of the people may be trivial or highly significant. The other criteria are that the information should be easily obtained by research people who can recognize and describe the significant facts without a long period of training. The greater number of characteristics that can be used in the Index, the greater the ease in using it in all kinds of social research.

whether it has aspirations "for higher things," doesn't care, or prefers a day-to-day existence which flouts the values of social mobility.

It is obvious that once an individual's characteristics have been determined, their scoring need not be done by an expert in social class analysis, for anyone who is accurate, careful, and has had experience can compute an I.S.C. But the interpretation of its meaning and implications needs an understanding of our class system and the skills and insight gained by such knowledge. The next chapter is designed to give the reader some of this knowledge and, where necessary, to introduce him to books and articles which will tell him what is known about social class and social mobility in America.

SPECIAL READINGS

Select appropriate publications from the last chapter.

CHAPTER 15

Instructions for, and Commentary about, Further Reading on Social Class

ART AND SCIENCE, MIRRORS OF SOCIAL CLASS IN AMERICA

DURING the last ten or fifteen years, a substantial and growing literature on social class based on field research on American life and founded on observed facts has accumulated. Much of it is significant and important to all those who wish to understand American culture, particularly to those who are interested in using the methods of Evaluated Participation and the Index of Status Characteristics. This chapter comments on some of the more useful scientific and literary publications which emphasize social class, social mobility, and how they function in American life. It is not intended to cover all references, but only the books and articles most useful for implementation of the methodological chapters. The comments, some of them quite extended, provide a guide for further reading, or they may function as a survey of findings for those who do not expect to read the references cited.

Perhaps the greatest value of this chapter will be found in the instruction given on how to analyze some of the contemporary novels by the general use of symbolic analysis and the techniques of E.P. and I.S.C.

Scientific documentation about the nature of our status system is greatly strengthened by the contemporary novels which have reported realistically on the current American scene. Some of them give their attention to the phenomena of social inequality—the tragic or comic, but always strained, relations between the members of different social strata, and the rise and fall of individuals and families, particularly emphasizing the strivings of people to climb into the class above and the efforts of those above to keep them out. Names of authors and their books immediately come to mind: Marquand and his *The Late George Apley, H. M. Pulham, Esquire, Wickford Point, So Little Time* and *Point of No Return;* John O'Hara's *Appointment in Samarra,* and many of his stories in *The New Yorker;* or Sinclair Lewis' *Babbitt, Dodsworth,* and *Main Street;* and the novels of Theodore Dreiser and Booth Tarkington. The story of the lower half of the social scale is told by such novels as James Farrell's *A World I Never Made* and those of William Faulkner and Erskine Caldwell in the South.

It is possible to read such novels, as many critics do, and see no more in them than character delineations and studies of personalities acting in a modern milieu. For the class analyst, they often are springs of information, occasionally graced with the magic insight of sensitive observers. By manipulating character, scene, and plot, the literary artist reports on what he feels and thinks about social reality; the social scientist, partly controlled by the discipline of his training, observes many of the same facts and reports in direct statement what he has discovered. To use the materials from the novel, the social scientist must analyze its symbols and translate them into the data of science.

Before continuing with this commentary and brief review of the literature on social class and mobility, for purposes of instruction, we will illustrate how status novels can be analyzed by the I.S.C. and E.P. to yield exact knowledge about social class. A few scenes from Sinclair Lewis' best-known novel, *Babbitt,* will serve well for analysis. Lewis was acutely aware of social stratification and the problems of the mobile man in the Middle West long before scientific studies were made of them.

BABBITT AND SOCIAL CLASS IN ZENITH

For his stories to be effective and hold the interest of two generations of Americans, it is obvious that more is involved than his simple plots. In addition to Lewis' clear insight into certain American personality types, in *Babbitt* he shows basic understanding of American community life. Despite his caricatures and exaggerations of trivial detail for contrast or to make a point, the basic structure of his books, certainly the earlier ones, is founded on accurate knowledge of the structure of community life; above all he knows what the three classes above the Common Man level are and how they function in America.

The plot and principal themes of *Babbitt* can be quickly summarized. *Babbitt,* as most of us know, is the story of George F. Babbitt, who is a partner in the Thompson-Babbitt firm, one of the most successful real estate offices in Zenith. The story is essentially of how Babbitt becomes a prominent citizen but fails in his efforts to be accepted by the top class of Zenith. Babbitt strays from the paths of righteousness, and momentarily loses his deep faith in the moral philosophy of business, but ostracism and social pressure soon make him willing to return from the wilderness. He again becomes a Prominent Citizen and leading businessman in Zenith.

Some of the principal characters in the book are William Eathorne, whom the authors of this volume class (with Lewis) as old-family and upper-class, Charles McKelvey, newly arrived and lower-upper class, both above upper-middle-class Babbitt, and Ed Overbrook, below Babbitt, in the lower-middle class. We will present direct quotations to establish their E.P. ratings. Before giving and analyzing the evidence to establish their I.S.C.'s, we will anticipate the results by saying that the I.S.C. of Babbitt is 26, McKelvey's score is 16.5, and Eathorne's, 14. The unfortunate Overbrook scores a 40. Each man's I.S.C. score confirms his E.P. rating.

Let us now test these conclusions by first presenting the evidence and then analyzing it by both methods. We will start with a brief picture of Zenith, follow it with the evidence for the four characteristics, principally residence and house type, and follow up with material on Institutional Membership, Symbolic Placement, and Status Reputation.

To interfere as little as possible with Lewis' art in telling his story of American status, the quotations from *Babbitt* will not be interrupted by analysis until all of them are given.

The city of Zenith with a population of "three hundred and forty or fifty thousand ordinary people" in 1920, founded in the 1790's, is located in one of the eastern states of the Middle West. It was considered an ancient settlement in the late 1890's, during Babbitt's years at State University, and with its two hundred thousand population, it was even then the wonder of all the state. A market town with a diversified industry, its "factories producing condensed milk, paper boxes, lighting fixtures, motor cars," its business center large and old, it now supports several skyscrapers.

Babbitt lived in the "residential district of Zenith known as

Floral Heights" in a green and white Dutch Colonial house. It was a residential settlement located in a region of large houses and bungalows with neat, well-cared-for gardens and lawns bordering on winding roads. Floral Heights, although a new development, supported several old mansions belonging to old families.

> The Babbitts' house was five years old. . . . It had the best of taste, the best of inexpensive rugs, a simple and laudable architecture, and the latest conveniences. Throughout, electricity took the place of candles and slatternly hearth-fires. Along the bedroom baseboard were three plugs for electric lamps, concealed by little brass doors. In the halls were plugs for the vacuum cleaner, and in the living-room plugs for the piano lamp, for the electric fan. The trim diningroom (with its admirable oak buffet, its leaded-glass cupboard, its creamy plaster walls, its modest scene of a salmon expiring upon a pile of oysters) had plugs which supplied the electric percolator and the electric toaster.

The bedroom "displayed a modest and pleasant color-scheme, after one of the best standard designs of the decorator who 'did the interiors' for most of the speculative-builders' houses in Zenith."

Babbitt belonged to a number of clubs. The principal one was the Zenith Athletic Club where he lunched daily. Lewis informs us that

> . . . the Zenith Athletic Club is not athletic and it isn't exactly a club, but it is Zenith in perfection. It has an active and smoke-misted billiard room, it is represented by baseball and football teams, and in the pool and the gymnasium a tenth of the members sporadically try to reduce. But most of its three thousand members use it as a cafe in which to lunch, play cards, tell stories, meet customers, and entertain out-of-town uncles at dinner. It is the largest club in the city, and its chief hatred is the conservative Union Club, which all sound members of the Athletic call "a rotten, snobbish, dull, expensive old hole—not one Good Mixer in the place—you couldn't hire me to join." Statistics show that no member of the Athletic has ever refused election to the Union, and of those who are elected, sixty-seven percent resign from the Athletic and are thereafter heard to say, in the drowsy sanctity of the Union lounge, "The Athletic would be a pretty good hotel, if it were more exclusive."
>
> In Zenith it was as necessary for a Successful Man to belong to a country club as it was to wear a linen collar. Babbitt's was the Outing Golf and Country Club, a pleasant gray-shingled building with a broad porch, on a daisy-starred cliff above Lake Kennepoose. There was another, the Tonawanda Country Club, to which belonged Charles McKelvey, Horace

Updike, and the other rich men who lunched not at the Athletic but at the Union Club. Babbitt explained with frequency, "You couldn't hire me to join the Tonawanda, even if I did have a hundred and eighty bucks to throw away on the initiation fee."

The association which inspired the most generous efforts of Babbitt and all members of both the Union and Zenith Athletic Clubs was the Good Citizens' League.

To the League belonged most of the prosperous citizens of Zenith. They were not all of the kind who called themselves "Regular Guys." Besides the hearty fellows, these salesmen of prosperity, there were the aristocrats, that is, the men who were richer or had been rich for more generations: the presidents of banks and of factories, the land-owners, the corporation lawyers, the fashionable doctors, and the few young-old men who worked not at all but, reluctantly remaining in Zenith, collected luster-ware and first editions as though they were back in Paris. All of them agreed that the working classes must be kept in their places; and all of them perceived that American Democracy did not imply any equality of wealth, but did demand a wholesome sameness of thought, dress, painting, morals, and vocabulary.

In this they were like the ruling-class of any other country, particularly of Great Britain, but they differed in being more vigorous and in actually trying to produce the accepted standards which all classes, everywhere, desire, but usually despair of realizing.

The relations between the two upper and two middle classes are magnificently dramatized by Lewis in his account of the annual dinner of his university class and its disastrous after effects on Babbitt's social aspirations.

Fame [as a prominent citizen] did not bring the social advancement which the Babbitts deserved. They were not asked to join the Tonawanda Country Club nor invited to the dances at the Union. Himself, Babbitt fretted, he didn't "care a fat hoot for all these highrollers, but the wife would kind of like to be Among Those Present." He nervously awaited his university class-dinner and an evening of furious intimacy with such social leaders as Charles McKelvey the millionaire contractor, Max Kruger the banker, Irving Tate the tool-manufacturer, and Adelbert Dobson the fashionable interior decorator. Theoretically he was their friend, as he had been in college, and when he encountered them they still called him "Georgie," but he didn't seem to encounter them often, and they never invited him to dinner (with champagne and a butler) at their houses on Royal Ridge.

All the week before the class-dinner he thought of them. "No reason why we shouldn't become real chummy now!"

McKelvey had been the hero of the Class of '96; not only football captain and hammer-thrower but debater, and passable in what the State University considered scholarship. He had gone on, had captured the construction-company once owned by the Dodsworths, best-known pioneer family of Zenith. He built state capitols, skyscrapers, railway terminals. . . . He was baronial; he was a peer in the rapidly crystallizing American aristocracy, inferior only to the haughty Old Families. (In Zenith, an Old Family is one which came to town before 1840.) . . .

When Babbitt and McKelvey meet at the dinner, McKelvey is affable:

"Why, hello, old Georgie! Say, George Babbitt is getting fatter than I am!"

"Planning to sit anywhere special, George? Come on, let's grab some seats. Come on Max. Georgie, I read about your speeches in the campaign. Bully work!"

Babbitt was thrilled, but not so weighted with awe as to be silent. If he was not invited by them to dinner, he was yet accustomed to talking with bank-presidents, congressmen, and clubwomen who entertained poets.

During the dinner he said to McKelvey: "It's a shame, uh, shame to drift apart because our, uh, business activities lie in different fields. I've enjoyed talking over the good old days. You and Mrs. McKelvey must come to dinner some night."

Vaguely, "Yes, indeed—"

"Like to talk to you about the growth of real estate out beyond your Grantsville warehouse. I might be able to tip you off to a thing or two, possibly."

"Splendid! We must have dinner together, Georgie. Just let me know. And it will be a great pleasure to have your wife and you at the house," said McKelvey, much less vaguely.

The Babbitts invited the McKelveys to dinner, in early December, and the McKelveys not only accepted but, after changing the date once or twice, actually came.

The dinner was well cooked and incredibly plentiful, and Mrs. Babbitt had brought out her grandmother's silver candlesticks. Babbitt worked hard. He was good. He told none of the jokes he wanted to tell. He listened to the others. He started Maxwell off with a resounding, "Let's hear about your trip to the Yellowstone." He was laudatory, extremely laudatory.

But he could not stir them. It was dinner without a soul. For no reason that was clear to Babbitt, heaviness was over them and they spoke laboriously and unwillingly.

At a quarter to ten McKelvey discovered with profound regret that his wife had a headache. He said blithely, as Babbitt helped him with his coat, "We must lunch together some time, and talk over the old days."

The Babbitts waited for a return dinner invitation which never came.

Ed Overbrook was a classmate of Babbitt who had been a failure. He had a large family and a feeble insurance business out in the suburb of Dorchester. He was gray and thin and unimportant. He had always been gray and thin and unimportant. He was the person whom, in any group, you forgot to introduce, then introduced with extra enthusiasm. He had admired Babbitt's goodfellowship in college, had admired ever since his power in real estate, his beautiful house and wonderful clothes. It pleased Babbitt, though it bothered him with a sense of responsibility. At the class-dinner he had seen poor Overbrook, in a shiny blue serge business-suit, being diffident in a corner with three other failures. He had gone over and been cordial: "Why, hello, young Ed! I hear you're writing all the insurance in Dorchester now. Bully work!"

They recalled the good old days when Overbrook used to write poetry. Overbrook embarrassed him by blurting, "Say, Georgie, I hate to think of how we have been drifting apart. I wish you and Mrs. Babbitt would come to dinner some night!"

Babbitt boomed, "Fine! Sure! Just let me know. And the wife and I want to have you at the house." He forgot it, but unfortunately Ed Overbrook did not. Repeatedly he telephoned to Babbitt, inviting him to dinner.

He accepted Overbrook's next plaintive invitation, for an evening two weeks off. . . . They had to change the date, because of their own dinner to the McKelveys, but at last they gloomily drove out to the Overbrook's house in Dorchester.

It was miserable from the beginning.

The Overbrook house was depressing. It was the second story of a wooden two-family dwelling; a place of baby-carriages, old hats hung in the hall, cabbage-smell, and a Family Bible on the parlor table. Ed Overbrook and his wife were as awkward and threadbare as usual, and the other guests were two dreadful families whose names Babbitt never caught and never desired to catch.

Babbitt tried to be jovial; he worked at it; but he could find nothing to interest him in Overbrook's timorousness, the blankness of the other guests, or the drained stupidity of Mrs. Overbrook, with her spectacles, drab skin, and tight-drawn hair. He told his best Irish story, but it sank like soggy cake.

Babbitt was sorry, but there was no hope; the dinner was a failure. At ten, rousing out of the stupor of meaningless talk, he said as cheerily as he could, " 'Fraid we got to be starting, Ed. I've got a fellow coming to see me early tomorrow." As Overbrook helped him with his coat, Babbitt said, "Nice to rub up on the old days! We must have lunch together, P.D.Q."

For a week they worried, "We really ought to invite Ed and his wife, poor devils!" But as they never saw the Overbrooks, they forgot them, and after a month or two they said, "That really was the best way, just to let it slide. It wouldn't be kind to *them* to have them here. They'd feel so out of place and hard-up in our home."

They did not speak of the Overbrooks again.

Babbitt, finding his campaign for social acceptance had failed to transform his Position of Prominence into social acceptance by the McKelvey set of Royal Ridge, turned his attention to leading a new venture, making the Sunday School of the Presbyterian Church the largest in the city. The secular leader and most powerful member of the church was William W. Eathorne. Babbitt, Mr. Eathorne, and the minister and one other prominent citizen were the directing committee of the campaign. The committee gave Babbitt face-to-face relations with Eathorne.

Mr. Eathorne was the seventy-year-old president of the First State Bank of Zenith. He still wore the delicate patches of side-whiskers which had been the uniform of bankers in 1870. If Babbitt was envious of the Smart Set of the McKelveys, before William Washington Eathorne he was reverent. Mr. Eathorne had nothing to do with the Smart Set. He was above it. He was the great-grandson of one of the five men who founded Zenith, in 1792, and he was of the third generation of bankers.

After their first meeting in the Eathorne mansion:

Babbitt did not drive home, but toward the center of the city. He wished to be by himself and exult over the beauty of intimacy with William Washington Eathorne.

He loved his city with passionate wonder. He lost the accumulated weariness of business-worry and expansive oratory; he felt young and potential. He was ambitious. . . . He was going to be an Eathorne; delicately rigorous, coldly powerful.

He drove happily home, and to Mrs. Babbitt he was a William Washington Eathorne, but she did not notice it.

So much for the evidence. We will now analyze it to establish the I.S.C. for the four men.

I.S.C.'S AND E.P.'S OF BABBITT AND HIS FRIENDS

Eathorne's I.S.C. is not difficult to compute. He is director of several large corporations including a bank. This gives him a rating of 1 for occupation. His principal source of income is from several generations of inherited wealth giving him a 1 for this characteristic. He lives in a mansion in Floral Heights, for which he scores a 1 for house type and a 2 for the area in which he lives. After multiplying each score by its proper weight he achieves the high total of 14, only two points below a perfect 12. The fact that he and a few others like him preferred to live in Floral Heights after it had become a new development filled with Babbitts and their Dutch Colonial bungalows pulls down his I.S.C., but not sufficiently to change his score from near the top of the upper-class range.

Charles McKelvey also is owner and manager of large corporations giving him an occupational rank of 1; his source of income is a combination of profits (3) and invested money (2) or 2.5; his house, baronial in its grandeur, is easily a 1; and he lives on "aristocratic" Royal Ridge, giving him another 1, and a final rating of 16.5. He is clearly upper-class in Zenith.

Babbitt does not do quite so well. He gets a 1 with them as a proprietor for occupation; a 3 for profits as his source of income; a 3 for his Dutch Colonial bungalow, which is above average but not a 2; and he rates a 2, as did Eathorne, for living in Floral Heights. His final score is 26, putting him at the high end of the I.S.C. range for upper-middle class.

Ed Overbrook, who longed for Babbitt's society, gets a ranking of 2 as an insurance salesman; his commission form of salary is a 4; his house type no better than a 4 (and possibly a 5); the area, Dorchester, above the workingmen's but no more than average (by inference), is a 4. His final rating is 40, possibly a little above, probably a little below; but, in any case, still lower-middle class.

In *Babbitt*, and, in fact, all of Lewis' novels, he does not give sufficient descriptive detail to permit the use of an I.S.C. for ranking individuals below lower-middle. He is content to refer generally to the masses of respectable workers and their workingmen's houses (most of them upper-lower class) and to the nonrespectable lower-lower class living in "a morass of lodging houses, tenements, and brothels." Zenith, it would appear, has a six-class system.

We will now analyze some of the rich and decisive evidence for establishing the social class of each of the four men supplied by Lewis while telling his story of the life and time of George Babbitt.

Eathorne and the few like him are remote and hardly known to exist by the vast majority of the citizenry of Zenith. Lewis tells us they are Old Family and superior to the McKelveys with their new wealth. Conspicuous spending of their wealth by the McKelveys and the feverish activities which keep them on the society page mark this family as below the Old Family upper-upper class which prefers to live in the quiet, sacrosanct orbit of the very select few. Babbitt looked up to and envied the McKelvey level, but he had a "reverence" for the Eathorne Old Family group.

Babbitt and the men of his level are often the social fronts for the two upper classes. They know them and are sometimes with them, but they are never of them. They belong to such social clubs as the Zenith Athletic Club and the Outing Golf and Country Club, but never the Union Club and Tonawanda Country Club. They are never admitted into the intimacy of members of the upper-class cliques.

To revert to the terminology of Evaluated Participation, if a personality card were scored for Eathorne's E.P., he would rank upper for Symbolic Placement (Old Family, etc.); a 1 for Status Reputation; a 1 for Comparison (said to be above the lower-upper McKelveys, etc.); 1 for Institutional Membership (family and clique). McKelvey rates a 1 for Institutional Membership (clique and association); a 1 for Status Reputation; and a 1 for Comparison (above Babbitt and below Eathorne).

Babbitt rates a 2 for Status Reputation; possibly a 2 for Symbolic Placement (a prominent citizen); and 2 for Institutional Membership (his clubs and cliques and his inability to rate a clique relation with McKelvey's or Eathorne's group).

Overbrook is less clearly drawn; but he gets a 3 for Status Reputation (by inference); a 3 for Institutional Membership (unsuccessful efforts to get into Babbitt's level); and a 3 for Comparison (rated by Babbitt and his kind as below them and Overbrook's tacit acceptance of this rating).

Thus we see that the I.S.C.'s and E.P.'s for all four men and their families agree. We said earlier that an I.S.C. would not distinguish between the two upper classes, and that only an E.P.

would; we also said they were so few and, when the researcher used a good informant, so easily identified and listed that the problem raised by this lack was not serious. *Babbitt* also demonstrates this point: Eathorne's and McKelvey's classes, clearly demarked by E.P., are not distinguished by their I.S.C.'s. The agreement of I.S.C. and E.P. indicates how clearly Lewis observes the American scene and is able to report to his readers about it. It also demonstrates how the I.S.C. and E.P. analyses can be used on the American social novel and permit scientific comparison of the contents of the novels as well as enabling us to use evidence from the novels to further our understanding of American social class.

THE NOVELIST AND SOCIAL CLASS

The general conclusions from scientific field studies of social status in the several regions of America correspond very closely with what novelists, such as Edith Wharton, Theodore Dreiser, John Marquand, and others, report about status in America.

Lewis' George Babbitt, McKelvey, and Eathorne are perfect symbols of the "ideal type" of the several classes they are designed to represent. In the Durkheimian sense, Babbitt is a "collective representation" of some of the meanings and feelings we ascribe to the upper-middle-class businessman who is striving to improve his position.

John Marquand's characters, such as George Apley and H. M. Pulham, Esquire, symbolize the old-family or upper-upper group in New England. Many *Wickford Point* characters are "old-family" and "new-family" representations. In their major outlines, they correspond almost exactly with some of the scientific characterizations of the people of these two classes made by the Yankee City field study. This is not too surprising since Marquand's home is in the town we have called Yankee City and much of the material in his novels is clearly taken from the town he knows from intimate, personal experience. Marquand, being "old family" in Yankee City, views it from the heights of his perspective and reflects many attitudes of this class, including a dislike of the striver from the "new-family" class or the recent arrival from even more submerged levels. (For example, see the character of the foreign correspondent in *So Little Time.*)

Although these comments (perhaps somewhat too personal)

are made about Marquand, in slightly different form they could have been said about any novelist. The novelist usually sees the society from the place where he fits into it. Any social analyst using the novel must take account of the status of the author—what it is today and what it was yesterday. Unfortunately, the analyst cannot always account for what the author hopes his status will be, a set of attitudes which very often colors the writers of novels. It should be remembered that some writers like their social place; others hate it and write accordingly. Some writers, of less integrity than those who have been mentioned on these pages, fawn upon their social betters by expressing their great admiration for people of a higher level and their contempt for those at their own by making their favorable characters men and women from the superior classes and their unfavorable ones from their own class level.

The middle-class writers of this generation who have been in revolt against their society, who have been called the "proletarian writers," have reversed this process. People from their own class are presented unfavorably and as villains, and those from the lower classes are turned into secular saints. The class analyst must know and always take account of the author's biases, for the best of authors may take sides and load his dice against his characters and the behavior of particular classes.

Although the use of novels and the principal problems involved in their use must be raised, they cannot be fully dealt with here. (The fifth and next volume of the "Yankee City Series" on American symbols and their function in American life will be devoted in part to the use of this form of symbolism in the American community.)

"PROFILES FROM YANKEE CITY"

Previous chapters (particularly Chapter 1) summarized some of the general results of the various scientific field studies that have been done on social status in America. These summaries did not tell what was found out about the personalities in the several classes and the relations between them. They tended to be statistical statements about averages and means. Brief excerpts from "Profiles from Yankee City" [1] which are composite drawings of actual people will be given here to provide the reader with the material to test the validity of

[1] See Warner and Lunt, *The Social Life of a Modern Community*, pp. 127-201.

the evidence from the novel and to permit comparison between the two methods.

After presenting the profiles, we will use the I.S.C. to analyze the position of each character to enable us to compare each of these individuals in the profiles with the characters from Babbitt.

The opening profile is called "They All Came."

On that autumn evening Mrs. Henry Adams Breckenridge was sitting in a large wing chair by the fireplace whose dying embers occasionally flared and lighted her pale face and white hair. Behind her, numerous used teacups were scattered on the table. Of her fifty-odd guests all but two had departed. Their automobiles, which had spread out along Hill Street and overflowed down the side streets, had disappeared.

The home of Mr. and Mrs. Henry Adams Breckenridge (upper-upper) where the tea had been given is a square white house which sits well back from the street. It has three stories and is topped by a captain's walk which increases its height. During most of the year large trees and a tall thick hedge obscure the house from the street. A gravel drive cuts through the center of the hedge and, passing the front of the house, continues to a large barn (now a garage) one hundred yards to the rear. In front of the house the drive forms a circle almost too sharp to allow automobiles to turn. Mrs. Breckenridge has often commented that the "circle" was made for carriages and should now be enlarged to accommodate automobiles; "but I like it the way it is and I won't have it changed."

The lawn runs from the hedge back to the barn. The garden stretches one hundred yards from the front circle on one side of the house to the adjoining property, owned and occupied by Mr. Breckenridge's brother and his family (UU). The latter grounds are also well kept, but they do not have an elaborate garden.

There are many old rose bushes in the Breckenridge garden, in which Mr. Breckenridge shows some interest. He occasionally picks off dead flowers and sprays the roses with a homemade solution to kill the rose bugs. Mrs. Breckenridge very rarely cares for the garden although she enjoys walking through it and telling visitors about the flowers. Back of the barn lie apple orchard and meadow. The trees are sprayed occasionally, but little effort is made to make them produce.

For years Mrs. Breckenridge and her sister drove about the town in horse-drawn carriages as did their friends, the Marshalls (UU). Mrs. Breckenridge's chief girlhood interest, in fact, was in horses; and she is still so fond of them that she grudgingly accepts the automobile as a necessary convenience.

Inside the house "very good colonial furniture" is mixed indiscriminately with mid-Victorian. This is a common occurrence in the houses of families whose means made it possible to add furniture during the period when the Victorian superseded the earlier colonial style. There are no reproductions. A few family portraits—two signed by famous artists—have prominent places.

When inspecting the shiny appearance of a new house built by a lower-upper, Mrs. Breckenridge said that one of the things she liked about her own home was that it always had the feeling of having been lived in. This is perhaps the first and most lasting impression that one has of the Breckenridge residence.

"It was nice of you to stay on," she said to the woman and man who sat with her by the fireplace. "I find these large teas a little exhausting. I always hate to give them but I couldn't get out of this one. Several of the members of the committee had given teas and they were afraid that Mrs. Starr [LU] would try to give the last one. She always gives the most perfect and elaborate ones but I am afraid everyone talks about them because they're just a little too-too."

"Of course, the Starrs are new shoe people," said Mrs. Wentworth (UU). "No one ever heard of him until he made his fortune manufacturing shoes."

"All of John's knowledge about the days of the sailing ships," remarked Mrs. Breckenridge, "came from his father and his grandfather. And I suppose he heard some of it from my father [UU] and from Uncle George [UU]. You could tell that all of what Mrs. Starr said she had learned from books she had read. Somehow it annoys me. I just can't help it. You could almost see her memorizing it all so she could use it on people like John and my brothers. I wouldn't mind so much if I thought she really cared about such things, but I know that she doesn't. She thinks it will help her socially to talk to them about things in which they have a genuine interest.

"Mrs. Starr is a social climber. I don't think that the fact of her recent arrival in Yankee City has anything to do with it. She is too aggressive—she is a social climber. She can be very nice, though, and her children are nice. Some of them are very good-looking, but the daughter isn't so much now because she is beginning to look like her mother."

Mrs. Breckenridge continued, "Mrs. Starr is very pushy and she tries to get into everything. I don't dislike her just because she's new. Everybody in the House and Home Club [UU-LU] hates her. If it hadn't been for Miss Churchill [UU] she would never have got in, but she was always very nice to Miss Churchill. When we started the club and sent out invitations, Mrs. Starr was not included; and when I was having it at my house, she called up just as if she were a bosom friend of mine, which she never was, and asked if she could come. I was embarrassed to death and I said, 'Why, no, Mrs. Starr. Mrs. Marshall started the club, and I don't feel I have any right to ask anyone, but if you would like to send in your name you may.' She said, 'All right, very well,' and she sent in her name. Everyone objected, but they all liked Miss Churchill so they said all right."

"I've always made fun of birth and old families, but they do mean something. Mrs. Starr has learned a lot from her books and by being on the *qui vive;* but breeding is something that doesn't come out of a book or by imitating your betters."

"You should have learned a lot about our city this afternoon," the hostess said to the man. "All sorts of people were here. People one hardly knows. Wouldn't you know, not one of the women on the committee or their husbands stayed away. They all came. The Camps [UM], the Frenches [UM], and the Flahertys [UM] were here. They were the people who stood off in one corner pretty much by themselves. They were the ones who were so polite when you tried to talk to them. They always agreed with everything you said. You know, I was just thinking that this is the first time that any of those three women has ever been in my house."

All the above evidence demonstrates how an ambitious, socially mobile person can manipulate an associational structure for the purpose of climbing in the community. It also shows how a given association can be used by an individual to climb and by the society to prevent further mobility. In the case of Mrs. Starr, there was a definite progression in the associations which she joined as she moved upward in the social hierarchy. She was at first active in an organization which included the three uppermost classes. As she became more successful in achieving social status, she lost interest in this association. She later joined another organization which had a smaller number of UM people and finally became a member of an organization which had no one outside of the two upper classes. Her interests decreased in the first two organizations and increased in the last.

The Phillip Starrs drove home from the tea in an oversized, custom-built limousine. John Alton had once remarked sarcastically that if Phillip ever lost his money he could put his stove in his car and camp out for the winter. And his hearer is reported to have said, "Or install a calliope in it and join the circus."

The Starrs were one of a small group of families who recently had purchased Georgian houses in one of the more handsome sections on Hill Street.

The large, square house is one of the old ones on Hill Street. Two well-known architects have declared it to be "one of the most beautiful surviving examples of Federal architecture." Several members of certain old families admitted that it was a beautiful home, but they said, "She's made a museum out of it. It's too perfect. She spent thousands of dollars to remodel it and make it a perfect example of Federal architecture. The trouble with her is she imitates and always overdoes it." Only a few feet of well-clipped grass separate the house from the sidewalk, but in the rear an expansive lawn, flanked by meticulously tended gardens, glistens in the sunlight. Some people feel that the gardens are overcared for, that the gardener has been too scrupulous, and that the house has been so frequently painted that it shines just a little too much.

Mrs. Starr's furniture had been purchased with the aid of an expert on New England antiques. There was nothing in her house that was not called "authentic Adams," or "a perfect example of Queen Anne." And her garden, one soon learned, had won numerous prizes.

Mr. and Mrs. Starr went into the library and waited dinner there before an open fire. Mr. Starr read the editorials of the Boston *Transcript* and re-examined the financial pages of the Boston *Herald.* He found nothing in the editorials but "good sound sense."

Mrs. Starr looked over the magazines on the library table. Those of her husband and son were arranged in a neat row on one side. They included *Fortune, Time, National Geographic,* and *Sports Afield.* Mr. Starr kept the *Saturday Evening Post* by his bedside and Mrs. Starr read the *Pictorial Review* in her own room. Such magazines, not considered fitting symbols of one's social place and intellectual level, were kept away from the view of casual—perhaps critical?—guests.

Mrs. Starr glanced idly through the magazines to which she and her husband subscribed: *Atlantic Monthly, House Beautiful, Harper's,* and *Vogue.*

After dinner Mr. Starr took his own car and drove down to the Lowell Club (UU to UM). The Lowell Club was called the "House of Lords" in local speech, while the Out-of-Doors Club was known as the "House of Commons." This was one way of saying that the Lowell Club was "more choosy" about its members—"no Catholics, and only the best people" are allowed in; but "the House of Commons takes in more fellows from the side streets."

The clubhouse of the Lowell Club had been the home of one of the old families. When Mr. Starr entered it that evening, he met many of the men whom he had seen at the tea. He talked with a broker, a manufacturer, and a banker about investment problems and found out from them what Jonathan Wentworth (UU) and John Breckenridge, the directors of several large institutions, had said on the subject. Mr. Wentworth and Mr. Breckenridge did not belong to the Lowell Club. Mr. Starr listened to Alexander French who talked about what the "classes and the masses" were going to do in the coming election. He heard Mr. French express surprise that there was social "class consciousness now among the people." French said that "the solid people like the men in the Chamber of Commerce and the Rotary Club and our own club can be depended on, but one can't always tell about some of the fellows in the Antlers [UU to LM] and the Caribou (UM to LL). And most of those foreigners down on River Street are the ringleaders in the unions, and they'll vote the other way."

As Mr. and Mrs. Alexander French drove home from the Breckenridge tea, each viewed in silence the events of the afternoon. Mrs. French had been very busy talking to Mrs. Starr, whom she disliked, and Frederica Alton, whom she admired. When she had felt herself being edged out by other ladies who engaged these two in conversation, she had sought out one of her cliquemates, Mrs. William Camp, and discussed the details of the coming Women's Club play. They were both to have parts in it. Mrs. Starr and Mrs. Alton had made it rather difficult to enter into their conversation because they were repeating some of the things that were said at the last meeting of the House and Home Club (UU to LU). Mrs. French would have liked to belong to the House and Home Club, but all her efforts in this direction had met with failure—just as her husband's hope for membership in the February Club had never been fulfilled.

Mr. French turned his car into his driveway and the two of them got out. The Frenches live in a modern six-room colonial house just off Hill Street in Homeville. It is a house with all of the most modern plumbing and mechanical conveniences built into it. There is a stained-shingle exterior which does not have to be repainted or stained again. The trim around the windows is white with blue blinds. The walk to the front door from the sidewalk is concrete as are the front steps. This use of concrete is a departure from what is approved of by members of the higher classes. The middle-class Frenches follow out the same social pattern as others of their status and mix the latest of modern improvements with the old or with reproductions of the old.

The living room has polished hardwood floors and bright paper with a green background on the walls. Mr. French is very proud of several pieces of old furniture, but his pride seems to consist in how much they are worth and how much he could sell them for. Most of the pieces are reproductions of antiques. The bellows hanging by the fireplace are new and an improvement on the old models. The lawn has small well-cut evergreen trees planted in front of the house and the small shrubs are carefully trimmed.

The life and surroundings of Mrs. Henry Adams Breckenridge, old-family and upper-upper, remote from the existence of the common people of Yankee City, correspond with the life of Mr. Eathorne in Zenith. Her ratings for the characteristics of her I.S.C. give her a final score of 12, or perfect, a little above Mr. Eathorne, higher because an old, slowly developing city like Yankee City preserves the quality of its "superior regions," unlike Zenith, where Mr. Eathorne lived in Babbitt's Floral Heights because his house, once remote and distant, was now surrounded by the houses of George Babbitt and Babbitt's friends. In tradition-bound Yankee City the Hill Street of

1800 and the Hill Street of 1948 are one and the same in quality and position.

Phillip Starr, McKelvey's counterpart in Yankee City, gets a final score of 15, very close to McKelvey's. Although he receives a rating of 1 for three characteristics, his Source of Income rates as 2; it is not inherited wealth but "newly-earned shoe money."

Alexander French, occupying Babbitt's place in Yankee City, rates a 3 for House Type and 2 for Area (see pages 227-55 of *The Social Life of a Modern Community* for the ecological areas and houses of Yankee City). His Occupation and Source of Income are not given in the few lines presented here but it is a 1 for occupation (real estate) and a 3 for Source of Income (profits). His score is 26, almost the same as Babbitt's.

The scores of Babbitt and French, McKelvey and Starr, Eathorne and Breckenridge are close, not by mere chance or by reason of careful and unrepresentative selection on the part of the authors of this volume, but because the novel's three characters are symbols and collective representations of their classes, and the three characters in the "Profiles from Yankee City" are also representations of the same three levels above the Common Man in New England.

Through careful study, the American novels and scientific monographs are capable of yielding valuable knowledge and contributions to what we must learn about the behavior of Americans.

Part Five

THEORY AND METHOD FOR THE COMPARATIVE STUDY OF SOCIAL STRATIFICATION

CHAPTER 16

The Several Types of Rank

SOCIAL class in America is but one of the many forms of rank found here and elsewhere. The foregoing chapters largely dealt with the techniques for its observation and analysis.[1] This chapter presents theory and method for the comparative study of all forms of social stratification. Social class in the United States is but one instance of one variety of rank; and to be understood and interpreted, it must be viewed comparatively. The contemporary study of the several varieties of social stratification is blessed (although at times confused) by an increasing use of evidence directly derived from field researches on human behavior and by the steady accumulation and use of statistical facts.[2] These studies test theory, develop methods and techniques, and help establish the empirical foundations for understanding how the varying orders of rank operate in the lives of individuals in all types of society. Territorially, these studies range throughout the world, through the literate and nonliterate societies.[3]

[1] The authors wish to thank Professor Joseph Gittler of the University of Rochester, the editor of *Review of Sociology* and John Wiley & Sons, Inc., for their generous permission to use most of a chapter from that book. The Gittler volume includes reviews and commentaries of the contemporary literature about the several fields of sociology.

[2] The previous discussion is concerned with how to study social class and does not concern itself with theoretical considerations and the broader concerns of method. Part V and the bibliography which follows it put the earlier chapters in this broader framework. The sources are many but primarily social anthropology and sociology.

[3] Class studies are being pursued throughout most of the western world, particularly in the United States (7, 18, 47, 49, 75, 106, 128, 136, 159, 176, 221, 248, 249, 261) and in England and the Commonwealth (100, 215). Other areas that might be mentioned are Burma (165), Africa (174), India (188, 189, 228), and Latin America (23).

The recent literature on social mobility and stratification on China and Japan provides valuable comparative material. Several studies on social mobility and the play of such factors as education, the acquisition of property, political achievement, and personality have been examined (87, 145, 147). Studies of the gentry, peasantry, and other ranks now make it possible to substitute evidence for speculation and doctrine for the comparative analysis of stratification (56, 268). Social change, conflict,

The economic determinists, Marxian and non-Marxian, have their own theories of rank. The latter, lineal descendants from earlier English and American theorists, in making assumptions about men as social beings tend to see the whole problem of status and rank in purely economic terms. Moreover, following the assumptions of their progenitors, they often view social and group behavior in individual terms (5, 10, 48, 222).[4] Individuals are not seen as interconnected parts of a social web of super- and subordinate relations, but as separate economic units to be reassembled by the investigator into economic categories which are evaluated as superior or inferior. Such studies are valuable and necessary, but they are not sufficient. They do not cover the whole area of man's group life in a status order, although many try to make them do so. Economic stratification is of first importance in any complex social system, and understanding it as such is of equal importance, but such behavior must also be examined as *one* part of the larger system of rank. Occupational studies can be treated separately, but ultimately to understand their social place they must be related by structural studies to the structure of collective life.

Although there have been a number of recent investigations of the social and status structures of communities (136, 249, 260) and still others on the hierarchies of institutions in this and other societies (86, 87, 268), there has been no general statement about the assumptions, the methodology, and theory of *structural* and comparative analysis of the forms of social stratification or of its relation to the study of occupational stratification.[5] With the results of present and previous research on which to build, it is now possible to present some of the basic principles involved. While examining the results of contemporary research, the present enterprise will do no more than make a beginning at such an undertaking.

---

and co-operation have been treated (235). Some of the principal issues about vertical mobility in the United States are argued in the recent studies of Warner and Abegglen (252, 853), Sjoberg (237), Rogoff (222), Hatt (125, 127), Centers (48, 51), Adams (5), and many others (10, 57, 190, 267). Those for England are (100, 101, 102, 120, 123, 201, 202, 203, 215).

[4] The numbers in parentheses found in the text refer to the numbered references in the bibliography which follows. Numbers without parentheses refer to the footnotes.

[5] The limitations of community analysis are numerous, including the difficulty of determining how representative the communities are of the national community (77, 79, 251, 259). Occupational studies are more easily used for national analysis, but this raises other problems, since they lose or disregard much of the significant life of the people at all levels of rank (163).

We may say briefly what is meant by structural studies and comparative analysis. The work of the structural analyst is similar to that of the biologist. The biologist studies the characteristics of an animal species as they are found in the animals themselves; he observes the relations of the characteristics to each other (taxonomy). He examines the genetic relations of the generations of animals and learns about the modifications and persistence of the several forms. The structural student of rank does likewise. He investigates the words and acts of men in relation to each other and observes uniformities and differences in these relations. He determines norms and modalities of behavior about what does happen and "ideally" what "ought" to happen, while learning the extent of the variations. Where possible he studies persistence and change (214).

For the structural analyst, "status is the most general term used to refer to the location of the behavior of individuals or the social positions of individuals themselves in the structure of any group. It is a defined social position located in a social universe. The term is synonymous with social position, social place, or social location. Statuses may or may not be ranked as superior or inferior." Therefore, they fall into two general types—the ranked and nonranked (251). We are dealing with the former only.

The form of a particular status in a rank order is defined operationally by answering the following questions: What are the rights and privileges enjoyed by those who occupy it? What are the rights and privileges of members of *other* statuses that are directly or indirectly related to it? What are the duties and obligations of those who occupy a given status and what are the duties and obligations of others who are in statuses which are related to it? To restate this in somewhat different terms, we need to know the rules of conduct and the appropriate symbols used by those who are in, or implicated with, a given status.

Status always implies and implicates the larger social universe in which it has its place. It is definable in large part explicitly or implicitly by reference to its relations with other parts of the social system. Ultimately, full understanding of a particular status can be gained not only by knowing what it is as a social object and how it is interrelated with other statuses but by understanding its relation to, and place in, the whole society (40, 108, 148, 218, 253, 256).

The comparison of particular status systems studied by this

method reveals general types (class, for example), varieties of the type (open and "closed" varieties of class systems), and particular instances (the class system of a community). The latter can be "broken down" into the observed acts of behavior out of which the status norms were built by the researcher. Thus, type, variety, the particular case and the observed acts of behavior, represent various levels of abstraction and generality. In discussions about status, not recognizing this fact has caused much difficulty and several needless controversies. If a *type* of status system such as caste is taken to mean, and is equated with, a *variety* or an *instance* or one observed bit of behavior, erroneous and improper comparisons are certain to be made. For example, if American Negro–white status relations are *typed* as caste (65, 77), it does not mean that they are necessarily the same as the several varieties of Indian or African caste (39, 63) or the classical type of Indian caste,[6] any more than when the biologist calls St. Bernards and Pomeranians dogs, he is saying they are identical. They are alike by the criteria of taxonomy.

Each of the several forms to which social stratification or the term rank refers is composed of interconnected statuses in relations of superordination and subordination and of superiority and inferiority. Power or prestige, or power and prestige are unequally distributed among the several statuses whose entirety comprises any given system (105, 162). All orders of rank distribute unequally the highly valued material and immaterial social objects as facts of power and symbols of prestige among the superior and inferior statuses. These systems persist and are modified through time, incorporating the members of each generation into their orderings of status. The methods by which forms of rank are transferred or not from generation to generation and the rules governing the relations of the generations constitute important parts of any of these orders. The processes which accomplish the task of socializing the young by the older with the status belief, values, and behavior of any given status system provide one of many places where structural and psy-

[6] The study of caste in India is being pursued by the several social sciences. Some of the problems examined and the issues now in debate are: What the roles of economic and ritual factors are in caste as a system of Indian ranking (188); how far social and economic class rather than caste determine a man's prestige and power; the degree to which tradition and social and economic change influence contemporary caste organization and behavior (189); what similarities and differences exist between Indian and other forms of caste (138). The comparative study of caste as a *type* of rank and all of its varieties has also been given attention (251).

chological analysis works effectively. The studies of the psychological effects of status on the learning abilities of the young and the research on performance by students at the different grade levels from different social classes have added much to our knowledge of how social class in America and Britain affects the lives of individuals and functions as a system of rank.

Since the varieties of rank differ in form and function and in their relations to the larger social systems in which they exist, all can be profitably compared and classified, and inferences drawn about the nature of the forms studied and the values they express. Fortunately a solid body of literature is now developing about the workings of status systems throughout the "civilized" and "primitive" societies of the world. The descriptive and explanatory generalizations about rank in the present chapter are built upon it.

Social stratification is a *type* of subsystem which exists in most, if not all, literate and nonliterate societies. Whether it exists in all or not is largely a matter of definition. Since the distinctions involved in the differences in definition are important, they need to be examined to help us better understand the principles involved in stratification. Stern's (242) recent paper (following similar distinctions of Hobhouse, Wheeler, and Ginsberg), as well as the publications of most anthropologists and sociologists, is not in accord with the position taken by writers like Sorokin. The latter includes such social systems as age and sex divisions among the forms of social stratification; the others do not. He declares in *Social Mobility* that "Any organized social group is always a stratified social body. There has not been and does not exist any permanent social group which is 'flat,' and in which all members are equal. Unstratified society, with a real equality of its members, is a myth which has never been realized in the history of mankind" (240, page 12).

Stratified society is manifested in various forms: "First, in the existence of the sex and age groups with quite different privileges and duties . . ." (240, page 13).

While it is true that age divisions place their members in super- and subordinate positions (32, 143, 220), the rules and principles involved are quite different from such forms of rank as social and economic class, or political, military, or ecclesiastical hierarchies, and others. Although they are socially defined and evaluated, age categories are essentially biologically founded and "fit" *everyone* during lifetime, the grades of age being statuses through which *all* maturing individuals must pass. There are no necessary invidious discriminations; age is a form that can be *commonly* shared at least by all those of the same sex. During their life development, members of the other systems of rank do not move inevitably through the higher and lower levels.

Because age grades do place people in orders of prestige and power, for our purposes they are treated as a major subtype of rank, rudimentary and nonspecialized, to be distinguished from all specialized and developed forms. They divide clearly into two basic varieties, those age divisions which are based entirely on social definitions of the aging processes and those which include other evaluative principles, such as economic, political, and birth distinctions. The second type of system is of particular importance in Africa which, with other status systems, is now being studied.

CRITERIA FOR THE STUDY OF RANK

Since the diversity of the forms of rank, even when limited to the specialized ones, is very great and, when taken on a world-wide basis, bewilderingly so, the question arises whether it is possible to make scientific sense out of the diversity and establish valid uniformities by use of classifications founded on criteria and principles basic to the behavior of men living in groups. Since all humans live in societies and since the societies are diverse in range and type, criteria adequate for this culture may not be so for others. The criteria used necessarily must be relevant to all systems of social stratification; they must be "culture free." Such criteria can only be said to be scientifically valid when founded on basic principles of human behavior and applicable at all times and places, including the *known* past of our own and other societies.

The *tests* for such guiding criteria are

a. They should be founded primarily on human adaptive behavior necessary everywhere for the maintenance and persistence of the social and biological life of all men in all groups.

b. They should be of vital significance to the life careers of individuals.

c. They should apply to all societies and all forms of rank.

d. They should come from, and be subject to, the evidence of actual observed behavior and not the armchair theories of ideologists or those primarily interested in constructing abstract philosophical theories.

e. From them and the evidence it should be possible and scientifically necessary to establish types of rank capable of testing by further evidence and analysis, which thus begin to assume a general and more abstract and less individual and unique conceptual character and are therefore subject to further analysis and testing.

f. From the several types it should be possible to build a coherent system incorporating the uniformities and the varieties into a conception of rank that comprehends the whole diversity yet refers to and places each individual form.

g. The taxonomic system of rank, consisting of interdependent logical categories referring to empirically derived individual systems, must be capable of yielding propositions about the nature of rank, its several forms, the conditions under which they exist, and the relations between the diverse forms and their surrounding conditions.

Two *kinds* of basic questions about the access to each other of the members of the species of any given group help us meet the demands of the several tests: First, are the statuses (or a status) within a system of rank open to movement to and from them so that those who might seek access or seek to leave them may do so? Is the system of assignment of status such that each individual's position is free so that he can move vertically or horizontally toward others and they to him? Can he and they compete for higher status or strive to maintain their own? Or is the status system closed so that men cannot move from status to status, their own individual positions thus being so fixed that their careers are confined to one status (or level of rank) and competition for any other status not possible? Some systems of rank conform to the first and some to the second type. In the first, individuals, families, and other groups through time move up or down from one status to another. Vertical mobility, social and occupational, are forms of this movement. Such a type can be called an open status system, subject to free competition. The second type is a system of closed status with the individual's life chances controlled by the rules governing the status he was assigned at birth. The principles of open and restricted competition for individuals and families and of free movement as well as social control over ingress and egress from ranked statuses are involved. Obviously these two are extreme polar forms; numerous mixed types intervene along the range between the two.

The second kind of basic question may be stated: To what extent is the life of a society and the activities of each individual controlled by any order of rank? Is the order's province *limited* to certain activities and not others? Is it limited to particular periods and times? Is it limited to certain individuals and not others? Does it regulate part of the lives of some people for part of the time but not all of it? What and how much does it control? In brief, and to apply terms, is it a *limited* hierarchy segmenting the membership and activities of the group, or is it inclusive, generally comprising everyone and all or most of the activities that make up the round of life of the group and each individual?

These two principles when used as criteria, the restriction of movement to and from statuses and the limitation and extent of the social and individual activities, are applicable to all systems and are of significance to each. Since systems of rank conforming to them order the several varieties of *status* which function to control the basic activities of man and determine who shall have or not have access to them, who shall have power and prestige or not, they clearly meet the demands of the tests previously set.

THE SEVERAL TYPES OF RANK

When the two polar types of status control, the closed form (not accessible to free competition) and the open (accessible to movement into it and allowing movement out) are combined with the two polar types of hierarchy (the general and all-inclusive one, which covers most or all of the activities of the individual and the society, and the segmentary or limited one whose controls are confined to a limited part of the society and its behavior) four basic forms of rank are logically recognizable. Each of the four logical types is now satisfied by empirical reality, there being numerous documented cases from contemporary research on civilizations and on the unlettered cultures of primitive society. Many varieties exist in the middle distances which can be arranged scientifically according to the two principles, the amount of control exercised over the free movement of peoples, and the extent of the control exercised over the total social activities.

The four extreme types are:

a. The inclusive (or general) system with open statuses where free competition prevails among individuals (and families) for position. Social class in the United States is but one variety.[7] Successful competition is expressed in social mobility.

b. The limited (segmentary) system within which the ranked statuses are open to free competition and there is movement in and out of the available statuses.

c. The inclusive (general) system whose statuses are closed and not open to competition. The position of the individual is fixed.

d. The *limited* (segmentary) system closed to free competition where, for the purposes of the hierarchy, the position of the individual is fixed and there is no movement from status to status.

The several types range from a high degree of freedom for the individual, with great fluidity of status, to a rigid, inflexible system with fixed life chances for the individual and his family.[8] The intermediate distances, ranging between the two extremes of the extent of the control of the variety of activities and the degree of closure of status, make it possible to recognize and place a number of intermediate or subtypes corresponding with the variations found by research in this and other societies. However, for our present purposes, only one intermediate type for each dimension will be introduced.

[7] Several issues about social and occupational mobility are now being profitably debated. Some of the principal ones are: How much movement is there (5, 17, 237)? Is there more or less than previously (252, 253)? Is American society becoming less or more rigid (134)? What are the factors involved in contemporary mobility: education, acquisition of skill, social and occupational imitation and modeling? Or are they personal and psychological (66, 133)? Do members of certain classes, the middle as compared with the upper or lower, move more (251)?

[8] Since in all or most societies there is a variety of ranked statuses, each with its own power and prestige, the same individual may be ranked differently. In some hierarchies he may have high status (a Brahmin) and in others low or high (economically or politically). For a discussion of the relation of an individual's status ratings in India see Marriott (188). By a careful study of the ratings of men of several castes by members of the community, he shows that different criteria are used by the villagers who evaluate them. Caste is but *one* system of rating. There was more disagreement about the prestige of the different men among the raters than among the members of the New York village studied by Kaufman (156, 157). *The Status System of a Modern Community* attacked the same problem (256).

Each system may be in a state of equilibrium, with opposition between the ranks organized or in a state of conflict. Partly as a result of the long reign of Marxian ideology among social scientists, the literature on class conflict is far greater than that on the study of cooperation among all levels on the common tasks of society, or than on organized opposition (in Simmel's sense) among those who collaborate. In fact, some writers would define the task of the analyst of rank as the study of the history of class conflict. Structural analysis disagrees; the histories of class and other forms of rank necessarily record periods of conflict and the nature of it, but such studies will be founded on the larger problem of status opposition where cooperation is an essential part of the class relations.

Inspection of Chart XI shows that the degrees of inclusion of activities have been arranged horizontally and the degrees of closure or openness of status vertically. The general and more inclusive type is at the upper left combined with free competition and the other extreme types (so numbered in one of the four corners) at the right; the mixed types are between them.

It will be noted that social class, which allows competition for the more prestigeful and powerful positions, is in the upper left (1) and that color caste, at the other extreme in status closure, which prohibits movement and competition, is in the lower left (2). The position of the individual and his family is *not* fixed in social class, for his life chances and those of his family can be (by the nature of the system) improved by competing freely (51) for higher position. The position of the individual and his family in a (classical) caste system is fixed and determined by birth. He is not free to compete for all or some of the prestige and power of the higher caste. His life chances (so far as caste is involved) are limited. The two forms of rank, however, are alike inasmuch as each covers the whole or most of the activities of those who are members of either system (246, 247, 266).

The publications on American, English,[9] and European[10] social

[9] English sociologists are rapidly developing a large body of literature on social class, social mobility, and other aspects of social stratification. The several classes and their composition have been recently reported on (3, 11, 37, 88, 89, 100, 169, 170). Occupational grading and succession are now being studied (52, 253). The relation of recent political, economic, and social change to changes in the status structure has been treated (215). The broad generalities of occupational grading in English-speaking culture now seem clear (59, 152, 186).

[10] Studies of stratification and social mobility in other European countries,

CHART XI

TYPES OF SOCIAL STRATIFICATION

THE DEGREE OF THE INCLUSION OF ACTIVITIES CONTROLLED BY A RANK ORDER

The degree of Openness or Closure of the Status Controls		General and Inclusive	Mixed: To General	Mixed: To Limited	Limited and Segmentary
Open With Free Competition		General and free (certain social classes and age grades) 1	Neither inclusive nor entirely limited, but free competition (ethnic group, certain occupations and professions) 8		Segmentary and free (certain factories, various military hierarchies, churches, etc., political) 3
Mixed	Open	General extension and with intermediate rules of closure	Neither inclusive nor limited, partly open		Segmentary, partly open
Neither Open nor Closed	Closed	(Certain ethnic groups. The middle classes more open, upper more closed) 5	(Certain occupations and professions; certain ethnic groups; degree of assimilation) 6		(Certain ethnic groups; degree of assimilation; certain factories, unions, associations, churches, etc.) 7
Status Closure With No Status Competition		General with status closure, no competition (color caste, certain castes in India, sex divisions) 2	Neither inclusive nor limited. Closed to competition (certain occupations and professions) 9		Segmentary with status closure. No competition (certain factories, unions, associations, etc.) 4

class and the issues being debated are endless. Some of them are methodological: Is American class no more than a statistical construct? Or is it a reality in group life? The number of classes has been discussed. The degree to which they exist and how they do

including France, Italy, Russia, the Netherlands, and the several Scandinavian countries, are being conducted and published (99, 120, 150, 177, 245).

in great metropolitan centers and the smaller cities and rural areas have been issues.

How sharply delineated or not the several levels are and the number involved in fact are interrelated problems. The present writer and those colleagues he has had the satisfaction of working with have at no time believed they were sharp and clearly distinct (251, 257). Nor has it been believed that everyone in a community sees them alike (251). In fact, the structural type of analysis (like the occupational one) depends on the analyst's examining his data and judging where the break-points are (for purposes of analysis and scientific representation of communicable reality). The technique of "matched agreement" clearly indicates that the scientific class construct refers to the norms of social reality. The class variations in an *open* system (with social mobility) necessarily make class "boundaries" indistinct. Only a classically defined caste system sharply separates two or more levels of rank.

The issue on the exact number of social classes existing in American (or English) society seems a false one. For some purposes there may be only three recognized by the participant or the informant, for example, the "Common Man Level" and those above and below it. The participant-informant may then redivide them in four, five, or six levels, running from upper down through the middle levels to the lowest class. Or he may see them as simply upper, middle, and working classes. Each system of classification exists in his mental life (beliefs and values) and behavior and among other members of the society. Analogous to these several divisions of class are those of age grades. The old, mature, and the young may be further divided or collapsed into the adult and subadult levels. Each is a reality.

The interrelations of the social classes have not had sufficient and proper attention. If they had, many of the false problems about the nature of American class would disappear. McCall's paper showing the amount of interaction of people in small groups among different class levels is most important (179). It indicates that for some purposes members of different classes are sometimes closer than those of the same level. This follows the approach set forth in the second volume of the Yankee City Series (256) where the interactions and relations of the six classes were measured for family, clique, and association.[11]

[11] Unfortunately for purposes of sensible debate of the real issues, this volume

Forms of rank in the segmentary positions are quite different from the general types (see chart, Positions 3 and 4). They are alike in so far as the control is limited; they are different since in the one the system is open, and in the other, closed to competition. The segmentary hierarchies, including political,[12] economic,[13] ecclesiastical,[14] military, and the like, in America (70, 78, 107) and many parts of Europe (231) may be open for competition for power and prestige to all those who enter them, or they may be partly closed or entirely so. The *accessibility* to the highly valued things and symbols of a society may be controlled by the rules governing such hierarchies. Salaries, wages, and other economic differences can be determined by such social rules governing movement. The distribution of goods and services and wealth is partly a function of position in the segmentary and general hierarchies.

---

has not been given the same attention as Volume I. On page 12 of the second volume it is said, "When the several internal structures of the community of Yankee City had been analyzed to determine the number and kind of positions [statuses] and relations, we sought to convert all the relations and positions of the separate structures into one general positional [status] system. If this were possible [as it was] we could dispense with the older class and structural analysis and depend entirely on the positional and relational system."

In brief, each class becomes a series of multiple statuses, and they are part of an interactive totality of statuses. All of them, for the individuals who participate in them, are as contexts of behavior "reference groups."

[12] Political hierarchies have their own separate bodies of literature. However, certain of them in the past have been of great influence in sociology and some in the present are of direct sociological significance. The nature of power in the hierarchy with its relation to community and individual affairs is one of them (27, 158, 185, 187, 223). The relation of the different kinds of personality to political behavior in hierarchical structures is another (161, 162). The study of the meaning of voting behavior, political parties, political attitudes, and socioeconomic and class levels and their significance for understanding national and community life is yielding valuable knowledge on which the sciences having to do with status can now depend (6, 12, 23, 30, 33, 84, 164).

[13] The literature on industrial hierarchies, including factories, corporations, and industries, as well as unions and other employer and employee groups, is exceedingly large and beyond the compass of this chapter. However, certain writers have emphasized the structural as well as the economic characteristics of these organizations. A few must be mentioned (19, 97, 98, 116, 196, 197, 244, 264). Others have stressed the personality as it functions in business enterprise (252).

The literature on industrial conflict has been examined in the history of structural change (115, 255).

[14] The varying ideologies of the church (218), the membership of the church (40, 41, 219, 266), and the place of churches in the class structure in the United States (219) have been studied. All show strong status relations, but they indicate that the effects of the entire community and democratic values are strongly felt by this institution (249). However, certain churches are heavily class-defined and are "store front," "middle-class," or "society" (77).

An inspection of the cases of rank in the mixed types is revealing. The American ethnic groups are not found in any of the polar types, but primarily in the three mixed types, according to their degree of assimilation (259, 266). They are not in Position 1 with social class because, although for a brief time the ethnic subsystem covers almost all or most of the activities of the individual and his family as does class, the system itself is a subsystem that does not include everyone in the society or all its activities. Only part of the society is involved. Yet, except in the broadest sense of the term, an ethnic group cannot be typed as segmentary since (unlike a job in a segmentary factory) most of the individual's and family's activities are ordered by it. Although in some respects certain American ethnic systems are like a caste (Position 2) in regard to closure, in fact there is always some movement and the group's ambivalent values partly encourage movement up and out. Consequently by *extent* it belongs in the mixed types. Most ethnic groups of two or three generations belong in the central position (6). They are partly general in their application of control but not entirely; they are partly open, yet there is a degree of closure beyond the rule of social class and the position of an individual is more often fixed than in an (open) social class. As an ethnic group such as the Irish Catholic becomes more assimilated, its members largely enter the general social system and confine their remaining ethnic activities (if any) to the hierarchy of the church (Position 7). Some of the members of ethnic groups who refuse to assimilate may become sects and develop a closed system (266).

When the two basic types of rank are combined, the rudimentary, universal one to which age grading belongs and the differentiated, specialized type in which social and economic class are varieties, it is then possible to cover all forms of rank existing in this and all societies. They all distribute power and prestige through the controls of the statuses which compose them.

The nature of power and its sources are concerns of fundamental importance and of necessary interest to contemporary students of rank. We need now to turn our attention to them.

CHAPTER 17

Power, Prestige, and the Human Adaptive Controls

POWER may be simply defined for our immediate purposes as the possession of control over other beings and objects in the social and natural environments, making it possible to act on them to achieve outcomes that would not take place if control were not exerted. Prestige is the kind and amount of value socially attributed to objects, activities, persons, and statuses (135, 155). The two are usually interrelated; power can derive from prestige and prestige from power. However, a man may have power with little prestige or high prestige with little power.[1] The kinds and amount of power and prestige vary from one territorial group to another. They also differ among the several forms of rank and status. The problem of how forms of rank are related to prestige and power as well as the nature of sources of power and prestige must be considered.

The Marxians and others have founded their system of class analysis on the assumption that power is *only* a product of *one* kind of status control over *one* kind of environment; that the statuses which control the means of production and the distribution of their products hold the power and are thus given the prestige which determine class alignments (61, 172); it is argued that since the technological adjustments to the natural environment are moving in a given, predetermined direction, the dependent society, its mental and cultural life, the class forms, their composition and relations are

[1] The problem of power and rank is of almost obsessive concern to Marxians. The followers of Max Weber are also greatly concerned with it, but conceived it more broadly and are less inclined to derive it entirely from one source (62, 187, 213, 214, 231). Others view it more in classical, political terms and with the ultimate use of force (73).

Lasswell, influenced by Freud and Pareto, as well as other psychologies and sociologies, views power broadly; but essentially he is concerned with the moral aspects of power as they are felt and expressed in the rewards and deprivations of the organism living in society (161, 162).

perforce moving in a predictable sequence to a classless society (28).

Clearly such economic determinists are correct in pointing out the importance of the statuses which control the natural environment and the real power inherent in such statuses or those superordinate statuses which control them. They are wrong, however, in assuming that technological control is the *only* source of power. The sources of power are *multiple,* not one. To properly understand the problems of power and prestige we must use the knowledge of sociology, social anthropology, and the psychological sciences that has accumulated since Marx and Engels. We must re-examine the whole question of the relation of power to the human adaptive controls of the several environments, and man's dependence on them.

Human survival universally depends on two and, it is believed, three environments. The first is the so-called natural environment which in varying degrees is controlled by the technology; the second, the human species environment which is controlled by (part of) the moral order, a system of social organization; and the third, real or not, the supernatural environment, ordered and controlled, it is believed, by the "myths" and rituals of religion and magic, a system of sacred symbols.

The very presence of these adaptive controls demonstrates: (a) that men are *dependent* on an adequate use of them for survival, each having the power of life and death over them; (b) that the controls exercised over the environments to reduce their control *over* men involve the use of several forms of power by individuals and groups; and (c) that, in exercising control, each adaptive mechanism employs real power. The tools and skills of the technology transform the natural world sufficiently to aid men in acquiring and producing food, shelter, and the other creature needs and comforts which increase the life chances (Weber's term more broadly used) of the adult individual, of the young to grow into maturity, and in a given group of the species to survive.

The second, the control over the species, by imposing the pressures of moral forms on animal behavior, regulates the discharge of species energy; it controls the interactions of individuals and structures their access to each other. Thus it orders the basic life-flow of the species and of each individual, including the procreative processes and the relations of the adult and immature; it orders the expression of hostility, aggression, and violence, the disposition of prized objects, and the imposition of unpleasant tasks among the members of the group. Control over the species environment means an exercise of real power; it also means the presence of power in every socially organized species group and a *sense* of social power (in Durkheim's sense) within the group among those who live in it. The meanings and social representations of what social power is vary from group to group; the forms by which it is utilized and expressed also vary enormously. The violent, not to say explosive, power of the emotions generated by the moral order's control over sexuality, individual growth and development, adult deterioration, and senility among the several family statuses has been given much attention. This focus, under the conceptual schemes of the psychoanalyst, has helped us understand emotion's great force but has tended to lose some of its deserved strength for status and power analysis because of too great reliance on individual psychology rather than on group and species foundations.

The *supernatural* adaptations controlling, it is believed, man's ultimate fate, govern those activities and outcomes over which the other two have insufficient power. Sickness, death, obliteration of the self, social disaster, and the ill or well being of man are in its compass. Each society has fashioned its own adaptive controls to meet as best it can the terrible and absolute power of this other world and thereby reduce human anxiety and dread.

Statuses function to order and coordinate the multiple activities involved in the control of each environment. They assign tasks and socially locate activities; they include and exclude the members of the society while placing them in a social universe. The statuses directly involved in the several adaptive activities, as integral parts of their ordering, possess, or are attributed, varying power and prestige according to the members of the society who feel their beneficial or harmful effects. Those with a high degree of adaptive control are likely to have high ranking; those believed to exercise low control are often given lower ranking.

Those statuses *not* directly involved in the mechanics of the adaptive processes, but which control those statuses that are, *share* some of their power with them, or they *remove* and *hold* it for themselves. Thus statuses are hierarchically arranged. The problem becomes why these secondary statuses in a rank order exercise control over the others and often accumulate more power and prestige than the primary ones directly involved in the adaptive tasks? This question is closely allied to another. Why do some societies possess specialized and developed rank orders of prestige and power and others only the rudimentary types? These questions will be dealt with in the following section.

The power of an adaptive status, or hierarchy of statuses, may be *intrinsic* and directly applied or *extrinsic* to its activities and functions. In other words, the force it possesses and applies may be an integral and necessary part of its adaptive activity, or it may be ("given") attributed to it by all, or some, members of the society. The power to kill a kangaroo with a spear by a hunter (who does or does not keep its meat for himself, his family, and clan) is at least partly intrinsic, but the man may also be accorded by his group increased power beyond his ability to kill and keep. The first is an intrinsic and integral part of his technical status as a hunter and of his moral status as a member of his family and clan; the latter power, not necessary for the execution of his technical and moral acts, is of course attributed to him.

The prestige of a status, the esteem in which it is held, or the derogation, is attributable and extrinsic. The values of the group, or some part of it, are projected upon the status and determine its social worth. Much of what are popularly and scientifically termed prestige and power are products of the larger group's feelings. The facts of the adaptive actions of a status become evaluated symbols which accumulate and attract other negative or positive social values that may have little to do with the activities of the status.

Since the statuses of adaptation are integral parts of a social system, they are in a position of mutual influence. No one system of adaptation is entirely free from the others. No one at *all* times and *all* places will necessarily dominate the others, the technological, the moral, or the social system, the other two. When the technology is complex the kinds and number of statuses (occupations, for example) are necessarily numerous and highly diverse. Such economic status systems may be scientifically classified into types and arranged along a continuum of simple to complex. In many primitive societies, occupations are largely undifferentiated. Each man performs many productive functions which are not classifiable occupationally. Occupational ranking is therefore not possible. In such a society as ours where the division of labor is exceedingly great, ranking of occupations is one of the principal forms of stratification; and the accumulation of wealth and the sources of wealth are also ranked in "separate" systems (257).

The several economic status orders found in different societies may be closed or open; they may be limited or general rank orders. In any given society the statuses associated with the technology may dominate the whole status order and all other types of status be subordinate to one or more orders of technological status. On the contrary, they may be under the control of, and subordinate to, the statuses which control the species or the myths and rituals which regulate the power of the supernatural and the unknown (32, 123, 165). Or the three may be in conflict (Russia seems to be a case in point).

The moral order's family, age, and sex statuses control and regulate some of the most powerful activities and energies of the species environment. The status of the parent, the father particularly, subordinates the statuses of the sons and daughters. The foundations of authority, its use by the one and submission to it by the other, are in this universal relation. The usual superordination of males and subordination of females and the similar relation of the mature to the young are forms of authority where social power is exercised. Rudimentary systems of rank are part of all family, kinship, and age grade systems (13, 139, 140, 178, 200, 263).

By extension or limitation of the usual rules of descent and marriage, the control of sexual accessibility or its prohibition and of descent of the offspring (together with economic controls) provides the powerful foundations for many general systems of rank. Crucial questions for understanding this problem of the relation of the moral statuses which control the species environment and rank order are: Are all unmarried males and females of mature sexuality potential mates, unfettered by any rules other than those of incest prohibitions? Or is the choice of mates bounded by, and limited to, sharply defined ranked categories? The general (inclusive) closed statuses which fix the position of the individual sharply divide the biological group by social prohibitions and boundaries. Full access between all members of the sexes for marriage purposes is forbidden. The physical life of the individual is confined within narrow boundaries; mates do not come from diverse but from socially similar statuses

(138). The open, inclusive type provides a "mating" system where the two members of the marriage pair may come from most diverse or very similar backgrounds.

Since the children are identified with the social status of the parents, both the closed and open general systems initially place the child's status in this system of rank. In the closed system like color caste the child remains by moral rule at the parents' and his ancestors' level; in the open he may stay or move out of it.

If the general inclusive type is an open system, the parent-child relation and the sibling relations often assume most diverse forms and are subject to great stress and distortion (68, 182). The son may move to superior position, or the daughter marry into one, thus subordinating the parent and placing the family's superior adult in an inferior position of rank. Some of the siblings may move up, others down, and still others remain at the parents' level. Open systems with free competition disperse the members of many families over distant parts of the rank order. Ordinarily they must if the systems are to continue. Closed fixed systems tend to hold the members of the family together and add their influence to maintaining family solidarity. In an open system the family of orientation quickly yields its maturing young to the larger world and to their own families of procreation; in a closed system the older generations are more likely to be related to the younger ones. The two families, often forming into a *grosse* family, hold together in primary interaction biologically, territorially, and socially. They provide the hard core of fixed position for their members and closure for movement beyond their limits (138).

The families of orientation and procreation are necessary and integral parts of the general, inclusive types of system (251). Their moral power, too, is an integral part of the power of these rank orders. It may be contained and held within the closed ranks of a caste or spread over the several ranks of a class system where there is freedom of movement.

The family may or may not be related to segmentary systems of rank. Political and ecclesiastical and other differentiated forms may derive part or most of their power and their structural form from the family, but such hierarchies can and do exist without the direct use of the family. Certain African political hierarchies are elaborations of superordinate heads of families; ecclesiastical hierarchies may be a scalar system of "fathers," but they may be built without direct use of family relations.

The statuses associated with the control of the unknown which reduce human anxieties about their life chances by the use of myth and ritual are religious and magical. They are ordinarily centered in the church. They include such ritual statuses as priests, magicians, some doctors and psychiatrists, and occasionally other statuses to which such power is attributed.

They, too, may be simple or complex. They, too, may be in societies where the religious life dominates, or is subordinate to, the technological or secular organization. In the simpler societies there may be no more than a temporary ritual leader with little power and prestige, his tenure being only during the ceremony. In many of the complex societies there may be a hierarchy of statuses from local ones up through a hierarchy that integrates and controls the supernatural activities of a whole nation or those of many nations. The vertical height may be exceedingly great or not, the area of social activity limited, or in a theocracy it may include the whole society.

The powers of the supernatural environment which can harm or benefit men are often dualistically conceived. The problem confronting the statuses related to these beings and the forces of sacred good and evil is to control them and to adapt their power to man's ends. The forces of good must be harnessed to assist men; the forces of evil must be diverted, quarantined, or weakened. When it is believed that the statuses manipulating myth and ritual accomplish these ends and they "control" the uncontrollable, the statuses of magicians, priests, and others like them are attributed some of the power of the environment they control. They and their statuses derive power and prestige both from their knowledge and ability to use the symbols effectively and from the power that comes from the sacred world itself. As Durkheim pointed out, supernatural forces are comparable to physical forces;[2] the words and objects of the rites of religion have social force and strength attached to them. They have the power to kill or cure. The priest or magician can

[2] The ethnologists early recognized these significant "sacred forces." Durkheim took his lead from Codrington, who identified and defined *mana* as he found it among the Melanesians. "There is," Codrington said, "a belief in a force altogether distinct from physical power, which acts in all ways for good and evil. . . . It is a power or influence . . . it shows itself . . . in any kind of power or excellence which a man possesses." (Robert H. Codrington, *The Melanesians.* Oxford: Clarendon Press, 1891, p. 118.)

benefit man or the sorcerer can cause sickness and death in his victim. They control the forces that can take or give life. The power that the sacred statuses possess tends to be absolute.

The generations of individuals arrive and disappear "but (spiritual) *force* [mana] always remains. . . . This force is an expression of the social power of the clan [the society]."[3] It awakens in all those who feel its force, all individuals in each society, an idea of an external force. According to Durkheim, the sign of the totem (the emblem of God) is a substitute for this abstract social force, allowing the sentiments of the group to be easily expressed. Since all religious symbols are signs expressing, and referring to, the forces of group life, the statuses which control (and manipulate) them exercise their power.

Since all men incorporate some of the society into their persons and since mana is power socially derived, all men necessarily possess some mana or social power. Weber's *charisma* seems to be little more than one form of personal mana. Charisma and mana, as parts of the value and meaning of objects and people, can be forms of attributed power. Ordinarily those in the more lowly statuses have less opportunity to acquire or express power than those advantageously placed in superior statuses. If *mana* (we use this term broadly as applicable to all societies) is largely a felt force deriving from the dominant values of the group being expressed in persons, objects, and actions, then in each society those possessing high mana are likely to be men and women who occupy one or more high-ranking statuses or, if the system be open and free, they will be candidates for achieved higher status. In a fixed and closed system there will be little or no legitimate opportunity (within that system) for those of low status to acquire high mana.

In a society where power primarily is *ritually derived* (attributed to ritual sources), if all men have access to sacred sources it is possible for men of high or low status to gain ritual mana (power and prestige). If the general systems of rank are closed and not open for vertical status movement, then the possessor of such power born to low status may become a very holy man of high spiritual worth, but remain in his same lowly *social* status. He may achieve high status in a formal or informal segmentary hierarchy of sacred sig-

[3] Chapter VI of Emile Durkheim, *The Elementary Forms of the Religious Life*. New York: Macmillan, 1915, pp. 188, 204.

nificance; at times his increased prestige and power may have such strong social influence that they will threaten the rules and sanctions of the social order. If the status order is open and free the spiritual power may be translated into vertical movement in one or more segmental or general hierarchies (church and association). If the ritual values are ascetic, it may be that lowly organizational and economic status (poor, deprived, and despised) may contribute to the conditions necessary for the acquisition of ritual power (a form of mana).

Since in the simple societies the degree of differentiation among the adaptive statuses is very low, and in the complex ones differentiation is exceedingly great, the powers of the technology and of the moral and sacred orders are accordingly combined and felt as one in the simple societies, and in the more advanced ones they divide into various political, economic, and religious categories and are felt to be many. Among the latter, including Western Europe and America, mana or social power takes on a rational as well as nonrational character. Superordinate statuses appear which often possess great power but which are not directly involved in the immediate adaptive activities.

The sources of power and prestige accordingly are multiple. They derive from all powerful environments and from their adaptive controls. The statuses which function to organize the activities of these controls possess their power. In all societies social power expressed in secular or sacred terms is present and distributed among statuses, persons, and things. Power, like prestige, may not be intrinsic to the activities of the status but attributed by the group to the status and its activities.

SOCIAL STRATIFICATION, SOCIAL CHANGE, AND STRUCTURAL CONDITION

All present research on the very simple societies confirms previous study that stratification there is largely confined to the universal, unspecialized types. However, earlier as well as more recent studies demonstrate that age and sex divisions unequally distribute property, sacred symbols, and other goods and services, and that power and prestige are attributed to certain and not other levels (32). The "advanced" forms of rank more often appear in the complex heterogeneous societies. It is in them that the adaptive statuses are reordered and placed in lineations of super- and subordination and inferiority and superiority. Social evolution in its broad sweep moves away from the nonspecialized forms of rank toward the specialized ones which place individuals and families in superior and inferior social orders.

The question is, why are these empirically founded generalizations true? Why does rank grow and luxuriate in the heterogeneous societies? We must analyze comparatively the conditions in the several societies which prohibit or contribute to the functioning and presence of rank orders. To do this we must examine within a time perspective the functional statuses, the environments they control, and the societies in which they are found. To guide our inquiry we shall offer an explanation founded on the established fact that greater specialization, heterogeneity, and higher division of labor are associated with a greater development of rank orders. Through the broad, long-term social changes, the emergent complexity of the social parts makes the use of rank orders necessary. If the highly differentiated statuses and activities of contemporary societies are to function properly for the common good, if the necessary social labor is to be performed, and if disorder is to be avoided and unified action among the necessary diverse statuses is to be maintained, hierarchies of segmentary and general types must be present to order and co-ordinate their diverse activities. The superordinate and subordinate levels exert power which serves common ends and achieves integration. As the number and variety of statuses among each of the three adaptive types increase and the relations among them become more numerous and complex, the total effect is to produce a society of hierarchies which coordinate the variety of statuses and their activities. The need for coordination in all complex societies produces rank orders which differentially distribute power and prestige (98). For the social labor of the society to be performed, ordering by coordination of the diverse activities must take place. The coordinating functions are hierarchically located in positions of power to direct and sanction activity. These positions accumulate actual and attributed power and prestige. Back of many of them is the sanctioned use of force (73). Those which coordinate the primary adaptive statuses are re-ordered by superior and superordinate levels (97, 264). Through time, vast hierarchies are often developed. Each may have its own province, political, economic, or ecclesiastical (223, 258).

When the family with its rules of marriage and descent is related to such hierarchies or is an integral part of their development, general types of stratification, open or closed, appear. The controls of the family serve to broaden the range of the hierarchy, as well as move the locus of power from the several adaptive primary statuses to one or more superior ones. Power is here inherent; those being controlled have their freedom of choice reduced, and those who control extend the social area of their own choice-making. The ordering of the relations of the statuses of the controlled and controlling takes the form of subordination and superordination (255).

The effect of coordination of complex statuses is not only (a) to produce superordinate statuses and subordinate position and (b) to distribute power differentially between them, but (c) to reduce the number of statuses which exercise control within the society, thereby creating a few statuses with more power than the others. This ordering of statuses produces an exclusive few in superordinate relations to an inclusive many. When the *few* exercise power over the many, they establish the foundations for the development of elites and aristocracies with lower rankings beneath them. When social change occurs rapidly the general closed types of rank are not adaptive, since they do not easily accommodate to the movement of individuals vertically or horizontally that is a necessary part of such change. The open system does (251). Color caste and all "fixed" forms are nonadaptive and likely to disappear.

Future research developments on rank, of course, will follow the interests of the investigators. It is certain if important advances are to be made and if we are to use present evidence more fruitfully and future knowledge more purposefully, we must follow MacRae's suggestion. He declares, "The most necessary and I believe the most valuable research open to us in the field of social stratification is synthetic, comparative and genetic" (186).

Many of the obsessive discussions of method, often betraying personal fears rather than scientific acumen, are likely to disappear when the several forms of American rank can be viewed by their investigators without the fear (or presence) of ethnocentrism.

Bibliography of Recent Literature

1. Aberle, D. F., and K. D. Naegele, "Middle-Class Father's Occupational Role and Attitudes Towards Children," *American Journal of Orthopsychiatry,* Vol. 22 (1952), pp. 366–378.

2. Abrahamson, Stephen, "Our Status System and Scholastic Rewards," *Journal of Educational Sociology,* Vol. 25 (1952), pp. 441–450.

3. Abrams, M., *The Condition of the British People.* London: Gollancz, 1945.

4. Adams, S., "Fact and Myth in Social Class Theory," *Ohio Journal of Science,* Vol. 51 (1951), pp. 313–319.

5. Adams, S., "Regional Differences in Vertical Mobility in a High-Status Occupation," *Amer. Soc. Rev.,* Vol. 15 (1950), pp. 228–235.

6. Almond, G., "The Political Attitudes of Wealth," *Journal of Politics,* Vol. 7 (1945), pp. 213–256.

7. Amory, C., *The Proper Bostonians.* Boston: Dutton, 1947.

8. Anastasi, A., and J. P. Foley, *Differential Psychology: Individual and Group Differences in Behavior* (rev. ed.). New York: Macmillan, 1949.

9. Anastasi, A., and S. Miller, "Adolescent 'Prestige Factors' in Relation to Scholastic and Socio-economic Variables," *Journal of Social Psychology,* Vol. 29 (1949), pp. 43–50.

10. Anderson, C. A., S. C. Brown, and M. J. Barman, "Intelligence and Occupational Mobility," *Journal of Political Economy,* Vol. 60 (1952), pp. 218–239.

11. Anderson, C. A., and M. Schapner, *School and Society in England: Social Backgrounds of Oxford and Cambridge Students,* Washington: Public Affairs Press, 1952.

12. Anderson, H. D., and P. E. Davidson, *Ballots and the Democratic Class Struggle.* Stanford Univ.: Stanford Univ. Press, 1943.

13. Anderson, W. A., "Family Social Participation and Social Status Self-Ratings," *Amer. Soc. Rev.,* Vol. 11 (1946), pp. 253–258.

14. Aron, R., "Social Structure and the Ruling Class," *Brit. J. Sociol.,* Vol. 1 (1950), pp. 1–17.

15. Ashmore, Harry S., *The Negro and the Schools.* New York: Van Rees Press, 1954 (copyright, 1954, Univ. of North Carolina Press).

16. Bailey, W. C., N. Foote, P. K. Hatt, R. Hess, R. T. Morris, M. Seeman, and G. Sykes, *Bibliography on Status and Stratification.* New York: Social Science Research Council, 1952.

17. Baltzell, E. Digby, "'Who's Who in America' and 'The Social Register': Elite and Upper Class Indexes in Metropolitan America," in Reinhard Bendix and S. M. Lipset (eds.), *Class, Status and Power.* Glencoe: The Free Press, 1953, pp. 172–184.

17a. Baltzell, E. Digby, *Philadelphia Gentlemen.* Glencoe: The Free Press, 1958.

18. Barber, B., and L. S. Lobel, "Fashion in Women's Clothes and the American Social System," *Social Forces,* Vol. 31 (1952), pp. 124–132.

18a. Barber, B., *Social Stratification: A Comparative Analysis of Structure and Process.* New York: Harcourt, Brace & Co., 1957.

19. Barnard, C. I., "Functions and Pathology of Status Systems," in W. F. Whyte, *et al., Industry and Society.* New York: McGraw-Hill, 1946.

20. Bascom, William R., "Social Status, Wealth, and Individual Differences among the Yoruba," *American Anthropologist,* Vol. 53 (1951), pp. 490-506.

21. Baudler, Lucille, and D. G. Patterson, "Social Status of Women's Occupations," *Occupations,* Vol. 26 (1947–1948), pp. 421–424.

22. Beales, H. L., "The Labour Party in Its Social Context," *Political Quart.,* Vol. 24 (1953), pp. 90–98.

23. Beals, R. L., "Social Stratification in Latin America," *Amer. J. Soc.,* Vol. 58 (1952–1953), pp. 327-340.

24. Becker, H., "Changes in Social Stratification in Germany," *Amer. Soc. Rev.,* Vol. 15 (1950), pp. 333–342.

25. Becker, Howard S., "Social-Class Variations in the Teacher-Pupil Relationship," *Journal of Educational Sociology,* Vol. 25 (1952), pp. 451–465.

26. Belcher, J. C., "Evaluation and Re-standardization of Sewell's Socioeconomic Scale," *Rural Sociol.,* Vol. 16 (1951), pp. 246–255.

27. Bendix, R., *Higher Civil Servants in American Society.* Univ. of Colorado Studies, Series in Sociology No. 2. Boulder: Univ. of Colorado Press, 1949.

28. Bendix, R., and Seymour Martin Lipset, *Class, Status and Power, A Reader in Social Stratification.* Glencoe: The Free Press, 1953.

29. Bennett, J. W., and M. M. Tumin, *Social Life.* New York: Knopf, 1948.

30. Benney, M., and P. Geiss, "Social Class and Politics in Greenwich," *Brit. J. Sociol.,* Vol. 1 (1950), pp. 310–327.

31. Berent, J., "Fertility and Social Mobility," *Popul. Stud.,* Vol. 5 (1952), pp. 224–261.

32. Bernardi, B., "The Age-System of the Nilo-Hamitic Peoples," *Africa,* Vol. 22 (1952), pp. 316–333.

33. Bonham, J., "The Middle Class Elector," *British J. Sociol.,* Vol. 3 (1952), pp. 222–231.

34. Bossard, J. H. S., "Ritual in Family Living," *Amer. Soc. Rev.,* Vol. 14 (1949), pp. 463–469.

35. Bossard, J. H. S., and E. S. Boll, "Rite of Passage—a Contemporary Study," *Social Forces,* Vol. 26 (1948), pp. 247-255.

36. Bott, Elizabeth, "The Concept of Class as a Reference Group," *Human Relations,* Vol. 7 (1954), pp. 259–285.

37. Bottomore, Thomas, "Social Stratification in Voluntary Organizations," in D. V. Glass (ed.), *Social Mobility in Britain.* Glencoe: The Free Press, 1954, pp. 349–382.

38. Bouriez-Gregg, Françoise, *Les Classes Sociales aux États-Unis.* Paris: Librairie Armand Colin, 1954.

39. Brooks, M. R., "American Class and Caste: an Appraisal," *Social Forces,* Vol. 25 (1946), pp. 201–211.

40. Brown, J. S., "Social Class, Inter-marriage and Church Membership in a Kentucky Community," *Amer. J. Soc.,* Vol. 57 (1951–1952), pp. 232-242.

41. Bultena, Louis, "Church Membership and Church Attendance in Madison, Wis.," *Amer. Soc. Rev.,* Vol. 14 (1949), pp. 384–389.

42. Burt, C., "Family Size, Intelligence and Social Class," *Popul. Stud.*, Vol. 1 (1947), pp. 177–187.

43. Burt, C., "The Trend of National Intelligence," *Brit. J. Sociol.*, Vol. 1 (1950), pp. 154–168.

44. Cantril, H., "Identification with Social and Economic Class," *J. Abnormal Soc. Psychol.*, Vol. 38 (1943), pp. 574–580.

45. Case, H. M., "An Independent Test of the Interest-Group Theory of Social Class," *Amer. Soc. Rev.*, Vol. 17 (1952), pp. 751–754.

46. Cauter, T., and J. D. Downham, *The Communication of Ideas.* London: Chatto and Windus, 1954.

47. Centers, R., "Class Consciousness of the American Woman," *Int. J. Opin. and Attit. Res.*, Vol. 3 (1949), pp. 399–408.

48. Centers, R., "Educational and Occupational Mobility," *Amer. Soc. Rev.*, Vol. 14 (1949), pp. 143–147.

49. Centers, R., "Marital Selection and Occupational Strata," *Amer. J. Soc.*, Vol. 54 (1948–1949), pp. 530–535.

50. Centers, R., "Motivational Aspects of Occupational Stratification," *Journal of Social Psychology*, Vol. 28 (1948), pp. 187–217.

51. Centers, R., "Occupational Mobility of Urban Occupational Strata," *Amer. Soc. Rev.*, Vol. 13 (1948), pp. 197–203.

52. Centers, R., *The Psychology of Social Classes: A Study of Class Consciousness.* Princeton: Princeton Univ. Press, 1949.

53. Centers, R., "Social Class, Occupation, and Imputed Belief," *Amer. J. Soc.*, Vol. 58 (1952–1953), pp. 543–555.

54. Centers, R., "Towards an Articulation of Two Approaches to Social Class Phenomena," *Int. J. Opin. and Attit. Res.*, Vol. 4 (1950), pp. 499–514.

55. Chambers, Rosalind C., "A Study of Three Voluntary Organizations," in D. V. Glass (ed.), *Social Mobility in Britain.* Glencoe: The Free Press, 1954, pp. 383–406.

56. Chen, T. A., "Basic Problems of the Chinese Working Classes," *Amer. J. Soc.*, Vol. 53 (1947–1948), pp. 184–191.

57. Chinoy, E., "The Traditions of Opportunity and the Aspirations of Automobile Workers," *Amer. J. Soc.*, (1951–1952), pp. 453–459.

58. Clark, R. E., "Psychoses, Income, and Occupational Prestige," *Amer. J. Soc.*, Vol. 54 (1948–1949), pp. 433–435.

59. Cole, G. D. H., "The Conception of the Middle Classes," *Brit. J. Sociol.*, Vol. 1 (1950), pp. 275–291.

60. Congalton, A. A., "Social Grading of Occupations in New Zealand," *Brit. J. Sociol.*, Vol. 4 (1953), pp. 45–60.

61. Cox, O. C., *Caste, Class and Race: A Study in Social Dynamics.* New York: Doubleday, 1948.

62. Cox, O. C., "Max Weber on Social Stratification: A Critique," *Amer. Soc. Rev.*, Vol. 15 (1950), pp. 223–227.

63. Cox, O. C., "Race and Caste: A Distinction," *Amer. J. Soc.*, Vol. 50 (1944–1945), pp. 360–368.

64. Davies, A. F., "Prestige of Occupations," *Brit. J. Sociol.*, Vol. 3 (1952), pp. 134–147.

65. Davis, A., "Caste, Economy and Violence," *Amer. J. Soc.*, Vol. 51 (1945–1946), pp. 7–15.

66. Davis, A., "The Motivation of Underprivileged Workers," in W. F. Whyte *et al., Industry and Society.* New York: McGraw-Hill, 1946, pp. 84–106.

67. Davis, A., *Social-Class Influences Upon Learning.* Cambridge: Harvard Univ. Press, 1948.

68. Davis, A., and R. J. Havighurst, *Father of the Man.* Boston: Houghton Mifflin, 1947.

69. Davis, A., and R. J. Havighurst, "Social Class and Color Differences in Child Rearing," *Amer. Soc. Rev.*, Vol. 11 (1946), pp. 698–710.

70. Davis, K., *Human Society.* New York: Macmillan, 1949.

71. Davis, K., and W. E. Moore, "Some Principles of Stratification," *Amer. Soc. Rev.*, Vol. 10 (1945), pp. 242–249.

72. Deeg, M. E., and D. G. Patterson,"Changes in Social Status of Occupations," *Occupations,* Vol. 25 (1947), pp. 205–208.

73. de Jouvenal, Bertrand, *Power, The Natural History of Its Growth.* London: Batchworth, 1952.

74. Dobb, M., *Studies in the Development of Capitalism.* London: Routledge, 1946.

75. Dollard, John, "Drinking Mores of the Social Classes," in *Alcohol, Science and Society.* New Haven: Yale Univ. Press, 1945, pp. 95–104.

75a. Dollard, John, *Caste and Class in a Southern Town.* New York: Anchor Books, 1957.

76. Dotson, F., "Patterns of Voluntary Association among Urban Working-Class Families," *Amer. Soc. Rev.*, Vol. 16 (1951), pp. 687–693.

77. Drake, St. C., and H. Cayton, *Black Metropolis.* New York: Harcourt, 1945.

78. Drucker, P. F., *The New Society.* New York: Harper, 1949.

79. Duncan, O. D., "A Critical Evaluation of Warner's Work in Community Stratification," *Amer. Soc. Rev.*, Vol. 15 (1950), pp. 205–215.

80. Duvall, E. M., "Conceptions of Parenthood," *Amer. J. Soc.*, Vol. 52 (1946), pp. 193–203.

81. Eells, K., *et al.*, *Intelligence and Cultural Differences.* Chicago: Univ. of Chicago Press, 1951.

82. Ericson, M. C., "Child-rearing and Social Status," *Amer. J. Soc.*, Vol. 52 (1946–1947), pp. 190–192.

83. Ericson, M. C., "Social Status and Child-rearing Practices," in T. M. Newcomb and E. L. Hartley, *Readings in Social Psychology.* New York: Holt, 1947.

84. Eysenck, H. J., "Primary Social Attitudes as Related to Social Class and Political Party," *Amer. J. Soc.*, Vol. 57 (1951–1952), pp. 222–231.

85. Fei, Hsiao-Tung, "Peasantry and Gentry: An Interpretation of Chinese Social Structure and Its Changes," *Amer. J. Soc.*, Vol. 52 (1946–1947), pp. 1–17.

86. Fei, Hsiao-Tung, and Chih-I Chang, *Earthbound China: A Study of Rural Economy in Yunnan.* Chicago: Univ. of Chicago Press, 1945.

87. Fei, Hsiao-Tung and Yung-Teh Chow, *China's Gentry: Essays in Rural-Urban Relations* by Fei with Six Life-Histories of Chinese Gentry Families Collected by Chow. Chicago: Univ. of Chicago Press, 1953.

88. Floud, J., "The Educational Experience of the Adult Population of England and Wales as at July 1949," in D. V. Glass (ed.), *Social Mobility in Britain.* Glencoe: The Free Press, 1954, pp. 98–140.

89. Floud, J., "Educational Opportunity and Social Mobility," *Year Book of Education,* London, Evan Bros., 1950, pp. 117–136.

90. Foote, N. N., "Destratification and Restratification," *Amer. J. Soc.*, Vol. 58 (1952–1953), pp. 325–326.

91. Foote, N. N., "The Professionalization of Labor in Detroit," *Amer. J. Soc.*, Vol. 58 (1952–1953), p. 371.

92. Foote, N. N., and Paul K. Hatt, "Social Mobility and Economic Advancement," *American Economic Review,* Vol. 43, Supplement (May, 1953), pp. 364–378.

93. Foreman, P. B., and M. C. Hill, *The Negro in the United States: A Bibliography,* Oklahoma A. and M. College Bull. 44, Oklahoma A. and M. College, Stillwater, 1947.

94. Form, W. H., "Toward an Occupational Social Psychology," *Jour. of Social Psychology,* Vol. 24 (1946), pp. 85–99.

95. Friedson, E., "Relation of Social Situation of Contact to the Media in Mass Communication," *Public Opinion Quarterly,* Vol. 17 (1953), pp. 230–239.

96. Friedson, E., "Communications Research and the Concept of the Mass," *Amer. Soc. Rev.,* Vol. 18 (1953), pp. 313–317.

97. Gardner, Burleigh B., "The Factory as a Social System," in Wm. Foote Whyte (ed.), *Industry and Society.* New York: McGraw-Hill, 1946.

98. Gardner, Burleigh B., and David Moore, *Human Relations in Industry.* Homewood: Richard D. Irwin, 1955.

99. Geiger, T., "An Historical Study of the Origins and Structure of the Danish Intelligentsia," *Brit. J. Sociol.,* Vol. 1 (1950), pp. 209–220.

100. Glass, D. V. (ed.), *Social Mobility in Britain.* Glencoe: The Free Press, 1954.

101. Glass, D. V., and J. R. Hall, "A Description of a Sample Inquiry into Social Mobility in Great Britain," in D. V. Glass (ed.), *Social Mobility in Britain.* Glencoe: The Free Press, 1954, pp. 79–97.

102. Glass, D. V., and J. R. Hall, "Social Mobility in Britain: A Study of Inter-Generation Changes in Status," in D. V. Glass (ed.), *Social Mobility in Britain.* Glencoe: The Free Press, 1954, pp. 177–265.

103. Goffman, Erving, "Symbols of Class Status," *Brit. J. Sociol.,* Vol. 2 (1951), pp. 294–305.

103a. Goffman, Erving, *The Presentation of Self in Everyday Life.* New York: Anchor Books, 1959.

104. Gold, Ray, "Janitors versus Tenants: A Status-Income Dilemma," *Amer. J. Soc.,* Vol. 57 (1951–1952), pp. 486–493.

105. Goldhammer, Herbert, and Edward A. Shils, "Types of Power and Status," *Amer. J. Soc.,* Vol. 45 (1939–1940), pp. 171–182.

106. Goldschmidt, W. R., "America's Social Classes: Is Equality a Myth?" *Commentary,* Vol. 10 (1950), pp. 175–181.

107. Goldschmidt, W. R., *As You Sow.* New York: Harcourt, Brace and Co., 1947.

108. Goldschmidt, W. R., "Class Denominationalism in Rural California Churches," *Amer. J. Soc.,* Vol. 49 (1943–1944), pp. 348–356.

109. Goldschmidt, W. R., "Social Class in America: A Critical Review," *Amer. Anthropol.,* Vol. 52 (1950), pp. 483–499.

110. Goldschmidt, W. R., "Social Class in American Sociology," *Amer. J. Soc.,* Vol. 55 (1949–1950), pp. 262–268.

111. Goldschmidt, W. R., "A System of Social Class Analysis" (Drew Univ. Studies, No. 2), Madison, N. J., Drew Univ. Bulletin, 1951.

112. Goodwin, A. (ed.), *The European Nobility in the Eighteenth Century.* London: Adam and Charles Black, 1953.

113. Gordon, M. M., "Kitty Foyle and the Concept of Class Culture," *Amer. J. Soc.,* Vol. 53 (1947–1948), pp. 210–217.

114. Gordon, Milton M., *Social Class in American Sociology.* Durham: Duke University Press, 1958.

115. Gouldner, Alvin, *The Wildcat Strike.* London: Routledge and Kegan Paul, 1955.

116. Gouldner, Alvin, *Patterns of Industrial Bureaucracy.* London: Routledge and Kegan Paul, 1955.

117. Green, A., "The Middle Class Male Child and Neurosis," *Amer. Soc. Rev.*, Vol. 12 (1946), pp. 31–41.

118. Gross, L., "The Use of Class Concepts in Sociological Research," *Amer. J. Soc.*, Vol. 54 (1948–1949), pp. 409–422.

119. Haggard, E. A., "Social-Status and Intelligence: An Experimental Study of Certain Cultural Determinants of Measured Intelligence," *Genetic Psychology Monographs,* Vol. 49 (1954), pp. 141–186.

120. Hall, J. R., and W. Ziegel, "A Comparison of Social Mobility Data for England and Wales, Italy, France and the U.S.A.," in D. V. Glass (ed.), *Social Mobility in Britain.* Glencoe: The Free Press, 1954, pp. 260–265.

121. Hall, J. R., "A Comparison of the Degree of Social Endogamy in England and Wales and the U.S.A.," in D. V. Glass (ed.), *Social Mobility in Britain.* Glencoe: The Free Press, 1954, pp. 344–346.

122. Hall, J., and D. Caradog Jones, "Social Grading of Occupations," *Brit. J. Sociol.*, Vol. 1 (1950), pp. 31–55.

123. Hall, J. R., and D. V. Glass, "Education and Social Mobility," in D. V. Glass (ed.), *Social Mobility in Britain.* Glencoe: The Free Press, 1954, pp. 291–307.

124. Hatt, P. K., "Class and Ethnic Attitudes," *Amer. Soc. Rev.*, Vol. 13 (1948), pp. 36–43.

125. Hatt, P. K., "Occupation and Social Stratification," *Amer. J. Soc.*, Vol. 55 (1950), pp. 533–544.

126. Hatt, P. K., "Social Class and Basic Personality Structure," *Sociology and Social Research,* Vol. 36 (1952), pp. 355–363.

127. Hatt, P. K., "Stratification in Mass Society," *Amer. Soc. Rev.*, Vol. 15 (1950), pp. 216–222.

128. Hatt, P. K., and V. Ktsanes, "Patterns of American Stratification as Reflected in Selected Social Literature," *Amer. Soc. Rev.*, Vol. 17 (1952), pp. 670–679.

129. Havighurst, R. J., "Child Development in Relation to Community Social Structure," *Child Development,* Vol. 17 (1946), pp. 85–89.

130. Havighurst, R. J., and F. H. Breese, "The Relation between Ability and Social Status in a Midwestern Community. III. Primary Mental Abilities," *Journal of Educational Psychology,* Vol. 38 (1947), pp. 241–247.

131. Havighurst, R. J., and R. R. Rodgers, "The Role of Motivation in Attendance at Post-High School Educational Institutions," in *Who Should Go to College,* B. S. Hollingshead (ed.). New York: Columbia Univ. Press, 1952.

132. Havighurst, R. J., and Hilda Taba, *Adolescent Character and Personality.* New York: Wiley, 1949.

133. Henry, W., "The Business Executive: Psychodynamics of a Social Role," *Amer. J. Soc.*, Vol. 54 (1948–1949), pp. 286–291.

134. Hertzler, J. O., "Some Tendencies Toward a Closed Class System in the United States," *Social Forces,* Vol. 30 (1952), pp. 313–323.

135. Hildebrand, George H., "American Unionism, Social Stratification, and Power," *Amer. J. Soc.*, Vol. 58 (1952–1953), pp. 381–390.

136. Hill, M. C., and B. C. McCall, "Social Stratification in a Georgia Town," *Amer. Soc. Rev.*, Vol. 15 (1950), pp. 721–730.

137. Himmelweit, H. T., "Social Status and Secondary Education since the 1944 Act: Some Data for London," in D. V. Glass (ed.), *Social Mobility in Britain.* Glencoe: The Free Press, 1954, pp. 141–159.

138. Hocart, A. M., *Caste: A Comparative Study.* London: Methuen, 1950.

139. Hollingshead, A. B., "Class and Kinship in a Middle Western Community," *Amer. Soc. Rev.*, Vol. 24 (1949), pp. 469–475.

140. Hollingshead, A. B., "Class Differences in Family Stability," *Annals of the Amer. Acad. of Political and Social Science,* Vol. 272 (1950), pp. 39–46.

141. Hollingshead, A. B., *Elmtown's Youth: The Impact of Social Classes on Adolescents.* New York: Wiley, 1949.

142. Hollingshead, A. B., "Selected Characteristics of Classes in a Middle Western Community," *Amer. Soc. Rev.*, Vol. 12 (1947), pp. 385–395.

143. Hollingshead, A. B., "Status in the High School," in W. Lloyd Warner (ed.), *Democracy in Jonesville.* New York: Harper, 1949, pp. 193–213.

144. Hollingshead, A. B., "Trends in Social Stratification: A Case Study," *Amer. Soc. Rev.*, Vol. 17 (1952), pp. 264–285.

144a. Hollingshead, A. B., and F. Redlick, *Social Class and Mental Illness.* New York: John Wiley, 1959.

145. Hsiao-T'ung Fei, "Peasantry and Gentry in China," *Amer. J. Soc.*, Vol. 52 (1946–1947), pp. 1–17.

146. Hsi-En Chen, Theodore, "The Marxist Remolding of Chinese Society," *Amer. J. Soc.*, Vol. 58 (1952–1953), pp. 340–346.

147. Hsu, Francis L. K., "Social Mobility in China," *Amer. Soc. Rev.*, Vol. 14 (1949), pp. 764–771.

148. Hughes, E. C., "Dilemmas and Contradictions of Status," *Amer. J. Soc.*, Vol. 50 (1944–1945), pp. 353–360.

149. Hyman, H. H., "The Psychology of Status," *Archives of Psychology,* No. 269, 1942, pp. 1–94.

150. Inkeles, A., "Social Stratification and Mobility in the Soviet Union," *Amer. Soc. Rev.*, Vol. 15 (1950), pp. 465–480.

151. Janke, L. L., and R. J. Havighurst, "Relations Between Ability and Social Status in a Midwestern Community. 11. 16-year-old Boys and Girls," *Journal of Educ. Psychol.,* Vol. 36 (1946), pp. 499–509.

152. Jenkins, H., and D. Caradog Jones, "Social Class of Cambridge Alumni of the 18th and 19th Centuries," *Brit. J. Sociol.*, Vol. 1 (1950), pp. 93–116.

153. Kahl, Joseph A., "Education and Occupational Aspirations of 'Common Man' Boys," *Harvard Educational Review,* Vol. 23 (1953), pp. 186–203.

154. Kaufman, H. F., "An Approach to the Study of Urban Stratification," *Amer. Soc. Rev.*, Vol. 17 (1952), pp. 430–437.

155. Kaufman, H. F., *Defining Prestige in a Rural Community* ("Sociometry Monographs," No. 10). New York: Beacon House, 1946.

156. Kaufman, H. F., "Members of a Rural Community as Judges of Prestige Rank," *Sociometry,* Vol. 9 (1946), pp. 71–86.

157. Kaufman, H. F., *Prestige Classes in a New York Rural Community.* Ithaca: Cornell University Agricultural Experiment Station Memoir No. 260, 1944.

158. Kelsall, R. K., *Higher Civil Servants in Britain.* London: Routledge and Kegan Paul, 1955.

159. Kinsey, A. C., *et al., Sexual Behavior in the Human Male.* Philadelphia: Saunders, 1948.

160. Kluckhohn, C., and F. Kluckhohn, "American Culture: General Orientations and Class Patterns," in L. Bryson, L. Finkelstein, and R. M. MacIver (eds.), *Approaches to Group Understanding.* New York: Harper, 1947.

161. Laswell, H. D., *Power and Society: A Framework for Political Inquiry.* New Haven: Yale Univ. Press, 1950.

162. Lasswell, H. D., D. Lerner, and C. E. Rothwell, *The Comparative Study of Elites: An Introduction and Bibliography*. Stanford: Stanford Univ. Press, 1952.

163. Lastrucci, C. L., "The Status and Significance of Occupational Research," *Amer. Soc. Rev.*, Vol. 11 (1946), pp. 78–84.

164. Lazarsfield, P. F., B. Berelson, and H. Goudit, *The People's Choice*. New York: Columbia Univ. Press, 1948.

165. Leach, E. R., *Political Systems of Highland Burma: A Study of Kachin Social Structure*. London: G. Bell, 1954.

166. Lee, Shu-Ching, "Intelligentsia of China," *Amer. J. Soc.*, Vol. 52 (1946–1947), pp. 489–497.

167. Lenski, G. E., "American Social Classes: Statistical Strata or Social Groups?" *Amer. J. Soc.*, Vol. 58 (1952–1953), pp. 139–144.

168. Lerner, Max, *America as a Civilization*. New York: Simon & Schuster, 1957.

169. Lewis, R., and A. Maude, *The English Middle Classes*. London: Phoenix House, 1949.

170. Lewis, R., and A. Maude, *The English*. London: Phoenix House, 1949.

171. Lin, Yueh-Hwa, *The Golden Wing: A Sociological Study of Chinese Familism*. London: Kegan Paul, Trench, Trubner, 1947.

172. Lipset, S. M., and R. Bendix, "Social Mobility and Occupational Career Patterns. 1. Stability of Jobholding," *Amer. J. Soc.*, Vol. 57 (1952), pp. 366–374.

173. Lipset, S. M., and R. Bendix, "Social Status and Social Structure," *Brit. J. Sociol.*, Vol. 2 (1951), pp. 150–168, 230–257.

174. Little, K. L., "Social Change and Social Class in the Sierra Leone Protectorate," *Amer. J. Soc.*, Vol. 54 (1948–1949), pp. 10–21.

175. Little, K. L., "The Study of 'Social Change' in British West Africa," *Africa*, Vol. 23 (1953), pp. 274–284.

176. Loomis, C. P., J. A. Beagle, and T. W. Longmore, "Critique of Class as Related to Social Stratification," *Sociometry*, Vol. 10 (1947), pp. 319–337.

177. Lowie, R. H., *The German People*, New York, Farrar and Rinehart, 1945.

178. Maas, Henry, "Some Social Class Differences in the Family Systems and Group Relations of Pre- and Early Adolescents," *Child Development*, Vol. 22 (1951), pp. 145–152.

179. McCall, Bevode, "Social Status and Social Interaction, A Case Study" (manuscript shortly to be published).

180. MacDonald, M., C. McGuire, and R. Havighurst, "Leisure Activities and the Socio-Economic Status of Children," *Amer. J. Soc.*, Vol. 54 (1948–1949), pp. 505–520.

181. McGuire, C., "Family Life in Lower and Middle Class Homes," *Marriage and Family Living*, Vol. 14 (1952), pp. 1–6.

182. McGuire, C., "Social Mobility: The Rise and Fall of Families," in W. Lloyd Warner (ed.), *Democracy in Jonesville*. New York: Harper, 1949, pp. 55–76.

183. McGuire, Carson, "Social Status, Peer Status and Social Mobility" (Memorandum for the Committee on Human Development), Univ. of Chicago, Committee on Human Development, 1949.

184. McGuire, Carson, "Social Stratification and Mobility Patterns," *Amer. Soc. Rev.*, Vol. 15 (1950), pp. 195–204.

185. MacIver, R. M., *The Web of Government*. New York: Macmillan, 1947.

186. MacRae, D. G., "Social Stratification: A Trend Report," *Current Sociology*, Vol. 2 (1953–1954), pp. 5–74.

187. Mannheim, Karl, *Freedom, Power and Democratic Planning*. New York: Oxford Univ. Press, 1950.

188. Marriott, McKim, "Individual Prestige *versus* Caste Ranking in Some Hindu Villages," Unpublished paper read at the AAA meetings, Tucson, 1953.

189. Marriott, McKim (ed.), *Village India.* Chicago: Univ. of Chicago Press, 1955.

190. Marshall, T. H., *Citizenship and Social Class.* Cambridge: Cambridge Univ. Press, 1950.

191. Marshall, T. H., "The Nature and Determinants of Social Status," *The Year Book of Education.* London: Evan Bros., 1953, pp. 30-50.

192. Martin, F. M., "An Inquiry into Parents' Preferences in Secondary Education," in D. V. Glass (ed.), *Social Mobility in Britain.* Glencoe: The Free Press, 1954, pp. 160–174.

193. Meeker, Marchia, "Status Aspirations and the Social Club," in W. Lloyd Warner (ed.), *Democracy in Jonesville.* New York: Harper, 1949, pp. 130–148.

194. Miller, W., "The Business Elite in Business Bureaucracies," in W. Miller (ed.), *Men in Business.* Cambridge: Harvard Univ. Press, 1952, pp. 286–305.

195. Miller, W., "The Recruitment of the American Business Elite," *Quarterly Jour. of Economics,* Vol. 54 (1950), pp. 242–253.

196. Millis, C. W., "The American Business Elite: A Collective Portrait," *J. Econ. Hist.,* 5 (suppl. 5), 1945, pp. 20-45.

197. Mills, C. W., *The New Men of Power: America's Labor Leaders.* New York: Harcourt, 1948.

198. Mills, C. W., *White Collar: The American Middle Classes.* New York: Columbia Univ. Press, 1951.

199. Moser, C. A., and J. R. Hall, "The Social Grading of Occupations," in D. V. Glass (ed.), *Social Mobility in Britain.* Glencoe: The Free Press, 1954, pp. 29–50.

200. Motz, A. B., "Conceptions of Marital Roles by Status Groups," *Marriage and Family Living,* Vol. 12 (1950), pp. 136–162.

201. Mukherjee, Ramkrishna, "A Study of Social Mobility between Three Generations," *Social Mobility in Britain.* London: Routledge and Kegan Paul, Vol. 9 (1954), pp. 266–290.

202. Mukherjee, Ramkrishna, "A Further Note on the Analysis of Data on Social Mobility," in D. V. Glass (ed.), *Social Mobility in Britain.* Glencoe: The Free Press, 1954, pp. 242–259.

203. Mukherjee, Ramkrishna, and J. R. Hall, "A Note on the Analysis of Data on Social Mobility," in D. V. Glass (ed.), *Social Mobility in Britain.* Glencoe: The Free Press, 1954, pp. 218-241.

204. Mulligan, R. A., "Social Mobility and Higher Education," *Journal of Educational Sociology,* Vol. 25 (1952), pp. 476–487.

205. Mulligan, R. A., "Socio-Economic Background and College Enrolment," *Amer. Soc. Rev.,* Vol. 16 (1951), pp. 188–196.

206. Murdock, G. P., *Social Structure.* New York: Macmillan, 1949.

207. Neugarten, B., "The Democracy of Childhood," in W. Lloyd Warner (ed.), *Democracy in Jonesville.* New York: 1949, pp. 77–88.

208. Neugarten, B., "Social Class and Friendship among School Children," *Amer. J. Soc.,* Vol. 51 (1945–1946), pp. 305-314.

209. Newcomb, T. M., *Social Psychology.* New York: Dryden Press, 1950.

210. Newcomb, T. M., and E. T. Hartley (eds.), *Readings in Social Psychology.* New York: Holt, 1947.

211. North, C. C., and P. K. Hatt, "Jobs and Occupations: A Popular Evaluation," *Opinion News,* Vol. 1 (1947), pp. 3–13.

212. Parsons, T., "The Professions and Social Structure," *Social Forces,* Vol. 17

(1939), pp. 457–467, and in T. Parsons (ed.), *Essays in Sociological Theory: Pure and Applied.* Glencoe: The Free Press, 1949.

213. Parsons, T., "Social Classes and Class Conflict in the Light of Recent Sociological Theory," *Amer. Economic R.,* Vol. 34 (1949), pp. 16–26.

214. Parsons, T., *The Social System.* Glencoe: The Free Press, 1951, pp. 132, 172.

215. Pear, T. H., *English Social Differences.* London: G. Allen, 1955.

216. Pfautz, H. W., "The Current Literature on Social Stratification: Critique and Bibliography," *Amer. J. Soc.,* Vol. 58 (1952–1953), pp. 391–418.

217. Pfautz, H. W., and O. P. Duncan, "A Critical Evaluation of Warner's Work in Social Stratification," *Amer. Soc. Rev.,* Vol. 15 (1950), pp. 205–215.

218. Pope, L., *Millhands and Preachers* (Studies in Religious Education, No. 15). New Haven: Yale Univ. Press, 1943.

219. Pope, L., "Religion and Class Structure," *Annals of the Amer. Acad. of Political and Social Science,* Vol. 256 (1948), pp. 84–91.

220. Prins, A. H. J., *East African Age-Class Systems: An Inquiry into the Social Order of Galla, Kipsigis, and Kikuyu.* Groningen: J. B. Wolters, 1953.

221. Riesman, D., *The Lonely Crowd: A Study of the Changing American Character.* New Haven: Yale Univ. Press, 1950.

222. Rogoff, N., "Recent Trends in Urban Mobility," in P. Hatt and A. Reiss (eds.), *Reader in Urban Sociology.* Glencoe: The Free Press, 1951, pp. 406–420.

223. Rosenstein, Joseph, "Party Politics: Unequal Contests," in W. Lloyd Warner (ed.), *Democracy in Jonesville.* New York: Harper, 1949, pp. 213–235.

224. Ruesch, J., *Chronic Disease and Psychological Invalidism* (Psychosomatic Medicine Monographs). New York: Paul Hoeber, 1946.

225. Ruesch, J., "Social Technique, Social Status, and Social Change in Illness," in H. A. Murray and C. Kluckhohn (eds.), *Personality in Nature, Society and Culture.* New York: Knopf, 1948, pp. 117–130.

226. Ruesch, J., A. Jacobson, and M. B. Loeb, "Acculturation and Illness," *Psychological Monographs: General and Applied,* No. 292, Vol. 62 (1948).

227. Ruesch, J., *et al., Duodenal Ulcer: A Sociopsychological Study of Naval Enlisted Personnel and Civilians.* Berkeley: Univ. of California Press, 1948.

228. Ryan, B. F., *Caste in Modern Ceylon.* New Brunswick: Rutgers Univ. Press, 1953.

229. Schatzman, Leonard, and Anselm Strauss, "Social Class and Modes of Communication," *Amer. J. Soc.,* Vol. 60 (1954–1955), pp. 329–338.

230. Schlesinger, A. M., *Learning How to Behave.* New York: Macmillan, 1946.

231. Schumpeter, J. A., *Imperialism and Social Classes.* New York: Kelley, 1951.

232. Sellars, R. W., V. J. McGill, and M. Farber, *Philosophy for the Future.* New York: Macmillan, 1949.

233. Sewell, W. H., *The Construction and Standardization of a Scale for the Measurement of the Socio-Economic Status of Oklahoma Farm Families.* Stillwater: Oklahoma A. and M. College Technical Bulletin No. 9, 1940.

234. Sewell, W. H., and B. L. Ellenbogen, "Social Status and the Measured Intelligence of Small City and Rural Children," *Amer. Soc. Rev.,* Vol. 17 (1952), pp. 612–616.

235. Shih, Kuo-Heng, ed. and tr. by Hsiao-tung Fei, and Francis L. K. Hsu, *China Enters the Machine Age.* Cambridge: Harvard Univ. Press, 1944.

236. Shils, E., *The Present State of American Sociology.* Glencoe: The Free Press, 1948.

237. Sjoberg, G., "Are Social Classes in America Becoming More Rigid?" *Amer. Soc. Rev.,* Vol. 16 (1951), pp. 775–783.

238. Smith, Benjamin F., "Wishes of Negro High School Seniors and Social Class Status," *Journal of Educational Sociology*, Vol. 25 (1952), pp. 466–475.

239. Sorokin, Pitirim, *Society, Culture, and Personality*. New York: Harper, 1947, pp. 277–278.

240. Sorokin, Pitirim, *Social Mobility*. New York: Harper, 1927.

241. Stendler, Celia Burns, *Children of Brasstown* (Univ. of Ill. Bull., Vol. 46, No. 59). Urbana: Bureau of Research and Service of the College of Education, 1949.

242. Stern, Bernhard J., "Some Aspects of Historical Materialism," in R. W. Sellars (ed.), *Philosophy for the Future*. New York: Macmillan, 1949.

243. Stone, Gregory, "City Shoppers and Urban Stratification. Observations on the Social Psychology of City Life," *Amer. J. Soc.*, Vol. 60 (1954–1955), pp. 36–45.

244. Taft, P., *The Structure and Government of Labour Unions*. London: Geoffrey Cumberlege, and Cambridge: Harvard Univ. Press, 1955.

245. Timasheff, N. S., "Vertical Social Mobility in Communist Society," *Amer. J. Soc.*, Vol. 49 (1943–1944), pp. 9–22.

246. Tumin, M. M., *Caste in a Peasant Society*. Princeton: Princeton Univ. Press, 1952.

246a. Vidich, A., and J. Bensman, *Small Town in Mass Society*. Princeton: Princeton Univ. Press, 1958.

247. Vogt, E. Z., "Social Stratification in the Rural Middle West: A Structural Analysis," *Rural Sociology*, Vol. 12 (1947), pp. 364–375.

248. Vogt, E. Z., Jr., "Town and Country: The Structure of Rural Life," in W. Lloyd Warner (ed.), *Democracy in Jonesville*. New York: Harper, 1949, pp. 236–265.

249. Warner, W. Lloyd (ed.), *Democracy in Jonesville*. New York: Harper, 1949.

250. Warner, W. Lloyd, "A Methodological Note," in St. Clair Drake and Horace R. Cayton, *Black Metropolis*. New York: Harcourt, 1945.

251. Warner, W. Lloyd, *Structure of American Life*. Edinburgh: The University Press, 1952. (American title: *American Life: Dream and Reality*. Chicago: Univ. of Chicago Press, 1953.)

251a. Warner, W. Lloyd, *The Living and the Dead*. New Haven: Yale Univ. Press, 1959.

252. Warner, W. Lloyd, and J. Abegglen, *Big Business Leaders in America*. New York: Harper, 1955.

253. Warner, W. Lloyd, and J. Abegglen, *Occupational Mobility in American Business and Industry, 1928–1952*. St. Paul: Univ. of Minnesota Press, 1955.

254. Warner, W. Lloyd, and William E. Henry, "The Radio Daytime Serial: A Symbolic Analysis," *Genetic Psychology Monographs*, Vol. 37 (1948), pp. 3–72.

255. Warner, W. Lloyd, and J. O. Low, *The Social System of the Modern Factory*. New Haven: Yale Univ. Press, 1947.

256. Warner, W. Lloyd, and P. S. Lunt, *The Status System of a Modern Community*. New Haven: Yale Univ. Press, 1947.

257. Warner, W. Lloyd, M. Meeker, and K. Eells, *Social Class in America*. Chicago: Science Research Associates, 1949.

258. Warner, W. Lloyd, and Marchia Meeker, "The Mill: Its Economy and Moral Structure," in W. Lloyd Warner (ed.), *Democracy in Jonesville*. New York: Harper, 1949.

259. Warner, W. Lloyd, and Leo Srole, *The Social Systems of American Ethnic Groups*. Vol. III, Yankee City Series. New Haven: Yale Univ. Press, 1945.

260. Warriner, Charles K., "Leadership in the Small Group," *Amer. J. Soc.*, Vol. 60 (1955), pp. 361–369.

261. West, J., *Plainville, U.S.A.* New York: Columbia Univ. Press, 1945.

262. White, Clyde, *These Will Go to College.* Cleveland: Press of Western Reserve Univ., 1952.

263. Whyte, W. F., "A Slum Sex Code," *Amer. J. Soc.*, Vol. 49 (1943), pp. 24–31.

264. Whyte, W. F., "The Social Structure of the Restaurant," *Amer. J. Soc.*, Vol. 54 (1949), pp. 302–310.

265. Williams, Robin M., Jr., *American Society: A Sociological Interpretation.* New York: Alfred A. Knopf, 1951, pp. 78–135.

266. Wray, D., "The Norwegians: Sect and Ethnic Group," *Democracy in Jonesville.* New York: Harper, pp. 168–192.

267. Wohl, R. Richard, "The Rags to Riches Story: An Episode of Secular Idealism," in R. Bendix and S. M. Lipset (eds.), *Class, Status, and Power.* Glencoe: The Free Press, 1953.

268. Yang, Martin C., *A Chinese Village: Taiton, Shantung Province.* New York: Columbia Univ. Press, 1943.

Index

Selected titles: revised December, 1967

harper torchbooks

HUMANITIES AND SOCIAL SCIENCES

American Studies: General

LOUIS D. BRANDEIS: Other People's Money, *and How the Bankers Use It* ‡ TB/3081

HENRY STEELE COMMAGER, Ed.: The Struggle for Racial Equality TB/1300

CARL N. DEGLER, Ed.: Pivotal Interpretations of American History Vol. I TB/1240; Vol. II TB/1241

A. S. EISENSTADT, Ed.: The Craft of American History: *Recent Essays in American Historical Writing* Vol. I TB/1255; Vol. II TB/1256

CHARLOTTE P. GILMAN: Women and Economics. ‡ *Ed. by Carl N. Degler with an Introduction* TB/3073

MARCUS LEE HANSEN: The Atlantic Migration: 1607-1860. TB/1052

JOHN HIGHAM, Ed.: The Reconstruction of American History△ TB/1068

ROBERT H. JACKSON: The Supreme Court in the American System of Government TB/1106

LEONARD W. LEVY, Ed.: American Constitutional Law TB/1285

LEONARD W. LEVY, Ed.: Judicial Review and the Supreme Court TB/1296

LEONARD W. LEVY: The Law of the Commonwealth and Chief Justice Shaw TB/1309

HENRY F. MAY: Protestant Churches and Industrial America TB/1334

RICHARD B. MORRIS: Fair Trial: *Fourteen Who Stood Accused, from Anne Hutchinson to Alger Hiss. New Preface by the Author* TB/1335

RALPH BARTON PERRY: Puritanism and Democracy TB/1138

American Studies: Colonial

BERNARD BAILYN: The New England Merchants in the Seventeenth Century TB/1149

JOSEPH CHARLES: The Origins of the American Party System TB/1049

HENRY STEELE COMMAGER & ELMO GIORDANETTI, Eds.: Was America a Mistake? *An Eighteenth Century Controversy* TB/1329

CHARLES GIBSON: Spain in America † TB/3077

LAWRENCE HENRY GIPSON: The Coming of the Revolution: 1763-1775. † *Illus.* TB/3007

PERRY MILLER & T. H. JOHNSON, Eds.: The Puritans: *A Sourcebook* Vol. I TB/1093; Vol. II TB/1094

EDMUND S. MORGAN, Ed.: The Diary of Michael Wigglesworth, 1653-1657 TB/1228

EDMUND S. MORGAN: The Puritan Family TB/1227

RICHARD B. MORRIS: Government and Labor in Early America TB/1244

WALLACE NOTESTEIN: The English People on the Eve of Colonization: 1603-1630. † *Illus.* TB/3006

JOHN P. ROCHE: Origins of American Political Thought: *Selected Readings* TB/1301

JOHN SMITH: Captain John Smith's America: *Selections from His Writings* TB/3078

American Studies: From the Revolution to 1860

MAX BELOFF: The Debate on the American Revolution: 1761-1783 TB/1225

RAY A. BILLINGTON: The Far Western Frontier: 1830-1860. † *Illus.* TB/3012

GEORGE DANGERFIELD: The Awakening of American Nationalism: 1815-1828. † *Illus.* TB/3061

WILLIAM W. FREEHLING, Ed.: The Nullification Era: *A Documentary Record* ‡ TB/3079

JOHN C. MILLER: Alexander Hamilton and the Growth of the New Nation TB/3057

RICHARD B. MORRIS, Ed.: The Era of the American Revolution TB/1180

R. B. NYE: The Cultural Life of the New Nation: 1776-1801. † *Illus.* TB/3026

A. F. TYLER: Freedom's Ferment TB/1074

LOUIS B. WRIGHT: Culture on the Moving Frontier TB/1053

American Studies: Since the Civil War

MAX BELOFF, Ed.: The Debate on the American Revolution, 1761-1783: *A Sourcebook* TB/1225

W. R. BROCK: An American Crisis: *Congress and Reconstruction, 1865-67* ° △ TB/1283

A. RUSSELL BUCHANAN: The United States and World War II. † *Illus.* Vol. I TB/3044; Vol. II TB/3045

EDMUND BURKE: On the American Revolution. † *Edited by Elliot Robert Barkan* TB/3068

THOMAS C. COCHRAN & WILLIAM MILLER: The Age of Enterprise: *A Social History of Industrial America* TB/1054

WHITNEY R. CROSS: The Burned-Over District: *The Social and Intellectual History of Enthusiastic Religion in Western New York, 1800-1850* TB/1242

FOSTER RHEA DULLES: America's Rise to World Power: 1898-1954. † *Illus.* TB/3021

W. A. DUNNING: Reconstruction, Political and Economic: 1865-1877 TB/1073

HAROLD U. FAULKNER: Politics, Reform and Expansion: 1890-1900. † *Illus.* TB/3020

FRANCIS GRIERSON: The Valley of Shadows TB/1246

SIDNEY HOOK: Reason, Social Myths, and Democracy TB/1237

WILLIAM E. LEUCHTENBURG: Franklin D. Roosevelt and the New Deal: 1932-1940. † *Illus.* TB/3025

JAMES MADISON: The Forging of American Federalism. *Edited by Saul K. Padover* TB/1226

ARTHUR MANN: Yankee Reformers in the Urban Age TB/1247

GEORGE E. MOWRY: The Era of Theodore Roosevelt and the Birth of Modern America: 1900-1912 † TB/3022

R. B. NYE: Midwestern Progressive Politics TB/1202

JAMES PARTON: The Presidency of Andrew Jackson, *From Vol. III of the* Life of Andrew Jackson ‡ TB/3080

† The New American Nation Series, edited by Henry Steele Commager and Richard B. Morris.
‡ American Perspectives series, edited by Bernard Wishy and William E. Leuchtenburg.
* The Rise of Modern Europe series, edited by William L. Langer.
** History of Europe series, edited by J. H. Plumb.
¶ Researches in the Social, Cultural and Behavioral Sciences, edited by Benjamin Nelson.
§ The Library of Religion and Culture, edited by Benjamin Nelson.
Σ Harper Modern Science Series, edited by James R. Newman.
° Not for sale in Canada.
△ Not for sale in the U. K.

FRANCIS S. PHILBRICK: The Rise of the West, 1754-1830. † *Illus.* TB/3067
WILLIAM PRESTON, JR.: Aliens and Dissenters: *Federal Suppression of Radicals, 1903-1933* TB/1287
JACOB RIIS: The Making of an American ‡ TB/3070
PHILIP SELZNICK: TVA and the Grass Roots TB/1230
TIMOTHY L. SMITH: Revivalism and Social Reform: *American Protestantism on the Eve of the Civil War* △ TB/1229
IDA M. TARBELL: The History of the Standard Oil Company. *Briefer Version.* ‡ *Edited by David M. Chalmers* TB/3071
ALBION W. TOURGÉE: A Fool's Errand. ‡ *Ed. by George Fredrickson* TB/3074
GEORGE B. TINDALL, Ed.: A Populist Reader ‡ TB/3069
VERNON LANE WHARTON: The Negro in Mississippi: 1865-1890 TB/1178

Anthropology

JACQUES BARZUN: Race: *A Study in Superstition. Revised Edition* TB/1172
JOSEPH B. CASAGRANDE, Ed.: In the Company of Man: *Portraits of Anthropological Informants* TB/3047
W. E. LE GROS CLARK: The Antecedents of Man: *Intro. to Evolution of the Primates.* °△ *Illus.* TB/559
CORA DU BOIS: The People of Alor. *New Preface by the author. Illus.* Vol. I TB/1042; Vol. II TB/1043
DAVID LANDY: Tropical Childhood: *Cultural Transmission and Learning in a Puerto Rican Village* ¶ TB/1235
EDWARD BURNETT TYLOR: Religion in Primitive Culture. *Part II of "Primitive Culture."* § *Intro. by Paul Radin* TB/34
W. LLOYD WARNER: A Black Civilization: *A Study of an Australian Tribe.* ¶ *Illus.* TB/3056

Art and Art History

EMILE MÂLE: The Gothic Image. § △ *190 illus.* TB/44
MILLARD MEISS: Painting in Florence and Siena after the Black Death. *169 illus.* TB/1148
ERICH NEUMANN: The Archetypal World of Henry Moore. △ *107 illus.* TB/2020
DORA & ERWIN PANOFSKY: Pandora's Box: *The Changing Aspects of a Mythical Symbol* TB/2021
ERWIN PANOFSKY: Studies in Iconology: *Humanistic Themes in the Art of the Renaissance* △ TB/1077
ALEXANDRE PIANKOFF: The Shrines of Tut-Ankh-Amon. *Edited by N. Rambova. 117 illus.* TB/2011
OTTO VON SIMSON: The Gothic Cathderal △ TB/2018
HEINRICH ZIMMER: Myths and Symbols in Indian Art and Civilization. *70 illustrations* TB/2005

Business, Economics & Economic History

REINHARD BENDIX: Work and Authority in Industry TB/3035
GILBERT BURCK & EDITORS OF FORTUNE: The Computer Age: *And Its Potential for Management* TB/1179
THOMAS C. COCHRAN: The American Business System: *A Historical Perspective, 1900-1955* TB/1080
ROBERT DAHL & CHARLES E. LINDBLOM: Politics, Economics, and Welfare TB/3037
PETER F. DRUCKER: The New Society △ TB/1082
ROBERT L. HEILBRONER: The Limits of American Capitalism TB/1305
FRANK H. KNIGHT: The Economic Organization TB/1214
FRANK H. KNIGHT: Risk, Uncertainty and Profit TB/1215
ABBA P. LERNER: Everybody's Business TB/3051
HERBERT SIMON: The Shape of Automation: *For Men and Management* TB/1245

Education

JACQUES BARZUN: The House of Intellect △ TB/1051
RICHARD M. JONES, Ed.: Contemporary Educational Psychology: *Selected Readings* TB/1292
CLARK KERR: The Uses of the University TB/1264

JOHN U. NEF: Cultural Foundations of Industrial Civilization △ TB/1024

Historiography & Philosophy of History

JACOB BURCKHARDT: On History and Historians. △ *Intro. by H. R. Trevor-Roper* TB/1216
J. H. HEXTER: Reappraisals in History: *New Views on History & Society in Early Modern Europe* TB/1100
H. STUART HUGHES: History as Art and as Science: *Twin Vistas on the Past* TB/1207
ARNALDO MOMIGLIANO: Studies in Historiography ° △ TB/1288
GEORGE H. NADEL, Ed.: Studies in the Philosophy of History: *Essays from* History and Theory TB/1208
KARL R. POPPER: The Open Society and Its Enemies △ Vol. I TB/1101; Vol. II TB/1102
KARL R. POPPER: The Poverty of Historicism °△ TB/1126
G. J. RENIER: History: Its Purpose and Method △ TB/1209
W. H. WALSH: Philosophy of History △ TB/1020

History: General

WOLFGANG FRANKE: China and the West TB/1326
L. CARRINGTON GOODRICH: A Short History of the Chinese People. △ *Illus.* TB/3015
DAN N. JACOBS & HANS H. BAERWALD: Chinese Communism: *Selected Documents* TB/3031
BERNARD LEWIS: The Arabs in History △ TB/1029
BERNARD LEWIS: The Middle East and the West ° △ TB/1274

History: Ancient and Medieval

A. ANDREWES: The Greek Tyrants △ TB/1103
P. BOISSONNADE: Life and Work in Medieval Europe ° △ TB/1141
HELEN CAM: England before Elizabeth △ TB/1026
NORMAN COHN: The Pursuit of the Millennium △ TB/1037
CHRISTOPHER DAWSON, Ed.: Mission to Asia △ TB/315
ADOLF ERMAN, Ed.: The Ancient Egyptians TB/1233
HEINRICH FICHTENAU: The Carolingian Empire: *The Age of Charlemagne* △ TB/1142
GALBERT OF BRUGES: The Murder of Charles the Good. *Trans. with Intro. by James Bruce Ross* TB/1311
F. L. GANSHOF: Feudalism △ TB/1058
DENO GEANAKOPLOS: Byzantine East and Latin West △ TB/1265
MICHAEL GRANT: Ancient History ° △ TB/1190
W. O. HASSALL, Ed.: Medieval England: *As Viewed by Contemporaries* △ TB/120[illegible]
DENYS HAY: Europe: The Emergence of an Idea TB/1275
DENYS HAY: The Medieval Centuries ° △ TB/1192
J. M. HUSSEY: The Byzantine World △ TB/1057
SAMUEL NOAH KRAMER: Sumerian Mythology TB/105[illegible]
ROBERT LATOUCHE: The Birth of Western Economy: *Economic Aspects of the Dark Ages* ° △ TB/129[illegible]
NAPHTALI LEWIS & MEYER REINHOLD, Eds.: Roman Civilization Vol. I TB/1231; Vol. II TB/123[illegible]
FERDINAND LOT: The End of the Ancient World and th[illegible] Beginnings of the Middle Ages TB/104[illegible]
ACHILLE LUCHAIRE: Social France at the Time of Phili[illegible] Augustus TB/131[illegible]
MARSILIUS OF PADUA: The Defender of the Peace. *Trans with Intro. by Alan Gewirth* TB/131[illegible]
G. MOLLAT: The Popes at Avignon: 1305-1378 △ TB/30[illegible]
CHARLES PETIT-DUTAILLIS: The Feudal Monarchy i[illegible] France and England ° △ TB/116[illegible]
HENRI PIRENNE: Early Democracies in the Low Cour[illegible] tries TB/111[illegible]
STEVEN RUNCIMAN: A History of the Crusades △ *Vol. I* TB/1143; *Vol. II* TB/1243; *Vol. III* TB/12[illegible]
J. M. WALLACE-HADRILL: The Barbarian West △ TB/10[illegible]

History: Renaissance & Reformation

JACOB BURCKHARDT: The Civilization of the Renaissan[illegible] in Italy △ Vol. I TB/40; Vol. II TB/[illegible]

JOHN CALVIN & JACOPO SADOLETO: A Reformation Debate. *Edited by John C. Olin* TB/1239
G. CONSTANT: The Reformation in England △ TB/314
G. R. ELTON: Reformation Europe, 1517-1559 ** ° △ TB/1270
WALLACE K. FERGUSON et al.: The Renaissance: *Six Essays. Illus.* TB/1084
JOHN NEVILLE FIGGIS: Divine Right of Kings TB/1191
FRANCESCO GUICCIARDINI: Maxims and Reflections of a Renaissance Statesman *(Ricordi)* TB/1160
J. H. HEXTER: More's Utopia TB/1195
HAJO HOLBORN: Ulrich von Hutten and the German Reformation TB/1238
JOHAN HUIZINGA: Erasmus and the Age of Reformation.△ *Illus.* TB/19
JOEL HURSTFIELD: The Elizabethan Nation △ TB/1312
JOEL HURSTFIELD, Ed.; The Reformation Crisis △ TB/1267
ULRICH VON HUTTEN et al.: On the Eve of the Reformation: *"Letters of Obscure Men"* TB/1124
ROBERT LATOUCHE: The Birth of Western Economy. ° △ *Trans. by Philip Grierson* TB/1290
NICCOLÒ MACHIAVELLI: History of Florence and of the Affairs of Italy TB/1027
GARRETT MATTINGLY et al.: Renaissance Profiles. △ *Edited by J. H. Plumb* TB/1162
J E. NEALE: The Age of Catherine de Medici ° △ TB/1085
ERWIN PANOFSKY: Studies in Iconology △ TB/1077
J. H. PARRY: The Establishment of the European Hegemony: 1415-1715 △ TB/1045
BUONACCORSO PITTI & GREGORIO DATI: Two Memoirs of Renaissance Florence: *The Diaries of Buonaccorso Pitti and Gregorio Dati* TB/1333
J. H. PLUMB: The Italian Renasisance △ TB/1161
A. F. POLLARD: Henry VIII °△ TB/1249
A. F. POLLARD: Wolsey: *Church and State in 16th Century England* ° △ TB/1248
CECIL ROTH: The Jews in the Renaissance. *Illus.* TB/834
A. L. ROWSE: The Expansion of Elizabethan England. °△ *Illus.* TB/1220
GORDON RUPP: Luther's Progress to the Diet of Worms °△ TB/120
FERDINAND SCHEVILL: Medieval and Renaissance Florence. *Illus.* Vol. I TB/1090; Vol. II TB/1091
R. H. TAWNEY: The Agrarian Problem in the Sixteenth Century TB/1315
G. M. TREVELYAN: England in the Age of Wycliffe, 1368-1520 °△ TB/1112
VESPASIANO: Renaissance Princes, Popes, and Prelates: *The Vespasiano Memoirs* TB/1111

History: Modern European

MAX BELOFF: The Age of Absolutism, 1660-1815 △ TB/1062
EUGENE C. BLACK, Ed.: European Political History, 1815-1870: *Aspects of Liberalism* TB/1331
ASA BRIGGS: The Making of Modern England, 1784-1867: *The Age of Improvement* °△ TB/1203
CRANE BRINTON: A Decade of Revolution, 1789-1799. * *Illus.* TB/3018
D. W. BROGAN: The Development of Modern France. °△ Vol. I TB/1184; Vol. II TB/1185
ALAN BULLOCK: Hitler, A Study in Tyranny ° △ TB/1123
E. H. CARR: German-Soviet Relations Between the Two World Wars, 1919-1939 TB/1278
E. H. CARR: International Relations Between the Two World Wars, 1919-1939 ° △ TB/1279
E. H. CARR: The Twenty Years' Crisis, 1919-1939 °△ TB/1122
GORDON A. CRAIG: From Bismarck to Adenauer: *Aspects of German Statecraft. Revised Edition* TB/1171
DENIS DIDEROT: The Encyclopedia: *Selections. Ed. and trans. by Stephen Gendzier* TB/1299
FRANKLIN L. FORD: Robe and Sword: *The Regrouping of the French Aristocracy after Louis XIV* TB/1217
RENÉ FUELOEP-MILLER: The Mind and Face of Bolshevism TB/1188
ALBERT GOODWIN, Ed.: The European Nobility in the Eighteenth Century △ TB/1313
ALBERT GUÉRARD: France in the Classical Age △ TB/1183
CARLTON J. H. HAYES: A Generation of Materialism, 1871-1900. * *Illus.* TB/3039
STANLEY HOFFMANN et al.: In Search of France TB/1219
LIONEL KOCHAN: The Struggle for Germany: *1914-45* TB/1304
HANS KOHN: The Mind of Germany △ TB/1204
HANS KOHN, Ed.: The Mind of Modern Russia TB/1065
WALTER LAQUEUR & GEORGE L. MOSSE, Eds.: Education and Social Structure in the 20th Century ° △ TB/1339
WALTER LAQUEUR & GEORGE L. MOSSE, Eds.: International Fascism, 1920-1945 ° △ TB/1276
WALTER LAQUEUR & GEORGE L. MOSSE, Eds.: The Left-Wing Intellectuals between the Wars, 1919-1939 ° △ TB/1286
WALTER LAQUEUR & GEORGE L. MOSSE, Eds.: Literature and Politics in the 20th Century ° △ TB/1328
WALTER LAQUEUR & GEORGE L. MOSSE, Eds.: The New History: *Trends in Historical Research and Writing since World War II* ° △ TB/1327
WALTER LAQUEUR & GEORGE L. MOSSE, Eds.: 1914: *The Coming of the First World War* ° △ TB/1306
FRANK E. MANUEL: The Prophets of Paris: *Turgot, Condorcet, Saint-Simon, Fourier, and Comte* TB/1218
KINGSLEY MARTIN: French Liberal Thought in the Eighteenth Century TB/1114
ROBERT K. MERTON: Science, Technology and Society in Seventeenth Century England ¶ TB/1324
L. B. NAMIER: Facing East: *Essays on Germany, the Balkans, and Russia in the 20th Century* △ TB/1280
L. B. NAMIER: Personalities and Powers △ TB/1186
NAPOLEON III: Napoleonic Ideas: *Des Idées Napoléoniennes, par le Prince Napoléon-Louis Bonaparte* TB/1336
FRANZ NEUMANN: Behemoth: *The Structure and Practice of National Socialism 1933-1944* △ TB/1289
DAVID OGG: Europe of the Ancien Régime, 1715-1783 ** ° △ TB/1271
JOHN PLAMENATZ: German Marxism and Russian Communism. °△ *New Preface by the Author* TB/1189
PENFIELD ROBERTS: The Quest for Security, 1715-1740. * *Illus.* TB/3016
GEORGE RUDÉ: Revolutionary Europe, 1783-1815 ** ° △ TB/1272
LOUIS, DUC DE SAINT-SIMON: Versailles, The Court, and Louis XIV △ TB/1250
HUGH SETON-WATSON: Eastern Europe Between the Wars, 1918-1941 TB/1330
A. J. P. TAYLOR: From Napoleon to Lenin: *Historical Essays* ° △ TB/1268
A. J. P. TAYLOR: The Habsburg Monarchy, 1809-1918 ° △ TB/1187
G. M. TREVELYAN: British History in the Nineteenth Century and After: *1782-1919* △ TB/1251
H. R. TREVOR-ROPER: Historical Essays °△ TB/1269
ELIZABETH WISKEMANN: Europe of the Dictators, 1919-1945 ** ° △ TB/1273
JOHN B. WOLF: France: 1814-1919 TB/3019

Intellectual History & History of Ideas

HERSCHEL BAKER: The Image of Man TB/1047
R. R. BOLGAR: The Classical Heritage and Its Beneficiaries △ TB/1125
J. BRONOWSKI & BRUCE MAZLISH: The Western Intellectual Tradition: *From Leonardo to Hegel* TB/3001
NORMAN COHN: Pursuit of the Millennium △ TB/1037
C. C. GILLISPIE: Genesis and Geology: *The Decades before Darwin* § TB/51
FRANK E. MANUEL: The Prophets of Paris: *Turgot, Condorcet, Saint-Simon, Fourier, and Comte* TB/1218
BRUNO SNELL: The Discovery of the Mind: *The Greek Origins of European Thought* △ TB/1018

W. WARREN WAGAR, Ed.: European Intellectual History since Darwin and Marx TB/1297
PHILIP P. WIENER: Evolution and the Founders of Pragmatism. △ *Foreword by John Dewey* TB/1212

Literature, Poetry, The Novel & Criticism

JACQUES BARZUN: The House of Intellect △ TB/1051
JAMES BOSWELL: The Life of Dr. Johnson & The Journal of a Tour to the Hebrides with Samuel Johnson LL.D. ° △ TB/1254
ERNST R. CURTIUS: European Literature and the Latin Middle Ages △ TB/2015
A. R. HUMPHREYS: The Augustan World: *Society in 18th Century England* °△ TB/1105
RICHMOND LATTIMORE: The Poetry of Greek Tragedy △ TB/1257
J. B. LEISHMAN: The Monarch of Wit: *An Analytical and Comparative Study of the Poetry of John Donne* ° △ TB/1258
J. B. LEISHMAN: Themes and Variations in Shakespeare's Sonnets °△ TB/1259
SAMUEL PEPYS: The Diary of Samuel Pepys. ° *Edited by O. F. Morshead. Illus. by Ernest Shepard* TB/1007
V. DE S. PINTO: Crisis in English Poetry, 1880-1940 °△ TB/1260
ROBERT PREYER, Ed.: Victorian Literature TB/1302
C. K. STEAD: The New Poetic: *Yeats to Eliot* ° △ TB/1263
PAGET TOYNBEE: Dante Alighieri: *His Life and Works. Edited with Intro. by Charles S. Singleton* TB/1206
DOROTHY VAN GHENT: The English Novel TB/1050
BASIL WILLEY: Nineteenth Century Studies: *Coleridge to Matthew Arnold* °△ TB/1261
BASIL WILLEY: More Nineteenth Century Studies: *A Group of Honest Doubters* ° △ TB/1262
RAYMOND WILLIAMS: Culture and Society, 1780-1950 ° △ TB/1252
RAYMOND WILLIAMS: The Long Revolution °△ TB/1253

Myth, Symbol & Folklore

MIRCEA ELIADE: Cosmos and History § △ TB/2050
MIRCEA ELIADE: Rites and Symbols of Initiation: *The Mysteries of Birth and Rebirth* § △ TB/1236
THEODOR H. GASTER: Thespis: *Ritual, Myth & Drama in the Ancient Near East* ° △ TB/1281
DORA & ERWIN PANOFSKY: Pandora's Box △ TB/2021

Philosophy

G. E. M. ANSCOMBE: An Introduction to Wittgenstein's Tractatus. ° △ *Second edition, Revised* TB/1210
HENRI BERGSON: Time and Free Will °△ TB/1021
H. J. BLACKHAM: Six Existentialist Thinkers ° △ TB/1002
CRANE BRINTON: Nietzsche TB/1197
ERNST CASSIRER: The Individual and the Cosmos in Renaissance Philosophy △ TB/1097
FREDERICK COPLESTON: Medieval Philosophy ° △ TB/376
F. M. CORNFORD: Principium Sapientiae: *A Study of the Origins of Greek Philosophical Thought* TB/1213
F. M. CORNFORD: From Religion to Philosophy § TB/20
A. P. D'ENTRÈVES: Natural Law △ TB/1223
MARVIN FARBER: The Aims of Phenomenology TB/1291
PAUL FRIEDLÄNDER: Plato: *An Introduction* △ TB/2017
J. GLENN GRAY: The Warriors: *Reflections on Men in Battle. Intro. by Hannah Arendt* TB/1294
W. K. C. GUTHRIE: The Greek Philosophers: *From Thales to Aristotle* ° △ TB/1008
G. W. F. HEGEL: The Phenomenology of Mind ° △ TB/1303
F. H. HEINEMANN: Existentialism and the Modern Predicament △ TB/28
EDMUND HUSSERL: Phenomenology and the Crisis of Philosophy TB/1170
IMMANUEL KANT: The Doctrine of Virtue, *being Part II of the* Metaphysic of Morals TB/110
IMMANUEL KANT: Groundwork of the Metaphysic of Morals. *Trans. & analyzed by H. J. Paton* TB/1159
IMMANUEL KANT: Lectures on Ethics §△ TB/105
IMMANUEL KANT: Religion Within the Limits of Reason Alone. § *Intro. by T. M. Greene & J. Silber* TB/67
QUENTIN LAUER: Phenomenology TB/1169
MAURICE MANDELBAUM: The Problem of Historical Knowledge: *An Answer to Relativism* TB/1338
GABRIEL MARCEL: Being and Having △ TB/310
GEORGE A. MORGAN: What Nietzsche Means TB/1198
H. J. PATON: The Categorical Imperative: *A Study in Kant's Moral Philosophy* △ TB/1325
MICHAEL POLANYI: Personal Knowledge △ TB/1158
WILLARD VAN ORMAN QUINE: Elementary Logic. *Revised Edition* TB/577
WILLARD VAN ORMAN QUINE: from a Logical Point of View: *Logico-Philosophical Essays* TB/566
BERTRAND RUSSELL et al.: The Philosophy of Bertrand Russell Vol. I TB/1095; Vol. II TB/1096
L. S. STEBBING: A Modern Introduction to Logic △ TB/538
ALFRED NORTH WHITEHEAD: Process and Reality: *An Essay in Cosmology* △ TB/1033
PHILIP P. WIENER: Evolution and the Founders of Pragmatism. *Foreword by John Dewey* TB/1212
LUDWIG WITTGENSTEIN: The Blue and Brown Books ° TB/1211

Political Science & Government

JEREMY BENTHAM: The Handbook of Political Fallacies. *Introduction by Crane Brinton* TB/1069
C. E. BLACK: The Dynamics of Modernization: *A Study in Comparative History* TB/1321
KENNETH E. BOULDING: Conflict and Defense TB/3024
CRANE BRINTON: English Political Thought in the Nineteenth Century TB/1071
ROBERT CONQUEST: Power and Policy in the USSR: *The Study of Soviet Dynastics* △ TB/1307
ROBERT DAHL & CHARLES E. LINDBLOM: Politics, Economics, and Welfare TB/3037
F. L. GANSHOF: Feudalism △ TB/1058
G. P. GOOCH: English Democratic Ideas in Seventeenth Century TB/1006
SIDNEY HOOK: Reason, Social Myths and Demccracy △ TB/1237
DAN N. JACOBS, Ed.: The New Communist Manifesto & *Related Documents. Third edition, Revised* TB/1078
HANS KOHN: Political Ideologies of the 20th Century TB/1277
ROY C. MACRIDIS, Ed.: Political Parties: *Contemporary Trends and Ideas* TB/1322
KINGSLEY MARTIN: French Liberal Thought in the Eighteenth Century △ TB/1114
BARRINGTON MOORE, Jr.: Political Power and Social Theory: *Seven Studies* ¶ TB/1221
BARRINGTON MOORE, JR.: Soviet Politics—The Dilemma of Power ¶ TB/1222
JOHN B. MORRALL: Political Thought in Medieval Times △ TB/1076
KARL R. POPPER: The Open Society and Its Enemies △ Vol. I TB/1101; Vol. II TB/1102
JOHN P. ROCHE, Ed.: American Political Thought: *From Jefferson to Progressivism* TB/1332
CHARLES I. SCHOTTLAND, Ed.: The Welfare State TB/1323
BENJAMIN I. SCHWARTZ: Chinese Communism and the Rise of Mao TB/1308
PETER WOLL, Ed.: Public Administration and Policy TB/1284

Psychology

ALFRED ADLER: The Individual Psychology of Alfred Adler △ TB/1154
ARTHUR BURTON & ROBERT E. HARRIS, Editors: Clinical Studies of Personality Vol. I TB/3075; Vol. II TB/3076
HADLEY CANTRIL: The Invasion from Mars: *A Study in the Psychology of Panic* TB/1282
HERBERT FINGARETTE: The Self in Transformation ¶ TB/1177
SIGMUND FREUD: On Creativity and the Unconscious § △ TB/45

WILLIAM JAMES: Psychology: *Briefer Course* TB/1034
C. G. JUNG: Psychological Reflections △ TB/2001
KARL MENNINGER: Theory of Psychoanalytic Technique TB/1144
ERICH NEUMANN: Amor and Psyche △ TB/2012
MUZAFER SHERIF: The Psychology of Social Norms TB/3072

Sociology

JACQUES BARZUN: Race: *A Study in Superstition. Revised Edition* TB/1172
BERNARD BERELSON, Ed.: The Behavioral Sciences Today TB/1127
KENNETH B. CLARK: Dark Ghetto: *Dilemmas of Social Power. Foreword by Gunnar Myrdal* TB/1317
LEWIS A. COSER, Ed.: Political Sociology TB/1293
ALLISON DAVIS & JOHN DOLLARD: Children of Bondage ¶ TB/3049
ST. CLAIR DRAKE & HORACE R. CAYTON: Black Metropolis △ Vol. I TB/1086; Vol. II TB/1087
ALVIN W. GOULDNER: Wildcat Strike ¶ TB/1176
CÉSAR GRAÑA: Modernity and Its Discontents: *French Society and the French Man of Letters in the Nineteenth Century* ¶ TB/1318
R. M. MACIVER: Social Causation TB/1153
ROBERT K. MERTON, LEONARD BROOM, LEONARD S. COTTRELL, JR., Editors: Sociology Today: *Problems and Prospects* ¶ Vol. I TB/1173; Vol. II TB/1174
TALCOTT PARSONS & EDWARD A. SHILS, Editors: Toward a General Theory of Action TB/1083
ARNOLD ROSE: The Negro in America TB/3048
GEORGE ROSEN: Madness in Society: *Chapters in the Historical Sociology of Mental Illness* ¶ TB/1337
PHILIP SELZNICK: TVA and the Grass Roots TB/1230
HERBERT SIMON: The Shape of Automation △ TB/1245
PITIRIM A. SOROKIN: Contemporary Sociological Theories: *Through the first quarter of the 20th Century* TB/3046
WILLIAM I. THOMAS: The Unadjusted Girl: *With Cases and Standpoint for Behavior Analysis* ¶ TB/1319
EDWARD A. TIRYAKIAN, Ed.: Sociological Theory, Values and Sociocultural Change: *Essays in Honor of Pitirim A. Sorokin* ¶ ° △ TB/1316
W. LLOYD WARNER & Associates: Democracy in Jonesville: *A Study in Quality and Inequality* TB/1129
W. LLOYD WARNER: Social Class in America TB/1013

RELIGION

Ancient & Classical

J. H. BREASTED: Development of Religion and Thought in Ancient Egypt TB/57
HENRI FRANKFORT: Ancient Egyptian Religion TB/77
G. RACHEL LEVY: Religious Conceptions of the Stone Age *and their Influence on European Thought* △ TB/106
MARTIN P. NILSSON: Greek Folk Religion △ TB/78
ERWIN ROHDE: Psyche △ § Vol. I TB/140; Vol. II TB/141
H. J. ROSE: Religion in Greece and Rome △ TB/55

Biblical Thought & Literature

W. F. ALBRIGHT: The Biblical Period from Abraham to Ezra TB/102
C. K. BARRETT, Ed.: The New Testament Background: *Selected Documents* △ TB/86
C. H. DODD: The Authority of the Bible △ TB/43
M. S. ENSLIN: Christian Beginnings △ TB/5
JOHN GRAY: Archaeology and the Old Testament World. △ Illus. TB/127
JAMES MUILENBURG: The Way of Israel △ TB/133
H. H. ROWLEY: Growth of the Old Testament △ TB/107
GEORGE ADAM SMITH: Historical Geography of Holy Land. ° △ *Revised and reset* TB/138
WALTHER ZIMMERLI: The Law and the Prophets: *A Study of the Meaning of the Old Testament* △ TB/144

The Judaic Tradition

MARTIN BUBER: Eclipse of God △ TB/12
MARTIN BUBER: Hasidism and Modern Man. △ *Edited and Trans. by Maurice Friedman* TB/839
MARTIN BUBER: The Knowledge of Man △ TB/135
MARTIN BUBER: Moses △ TB/837
MARTIN BUBER: Pointing the Way △ TB/103
MARTIN BUBER: The Prophetic Faith TB/73
GENESIS: *The NJV Translation* TB/836

Christianity: General

ROLAND H. BAINTON: Christendom: *A Short History of Christianity and its Impact on Western Civilization.* △ *Illus.* Vol. I TB/131; Vol. II TB/132

Christianity: Origins & Early Development

AUGUSTINE: An Augustine Synthesis. △ *Edited by Erich Przywara* TB/335
W. D. DAVIES: Paul and Rabbinic Judaism: *Some Rabbinic Elements in Pauline Theology* ° △ TB/146
ADOLF DEISSMANN: Paul: *A Study in Social and Religious History* TB/15
EDWARD GIBBON: The Triumph of Christendom in the Roman Empire. § △ *Illus.* TB/46
EDGAR J. GOODSPEED: A Life of Jesus TB/1
ADOLF HARNACK: The Mission and Expansion of Christianity in the First Three Centuries TB/92
R. K. HARRISON: The Dead Sea Scrolls ° △ TB/84
EDWIN HATCH: The Influence of Greek Ideas on Christianity § △ TB/18
GERHART B. LADNER: The Idea of Reform: *Its Impact on Christian Thought and Action in the Age of the Fathers* TB/149
ARTHUR DARBY NOCK: St. Paul ° △ TB/104
ORIGEN: On First Principles △ TB/311
SULPICIUS SEVERUS et al.: The Western Fathers △ TB/309
JOHANNES WEISS: Earliest Christianity Vol. I TB/53; Vol. II TB/54

Christianity: The Middle Ages and The Reformation

ANSELM OF CANTERBURY: Truth, Freedom and Evil: *Three Philosophical Dialogues* TB/317
JOHN CALVIN & JACOPO SADOLETO: A Reformation Debate. *Edited by John C. Olin* TB/1239
G. CONSTANT: The Reformation in England △ TB/314
JOHANNES ECKHART: Meister Eckhart: *A Modern Translation by R. B. Blakney* TB/8
DESIDERIUS ERASMUS: Christian Humanism and the Reformation TB/1166

Christianity: The Protestant Tradition

KARL BARTH: Church Dogmatics: *A Selection* △ TB/95
KARL BARTH: Dogmatics in Outline △ TB/56
KARL BARTH: The Word of God and the Word of Man TB/13
RUDOLF BULTMANN et al.: Translating Theology into the Modern Age TB/252
NELS F. S. FERRÉ: Swedish Contributions to Modern Theology. *New chapter by William A. Johnson* TB/147
ERNST KÄSEMANN, et al.: Distinctive Protestant and Catholic Themes Reconsidered TB/253
SOREN KIERKEGAARD: On Authority and Revelation TB/139
SOREN KIERKEGAARD: Crisis in the Life of an Actress *and Other Essays on Drama* △ TB/145
SOREN KIERKEGAARD: Edifying Discourses △ TB/32
SOREN KIERKEGAARD: The Journals of Kierkegaard ° TB/52
SOREN KIERKEGAARD: The Point of View for My Work as an Author § TB/88
SOREN KIERKEGAARD: The Present Age § △ TB/94

SOREN KIERKEGAARD: Purity of Heart △ TB/4
SOREN KIERKEGAARD: Repetition △ TB/117
SOREN KIERKEGAARD: Works of Love △ TB/122
WALTER LOWRIE: Kierkegaard Vol. I TB/89
Vol. II TB/90
JOHN MACQUARRIE: The Scope of Demythologizing: *Bultmann and his Critics* △ TB/134
WOLFHART PANNENBERG, et al.: History and Hermeneutic TB/254
JAMES M. ROBINSON et al.: The Bultmann School of Biblical Interpretation: New Directions? TB/251
F. SCHLEIERMACHER: The Christian Faith. △ *Introduction by Richard R. Niebuhr* Vol. I TB/108; Vol. II TB/109
PAUL TILLICH: Dynamics of Faith △ TB/42
EVELYN UNDERHILL: Worship △ TB/10

Christianity: The Roman and Eastern Traditions

DOM CUTHBERT BUTLER: Western Mysticism § ° △ TB/312
A. ROBERT CAPONIGRI, Ed.: Modern Catholic Thinkers △ Vol. I TB/306; Vol. II TB/307
THOMAS CORBISHLEY, S. J.: Roman Catholicism TB/112
G. P. FEDOTOV: The Russian Religious Mind: *Kievan Christianity, the 10th to the 13th Centuries* TB/370
ÉTIENNE GILSON: The Spirit of Thomism TB/313
GABRIEL MARCEL: Being and Having TB/310
GABRIEL MARCEL: Homo Viator TB/397
FRANCIS DE SALES: Introduction to the Devout Life TB/316
GUSTAVE WEIGEL, S. J.: Catholic Theology in Dialogue TB/301

Oriental Religions: Far Eastern, Near Eastern

TOR ANDRAE: Mohammed § △ TB/62
EDWARD CONZE: Buddhism ° △ TB/58
ANANDA COOMARASWAMY: Buddha and the Gospel of Buddhism. △ *Illus.* TB/119
H. G. CREEL: Confucius and the Chinese Way TB/63
FRANKLIN EDGERTON, Trans. & Ed.: The Bhagavad Gita TB/115
SWAMI NIKHILANANDA, Trans. & Ed.: The Upanishads: *A One-Volume Abridgment* △ TB/114

Philosophy of Religion

NICOLAS BERDYAEV: The Beginning and the End § △ TB/14
NICOLAS BERDYAEV: Christian Existentialism △ TB/130
NICOLAS BERDYAEV: The Destinv of Man △ TB/61
RUDOLF BULTMANN: History and Eschatology ° TB/91
RUDOLF BULTMANN AND FIVE CRITICS: Kerygma and Myth: *A Theological Debate* △ TB/80
RUDOLF BULTMANN AND KARL KUNDSIN: Form Criticism: *Two Essays on New Testament Research* △ TB/96
MIRCEA ELIADE: Myths, Dreams, and Mysteries: *The Encounter between Contemporary Faiths and Archaic Realities* § ° △ TB/1320
MIRCEA ELIADE: The Sacred and the Profane TB/81
LUDWIG FEUERBACH: The Essence of Christianity § TB/11
ÉTIENNE GILSON: The Spirit of Thomism TB/313
ADOLF HARNACK: What is Christianity? § △ TB/17
FRIEDRICH HEGEL: On Christianity TB/79
KARL HEIM: Christian Faith and Natural Science △ TB/16
IMMANUEL KANT: Religion Within the Limits of Reason Alone. § *Intro. by T. M. Greene & J. Silber* TB/67
K. E. KIRK: The Vision of God △ TB/137
JOHN MACQUARRIE: An Existentialist Theology: *A Comparison of Heidegger and Bultmann* ° △ TB/125
EUGEN ROSENSTOCK-HUESSY: The Christian Future *or the Modern Mind Outrun. Intro. by Harold Stahmer* TB/143
PIERRE TEILHARD DE CHARDIN: The Divine Milieu ° △ TB/384
PIERRE TEILHARD DE CHARDIN: The Phenomenon of Man ° △ TB/383
PAUL TILLICH: Morality and Beyond TB/142

Religion, Culture & Society

WILLIAM A. CLEBSCH & CHARLES R. JAEKLE: Pastoral Care in Historical Perspective: *An Essay with Exhibits. New Preface by the Authors* TB/148
C. C. GILLISPIE: Genesis and Geology: *The Decades before Darwin* § TB/51
KYLE HASELDEN: The Racial Problem in Christian Perspective TB/116
WALTER KAUFMANN, Ed.: Religion from Tolstoy to Camus TB/123
H. RICHARD NIEBUHR: Christ and Culture △ TB/3
H. RICHARD NIEBUHR: The Kingdom of God in America TB/49
TIMOTHY L. SMITH: Revivalism and Social Reform: *American Protestantism on the Eve of the Civil War* △ TB/1229

NATURAL SCIENCES AND MATHEMATICS

Biological Sciences

CHARLOTTE AUERBACH: The Science of Genetics Σ △ TB/568
W. E. LE GROS CLARK: The Antecedents of Man ° △ TB/559
W. H. DOWDESWELL: Animal Ecology. △ *Illus.* TB/543
R. W. GERARD: Unresting Cells. *Illus.* TB/541
EDMUND W. SINNOTT: Cell and Psyche: *The Biology of Purpose* TB/546
C. H. WADDINGTON: The Nature of Life △ TB/580

History of Science

MARIE BOAS: The Scientific Renaissance, 1450-1630 ° △ TB/583
W. DAMPIER, Ed.: Readings in the Literature of Science. *Illus.* TB/512
A. HUNTER DUPREE: Science in the Federal Government: *A History of Policies and Activities to 1940* △ TB/573
ALEXANDRE KOYRÉ: From the Closed World to the Infinite Universe △ TB/31
A. G. VAN MELSEN: From Atomos to Atom: *A History of the Concept* Atom TB/517
STEPHEN TOULMIN & JUNE GOODFIELD: The Architecture of Matter ° △ TB/584
STEPHEN TOULMIN & JUNE GOODFIELD: The Discovery of Time ° △ TB/585

Mathematics

E. W. BETH: The Foundations of Mathematics △ TB/581
S. KÖRNER: The Philosophy of Mathematics △ TB/547
WILLARD VAN ORMAN QUINE: Mathematical Logic TB/558
FREDERICK WAISMANN: Introduction to Mathematical Thinking. *Foreword by Karl Menger* TB/511

Philosophy of Science

R. B. BRAITHWAITE: Scientific Explanation TB/515
J. BRONOWSKI: Science and Human Values △ TB/505
ALBERT EINSTEIN et al.: Albert Einstein: Philosopher-Scientist Vol. I TB/502; Vol. II TB/503
WERNER HEISENBERG: Physics and Philosophy △ TB/549
KARL R. POPPER: Logic of Scientific Discovery △ TB/576
STEPHEN TOULMIN: Foresight and Understanding △ TB/564
STEPHEN TOULMIN: The Philosophy of Science △ TB/513

Physics and Cosmology

JOHN E. ALLEN: Aerodynamics △ TB/582
P. W. BRIDGMAN: Nature of Thermodynamics TB/537
C. V. DURELL: Readable Relativity △ TB/530
ARTHUR EDDINGTON: Space, Time and Gravitation: *An Outline of the General Relativity Theory* TB/510
GEORGE GAMOW: Biography of Physics Σ △ TB/567
STEPHEN TOULMIN & JUNE GOODFIELD: The Fabric of the Heavens: *The Development of Astronomy and Dynamics.* △ *Illus.* TB/579